PRAISE FOR *HEAD OVER HEELS FOREVER*

Some books change your mind; this book can change your marriage! Chris and Melina are passionate about helping ordinary couples have extraordinary marriages. With keen insights and refreshing honesty, they supply truth, tools, and tough love to help any relationship thrive. The Hanns have a "realness" we can all relate to, and their book reads like they're sitting in your family room. If you want a vibrant and meaningful marriage, here's practical advice on how to rediscover, reenergize, and protect your love — and have a blast doing it.

> **Dave & Ann Wilson,** hosts of FamilyLife Today radio show, nationally known marriage teachers, Kensington Church pastors, authors of *Vertical Marriage: The One Secret That Will Change Your Marriage*

Want a "no regrets" marriage? Every page of this book offers wisdom and practical advice for couples. Chris and Melina have written one of the most authentic books I've ever read. A good and healthy marriage is all about being intentional. In life, it's either the pain of discipline or the pain of regret — and the Hanns will show you how to have a beautiful, "regret free" marriage.

> **Jim Burns,** PhD, president of HomeWord, author of *Creating an Intimate Marriage, Closer,* and *Getting Ready for Marriage*

After 38 years of working with couples, I've just discovered one of the best new resources to help develop and maintain a successful relationship. It's called *Head Over Heels Forever.* It's a down-to-earth, practical, and highly effective guide that will benefit any couple. I strongly recommend it — whether you're struggling in your marriage or just want to enjoy the best possible relationship.

> **Eva Kraus-Turowski,** MSW, LICSW.
> Marriage and family therapist

Chris and Melina reveal the launch code to take your marriage higher, deeper, and farther in their refreshing "tell all" kind of way. No sugar coating, no pie in the sky, just straight talk from a couple who've experienced the good, the bad, and the ugly ... and discovered how to make radical commitment work. This book is rocket fuel for your marriage. Fill up and watch your marriage soar!

> **Michael Komara,** author of *Life in the Balance,*
> and founder of Wisdom Works, LLC.

If only *Head Over Heels Forever* had been published during my dozen years working at Saddleback Church — what a difference it would've made. And not only in the hands of the counselors I managed, but as a powerful tool for the struggling couples who came to us daily seeking a breakthrough. Chris and Melina peel away the mask of their own marriage, immersing us in a vulnerable and honest conversation on the pitfalls and pleasures of marriage.

> **Mark Jordan Koeff**, Hall of Fame photographer, lay counselor-supervisor at Saddleback Church.

A life changer! Chris and Melina have put together a practical and inspiring manual on how to have a great marriage. No matter how long you've been married, this book will refresh and safeguard your relationship.

> **Juan Ortiz**, motivational speaker, author of *Never Forsaken*.

Nothing is off-limits, and their brutal honesty is as refreshing as it is brave. Chris and Melina have a unique way of keeping readers engaged while addressing relevant topics that truly matter — including the ones ignored by other self-help books.

> **Kevin Snyder**, estate planning & elder law attorney,
> Snyder Law, PC.

All marriages can mend. And anything is possible when two people are willing to put in the hard work. Chris and Melina are the proof! Despite life's challenges and obstacles, they've maintained a committed, loving relationship. Now they're sharing how — in a practical, honest, and encouraging guide to support couples with the tools to enhance and strengthen their marriage.

> **Julie Turvey**, MFT, BBSE. Marriage and family therapist

Finally! A book by real people living in the real world who've done marriage right (and are more in love than ever). I will use this book for premarital counseling, recommend it for small groups at churches, and assign it for homework to my clients. As a therapist, it's hard to find a book that's not too academic (boring), or written by super-spiritual people we can't relate to (and make us feel guilty). Chris and Melina are honest about their ups and downs — it's like you're in the living room talking to friends who're open, honest, and encouraging.

> **Douglas Williams**, MFT. Marriage and family therapist

Head Over Heels Forever

Save Your Marriage, Your Sanity, and Your Sex Life (Before It's Too Late).

Chris and Melina Hann
With Karl Nilsson

pacific coast press
Rancho Santa Margarita, CA

pacific coast press™

Head Over Heels Forever
Copyright ©2019 by Chris & Melina Hann

ISBN 978-1-7328623-0-2

Requests for information or speaking engagements should be addressed to:
Pacific Coast Press, 29851 Aventura, Suite K, PO Box 80525, Rancho Santa Margarita, CA 92688
or via *chrisandmelina.com.*

Anecdotal illustrations in this book are true to life. In some cases, names have been changed for privacy purposes.

ACKNOWLEDGEMENTS

"Faithful are the wounds of a friend who corrects out of love and concern."
— Proverbs 27:6 (AMP)

Candid feedback from our friends has been priceless.

Your honest critique has made the process of writing our first book a rewarding journey. Heartfelt thanks to Kevin and Alison Islip, John and Betsy Borglin, Mike and Mary Ann Komara, Steve Andrews, Dave Wilson, Sharon Elliott, Eva Kraus-Turowski, Mary Westerlund, Mike and Lynn Jakubik, Susan and John Haagen, Robert and Diane Van der Goes, Jim and Jude Zwierzynski, Julie and Kevin Turvey, Tom and Leeza Groters, Tamara and Curtis Crawford, Marcela and Albie Hahn, Kathi and Mike Jesse, Chris and Amy Breen, Alex and Sabrina Gulotta, Jeremy and Britt Byrne, Marilyn and Gerry Oestreich, Claudio and Kristine Junge, Bruce and Ingrid Greenfield, Matthew Mitchell, Dipak and Dolly Makwana, Mike and Liz Markowski, Dr. Ray Ganem, Juan and Becky Ortiz, Chris and John O'Conner, Sandeep and Megan Gugneja, Kevin and Carolyn Snyder, Mark and Kari Jordan Koeff, James Douglas Williams, and Jim Burns. We are humbled by your love; your encouragement kept us going. You are true friends.

Thanks to Karl Nilsson — your creative genius and editorial flair helped to make this project so much more than it was.

Additional thanks to Gil Lapastora for his design excellence and to Sakura Keast for her proofreading brilliance.

To our children, Samantha and Alex — you are the inspiration for our dreams. May you be blessed in your relationships and learn from the mistakes we've made along the way. We love you both so very much!

What's up with the ring thing?

A wedding ring isn't just jewelry. It's a symbol of radical commitment.

For the two of us, wearing our rings is a constant reminder of the ferocious, non-negotiable loyalty we have for each other and our relationship.

Because a circle has no beginning or end, a wedding ring is a symbol of infinity. It symbolizes the security of knowing that "for as long as we both shall live," we will each be an invaluable, inseparable part of the other.

(And it's also a code so you'll know which one of us is talking!)

> **INSIGHT**: We wrote our book from two different but equally important perspectives — *husband* and *wife*. We take turns teaching; you'll know "who's who" by observing our wedding rings. Enjoy!

CONTENTS

A raging epidemic.

You're hungry. In fact, you're starving.

Fortunately, you're seated at the best table in your favorite restaurant. You're looking over the menu when the waiter walks up.

He smiles and announces, "Today's special is our most popular entrée. It's delicious. It's exciting. It's the meal you've been dreaming about."

By now your mouth is watering. But before you can reply, the waiter adds, "I should mention there's a 50/50 chance it's poisoned. Half of all customers who eat it will die. And most who survive will be miserable. Are you ready to order?"

I'm guessing you get up and head out. Quick.

A person would be crazy to risk it all on such lousy odds. And yet millions of couples heading into marriage do exactly that — with the odds of succeeding no better than flipping a coin. If it's a second marriage, the stats are even worse.

But there is a way to beat the odds. A proven way to have a happy, healthy relationship that goes the distance. Before we look at the *solution*, let's take a hard look at the *problem*. Virtually every family has been touched by it. And it's taking an awful toll on our culture, our economy, even our life expectancy.

First, the good news: "In Western cultures, more than 90 percent of people marry." That's according to the American Psychological Association. Their studies show that strong marriages are good for our mental and physical health, and "protect children from mental, physical, educational, and social problems."

Now, the bad news: "However, about 40 to 50 percent of married couples in the United States divorce. The rate for subsequent marriages is even higher."

(Recent research suggests couples who attend church regularly *do* have a lower divorce rate — ranging from 15 to 37 percent, depending on the study. But that's *still* a significant chunk of marriages that don't make it, no matter how you slice it!)

It's said that California is a predictor for America's social trends. If so, marriage is in big trouble. In sunny California, the divorce rate is already 60 percent. Yikes.

That's not all. Writing for the *Orange County Register*, David Whiting says, "According to the California Association of Marriage and Family Therapists, in Orange County it's 70 percent."

We live in Orange County. This staggering 7-out-of-10 failure rate is happening in our backyard. We've had an up-close-and-personal look at the suffering:

• After a bitter legal battle, a court decided our friend's two sons were better off moving with their mom across the country. Cost of divorce proceedings? Over $300,000. Not counting the pain and confusion of ripping young boys out of their home and away from their father's care.

• A neighbor's three-year-old son is suffering from severe anxiety and insecurity. Why? Because his dad remarried and now has two "new" children from his second wife's previous marriage. This confused boy is struggling to figure out where he fits in.

• Our friend's husband ran off with his secretary, leaving her and three young kids in the wreckage. Years later, he told his ex-wife how sorry he was. He confessed that if he had put as much work into saving his *first* marriage as he put into his second marriage, they'd likely still be together.

> In sunny California, the divorce rate is already 60 percent. Yikes.

We could fill pages with similar examples. And so could you.

The real tragedy is that all this emotional and financial upheaval rarely *solves* anything. In most cases, issues that derailed the first marriage resurface in the second or third relationship. As our regretful friend said, if the same amount of effort expended in *dissolving* a marriage was applied to *saving* it, the majority of troubled marriages would survive.

I do, I did, I'm done.

Move over, bachelors. Take a backseat, bachelorettes.

The fastest-growing celebration in America is the divorce party.

A party planning company in Las Vegas says bookings for divorce parties are up 70 percent. According to a story in *Time*, the company can arrange dance outings, limo rides, and naughty VIP parties complete with a divorce cake.

In "The Booming Business of Divorce Parties," Martha White says party suppliers are raking it in on items like decapitated groom cake toppers. Hot sellers include "Down with Love" voodoo dolls (complete with pins) and stuffed piñatas made in the likeness of your former spouse.

> Move over bachelors and bachelorettes. The hot new celebration is the divorce party.

Flooded with requests, one company began churning out ex-husband toilet paper and cheeky doormats customized with photos of Mr. Wrong.

Divorcées can now buy party favors stamped, "No men? Amen!" And napkins reading, "Screw the ring, I want alimony!" Ready to advertise a change in status? Fashionable T-shirts proclaim, "Divorced and on the prowl."

Based in LA, entrepreneur Christine Gallagher plans divorce parties for $5,000 to $20,000 per soiree and often cannot keep up with demand. Gallagher says, "To me, it marks the changing societal acceptance of divorce. It's not like the old days where divorce was shameful and you were left out of the dinner party."

Perhaps the ultimate expression of the un-wedding is publicly burning your wedding dress. And it's catching on.

Recently, this shift in attitudes hit close to home. A friend of mine posted on Facebook that her divorce was final and she was "finally free." The gleeful responses from her gal pals were telling:

"Congrats on your divorce! Now it's time to start really living!"

"Way to go, girlfriend!"

"You'll be better off alone!"

There were dozens of similarly upbeat notes, but one post took a different approach that really caught my eye:

"Does anybody know of a marriage that actually works?"

Love conquers all, but if that fails, try hard work.

It might have been a cry for help. Or maybe just a flippant remark. Either way, I felt compelled to respond. Here's part of my reply:

"Marriage doesn't just 'work' — YOU have to work at your marriage. Without serious effort, no marriage is ever going to 'work' on its own."

That's our book in a nutshell.

I wish we could tell you the secret to a great marriage is scented candles or Barry White music. But the real secret is far more grit than glamour.

As someone said, "Love conquers all, but if that fails, try hard work."

That's a good formula for keeping your wedding dress off the BBQ pit.

High fidelity.

Paul Newman and Joanne Woodward were married for 50 years. And they were deeply in love until Paul died at age 83. But fidelity is rare in pop culture.

With a scarcity of positive role models, it's not surprising the young couples we meet are hesitant about tying the knot.

Today, 76 percent of newlyweds cohabit before marriage. And plenty of folks are skipping the wedding altogether. Sharing the bills and the bed without a trip down the aisle is the new normal. And it doesn't raise an eyebrow. A *USA Today Gallup* poll found that only 27 percent of Americans disapprove of shacking up.

We'd like to reverse that trend and move the needle closer to the "original" formula. We believe a solid marriage is like a shining light — a beacon that attracts others to one of the best ideas God ever gave mankind. That's our mission.

And it all started by people noticing that Melina and I were ... well, *different*.

Newlyweds forever?

Sun. Surf. Breathtaking scenery. We were in Ixtapa, Mexico, for a week of focused "couple time." Our resort was picture perfect, with panoramic views and a private beach. Rolling waves and the exotic beat of reggae music set the scene for relaxation and romance. One morning at breakfast, we were flirting and joking with each other when a young couple walked up. They smiled, "We've been watching you guys and figure you must be on your honeymoon like us."

We laughed and told them it was actually our tenth wedding anniversary! After the shock wore off, the newlyweds said they hoped to be just as in love as we were ten years down the road.

Fast-forward six years to a social event for our daughter's volleyball team. Melina was sitting on my lap while we chatted with the other parents. Suddenly, one of the moms looked at us and blurted out, "You guys seem like you're newlyweds." Then with a wink and a chuckle she added, "It's kind of disgusting."

A year later, it happened again while shopping for dinner. We were talking and holding hands up and down the grocery aisles, laughing and having a wonderful time. When the checkout girl rang us up, she asked if we were newlyweds! She was shocked to hear we'd been married 17 years at the time.

Events like these reinforced what we already knew — we're blessed to have something in our marriage that's special, rare, and hopefully contagious.

Eventually, so many people asked what made us "different" that we decided to answer the question in writing. This book was birthed while we were mentoring soon-to-be-married couples at our church. After counseling our very first duo, we both sensed we had a lot to offer from our life experiences (good and bad).

We felt almost obligated to share the insights we'd been given. Jesus said, *"To whom much is given, much is required."* And we've been given a ton. Keeping that kind of info to ourselves seemed selfish.

So soak it up. Use what you can. Then spread it around.

We're just like you. But worse.

Did you idolize someone growing up?

As kids, most of us looked up to a hero. But sooner or later, we inevitably found an imperfection. And we were sadly disillusioned.

When someone we admire turns out to have a character flaw, we say they have "feet of clay." Before you read our advice, we want you to understand that's us!

We fight, we argue, we pout. We struggle with forgiveness. We say things we later regret. Like all couples, we mess up, act selfishly, and take each other for granted. And when we blow it, we offer lukewarm apologies.

Our marriage looks bright and shiny to neighbors and friends, but we're self-absorbed and often overlook each other's needs.

Bottom line is we're *not* a perfect couple. Not even close.

Like most newlyweds, we had high hopes for a Disneyesque "happily ever after." We soon discovered that perpetual bliss is impossible, and experienced our share of conflict and chaos. But here's the difference — while many of our peers threw in the towel, we stuck it out. And more than just *surviving*, we've been *thriving*.

> Bottom line is we're not a perfect couple. Not even close.

This book is our humble effort to share principles that helped us make it against some mighty big odds. Hopefully, what we've learned will help you achieve the amazing marriage you envisioned together before you said "I do."

As you read, watch out for our big muddy footprints — they're from our feet of clay. If *we* can nurture a successful marriage, you can too.

INSIGHT: Maybe you had a rough start. Maybe things seem broken. Unfixable. Don't give up! Melina and I both came from broken homes with divorced parents. Statistically, that's a marriage killer. Risk of divorce is 50 percent higher when one spouse comes from a divorced home, 200 percent higher when both do. Worse yet, we each had a parent with *multiple* failed marriages. We're grateful proof that with God's help, you can overcome any background or obstacle.

CHAPTER 1

Together Forever:
A practical look at commitment

The longest marriage in America lasted 86 years, 9 months, and 16 days.

Herbert and Zelmyra Fisher of North Carolina were wed in 1924 and stayed married until Mr. Fisher passed away at 104 years old, leaving his 101-year-old bride for the first time since Calvin Coolidge was president.

On the other end of the spectrum, Kim Kardashian and Kris Humphries divorced after 72 days. But that's an eternity compared to Britney Spears. She dumped Jason Alexander after two days. The briefest Hollywood marriage? Rudolph Valentino and Jane Acker. The couple's marriage lasted just six hours.

Ever wonder *why* there's such a high failure rate? Were the couples not committed in the first place? Were they faking it when they pledged to love each other "till death do us part?" Did they plunk down huge amounts of money on a ceremony just to show off? (If you're wondering, Kardashian's wedding cost $10 million.) Did they invite family and friends just to witness a fraud?

Of course not. That doesn't make any sense.

It's far more likely the vast majority of couples enter marriage fully intending it to last.

> The briefest Hollywood marriage lasted six hours.

But if newlyweds *plan* to stay married, why do so many split up?

To be honest, no one knows for sure. But I do know this. You can replace the "cross-your-fingers" approach with a concept we call "radical commitment."

The dictionary defines *radical* as "very different from the ordinary, extreme." It defines *commitment* as "a promise to be loyal, a pledge."

Please understand you cannot be neutral. There are only two options: You can consciously choose to be proactive and protect your relationship. Or you can opt out. But by doing nothing, you are actually choosing to fail.

If you commit to work 24/7 on building a strong and lasting marriage, your odds of success increase exponentially. If you default and just let nature take its course, the pressures of life will crack your marriage into pieces.

If you don't intentionally take ownership of your relationship, you automatically default to the Las Vegas approach: *Let's roll the dice and see what happens.*

Unfortunately, the odds always favor the house, not the gambler.

Think about people you know with healthy, long-lasting marriages. I can almost guarantee this concept is woven into the daily fabric of their lives. Even if they don't use a fancy name like "radical commitment," the words and actions of a fanatically devoted couple are at the heart of their success.

Incidentally, we're not just after longevity. We're after joy and harmony and great sex and lasting romance! The idea of radical commitment is not just the key to a lengthy marriage — it's the key to a "keeps-getting-better" kind of marriage.

> By doing "nothing," you are actually choosing to fail.

They say love is blind. But is bumping into things and groping around a good way to navigate life?

The average person walks blindly into marriage, assuming things will just automatically work out. They see no need to put effort into it or change their behavior from when they were single. But that's not you. The fact you're reading this book is proof you're proactive and eager to succeed.

Let's get radical.

Maybe you've heard that marriage is a 50/50 proposition.

Wrong. Marriage is a 100/100 proposition.

Each partner must be 100 percent devoted to the other. You must give all of yourself to your partner without expecting anything in return. Incidentally, that's not something we dreamed up. The Bible sets a high bar. It says we should love each other *"as Christ loved the church."* And Jesus unselfishly gave up everything — including his very life on the cross.

That was the most radical commitment in the universe.

But what does that look like for ordinary humans like us?

First of all, a radically committed marriage is not about meeting each other halfway. It's about doing whatever it takes. Sometimes that means meeting your spouse completely on their side (100/0).

All with no grumbling or finger pointing.

That's not how the world operates, right? Let's unpack the concept. When you're at your job, it seems unfair if one employee does less work than the others. It seems discriminatory if one employee gets more perks or time off than the rest of the staff. Nobody wants a co-worker who isn't putting the same amount of time and effort into the work at hand.

> A radically committed marriage is about doing whatever it takes.

But a successful marriage is *different* from a vocation or even a friendship.

Unlike a job application or business contract, you made a promise that you will always remain committed to your spouse, no matter what happens, no matter how lopsided the workload (or the rewards) may appear.

This unselfish ideal originates in the Bible: *"Do nothing out of selfish ambition ... Rather, in humility value others above yourselves, not looking to your own interests"* (Phil. 2:3,4 NIV).

In today's "me-first" culture, that's pretty radical.

In this age of self-absorption, who brags about someone else? Who voluntarily plays second fiddle? Yet that's the unlikely sounding path to relational peace. Consider this modern language take on the same verse: *"Put yourself aside, and help others get ahead. Don't be obsessed with getting your own advantage. Forget yourselves long enough to lend a helping hand"* (Phil. 2:3,4 MSG).

Forget yourself. Put yourself aside. Lend a helping hand. What would the world (or our marriages) look like if we all practiced that?

Radical commitment is about being the first to apologize, even if you're not the guilty party. It's about being the first to seek resolution, even when your spouse is mostly (or even completely) in the wrong. It's about realizing that the health of the relationship is more important than individual egos.

Radical commitment is about changing behaviors or habits that hurt or irritate your spouse. It's about adjusting your actions, not because you're obligated, but because you're radically committed to each other and to having an exceptional, lifelong relationship.

Marriage is not a contest. Never keep score.

And finally, it's about saying "no" to anything and everything that might have the slightest chance of damaging or ending your relationship. This is the conscious decision by both spouses that there are *no other options* out there. Period.

The Fishers of Carolina stayed married for over 86 years. Their advice? "With each day that passed, our relationship was more solid and secure. Divorce was *never* an option or even a thought. Remember, marriage is not a contest — never keep score. God has put the two of you together on the same team to win."

INSIGHT: If you try to make marriage 50/50, somebody's going to come up short, which will cause resentment, which will lead to problems. You'll get hung up on keeping score and feeling competitive instead of loving. The Bible says there's no greater love than to lay down your life for somebody. That can mean actually dying, but in marriage it usually means letting your spouse have their way — putting their happiness and welfare above your own.

Purpose-driven marriage.

Melina here! Our family has attended Saddleback Church in Lake Forest since moving to Orange County about ten years ago. Pastor Rick Warren and his wife Kay have been open and transparent about the struggles they've endured in their marriage. By revealing their "feet of clay," they're an outstanding example of what a radical commitment to each other and to a marriage vow looks like.

Their marriage started off on the wrong foot from day one.

Even the honeymoon was disappointing. In *Christianity Today*, Kay Warren explained that on the way back from their honeymoon they already felt despair about their predicament. She recalls, "People would ask, 'So, did you guys have fun?' And we're like, 'Sure, it was great.' But inside we were just dying."

And things went downhill from there.

In an article for *Lifeway*, the Warrens said, "For a while, nothing worked — absolutely nothing!" Kay adds, "We fought about everything we could possibly fight about." Rick chimes in, "About big things. Communication, in-laws, sex, money, and children. And we were striking out on all five."

Kay declared it a disaster. "I just saw no hope … I had just consigned myself to a lifetime of misery. And so I wished that divorce was an option. I knew it wasn't for me, but I wished it was because I was so miserable."

People with marital problems sometimes tell Kay she can't imagine how bad things are for them. To that, she replies, "I do know what it's like to wish with my entire heart that either he (Rick) would die or that God would say divorce is okay. And I know what it feels like to believe there is no hope; it will never be different; we are doomed to live this way; things are unbearable; and there's no way out."

By the way, Rick and Kay have now been married for *over 40 years*!

So how did the Warrens' marriage survive such a miserable start?

They often share that the only thing that kept them together was agreeing that divorce would never be an option. They maintained a radical commitment to each other and to whatever it took to survive as a couple. To get help, they began seeing a marriage counselor — even though it

11

cost nearly half their monthly income. It took time and hard work, but avoiding divorce was worth the effort and cost. Over time, they learned to communicate and resolve conflict, eventually coming to deeply love and cherish each other.

Their example taught Chris and me that nobody's marriage is easy.

Rick Warren says, "When people ask, 'Why am I having all these problems?' I answer, 'Because this is earth! This is not heaven.'"

> **God is more interested in our character than our comfort.**

And that applies doubly to the stress of relationships. Rick adds, "God is far more interested in my character than in my comfort, and that's particularly true in marriage. The number-one way God makes me like Jesus is through marriage."

Incidentally, the first four words of Rick Warren's bestseller *The Purpose Driven Life* reveal the key to a good marriage: "It's not about you."

An affair to remember.

Mike and Lynn have a marriage we've long admired. In fact, we asked for their input on early drafts of this book. They told us that before they even got married they decided to never, ever use the "D-word" (divorce). Not even jokingly. They made the conscious decision it would never be an option. No matter what came up, they would always work through it.

In today's world of disposable marriages, that's radical. But because of it, they've been happily married for over three decades. During that time, they've dealt with stressful issues including infertility, financial problems, illness, and lawsuits. Life hasn't always been easy. But their radical commitment has resulted in a fruitful and lasting marriage that inspires others.

So what's the big deal? What's so "do-or-die" about radical commitment? Because without it, you run the risk of becoming part of a disturbing statistic.

Researchers say over 1-in-5 employees are sexually active with somebody from their workplace. A survey revealed 66 percent of

Americans believe people inevitably cheat on their spouses at out-of-town conferences. The CNET report says two-thirds assume infidelity is the "new normal" when away on business.

Closer to home, Melina and I have good friends whose lives were turned upside down by what started out as an innocent friendship between co-workers ...

Bill and Mary had a wonderful marriage. They had the normal ups and downs, but overall, they had great communication. In fact, Melina and I patterned our relationship after theirs.

Mary was in the habit of having lunch with people from her work. At first, the lunches were with an entire team, but over time the group dwindled down to just Mary and one other man. She wasn't especially attracted to him and didn't see any harm in it. Actually, it was nice to have a friend to talk to, especially when she and Bill had a fight or a problem at home. Mary never had any intention of having an affair, and yet one day she found herself looking back and wondering how she had ended up in bed with her male co-worker.

> Over 1-in-5 employees are sexually active with somebody from their workplace.

Both cheating parties were married with young children and because of their affair, both families broke up. Their former spouses and six innocent kids had their worlds completely shattered, and their own lives have become infinitely more complex, expensive, and difficult.

Today, Mary and her new hubby are juggling four households on the income of two. And they're stuck with the nightmare of child custody logistics. Not to mention the on-going guilt of causing people they love unbearable pain.

Could all this have been avoided by making a radical choice within their respective marriages? We'll never know, but it seems to us the downward spiral that started so slowly and so innocuously could have been prevented — *if* they had chosen to put preset, non-negotiable boundaries around their marriages.

Sex and the city (of Jerusalem).

The Bible provides a classic example of what can result from not having a radical commitment to the sanctity of marriage. In this story, Israel's King David is home from the battlefield and frankly, he's bored. One evening

David gets out of bed and wanders around the roof of his palace. From there he sees a beautiful young woman bathing. At that moment he had the chance to make a radical choice — to simply look away, walk away, and not let his eyes linger on her naked form.

If David had made the decision to avert his gaze, he might have broken the spell of temptation and avoided untold pain and suffering. Instead, David kept peeping, got aroused, and ended up summoning Bathsheba to his room. He had sex with her, got her pregnant, and wound up having her husband killed to try and avoid the consequences. Adultery and murder were the short-term results of David's decision to not make the radical choice. Ultimately, his sin also resulted in the infant's death, a bloody political coup, and the death of three adult sons.

Think it can't happen to you? Think you're strong enough to resist?

Earlier in David's life, God had called him *"a man after my own heart."* If this spiritual giant could not resist the pull, what about us? How much more should we be looking to make radical choices to avoid putting ourselves in risky situations? The way to avoid the wreckage of broken hearts and unforeseen consequences is by making up your mind well in advance — to look away, run away, and stay away. (Read about David's affair in 2 Samuel 11:1-13.)

> If *this* spiritual giant could not resist the pull, what about us?

INSIGHT: Guys, have you ever found yourself staring at a beautiful woman who's not your wife? In the gym? In the airport? Ladies, have you ever checked out an attractive man who's not your husband? At work? In the mall? Like David, we have a radical choice to make on the spot — avert our eyes and turn around.

Affair-proof your marriage.

In Chapter 9 we discuss how the success (or failure) of your marriage can depend on the power of peers — who you as a couple choose to spend time with. Early in our marriage we had the good fortune to hang out with happily married couples who'd been together anywhere from 5 to 25 years. They all agreed on one thing — a married man or woman should *not* spend time alone with someone of the opposite sex.

Around that time, I heard a pastor on the radio discussing how to have an affair-proof marriage. He echoed our point that most people who get married fully intend for it to last. "So why are there so many affairs out there?" he asked. "Because," he said, "most people never set boundaries in their marriage. Any time you're alone with the opposite sex, step back and ask yourself, 'If someone saw us together right now, could they wrongly assume we're having an affair?'"

> Most people never set boundaries in their marriage.

For example, suppose you're out to lunch with your boss. You're not attracted to each other in any way. He knows you're married, and vice versa. Maybe you even know his wife and kids. You both have great marriages and you're totally faithful. But here's the question: *Could someone who knows you walk by and see you eating and laughing, and possibly think you're having an affair?*

If the answer is "yes," do not put yourself in that situation.

This simple rule was a game changer. I realized that if I took the preacher's advice, I would *never* have an affair — because I would avoid any situation where something could ever develop. And that was his point. Also, he never traveled alone. That way if a temptation did arise, an associate (of his gender of course!) would remind him who he was and how happily married he was. His "accountability partner" would reinforce the boundaries he had intentionally put up to protect his marriage.

He had one additional safeguard. If he was forced to be out of town by himself, he had a standing appointment to call his wife at 9 p.m. If for some reason he was dining alone, and the waitress became a bit too "friendly," the mandatory phone call was a quick reminder he had someone at home waiting to hear his voice. This check-in would derail a potentially dangerous flirtation.

Chris and I hadn't been married long when I first heard this message. As I pulled into the driveway, I knew this kind of radical commitment was meant for us. I turned off the car and literally ran up to the door. I burst in and wrapped my arms around my husband's neck. Breathlessly I exclaimed, "I just heard something on the radio and I want us to make it a part of our marriage!"

We've been radically committed to each other ever since.

> **INSIGHT**: Stop rumors before they start. Don't ride alone in a car with a member of the opposite sex. Go with three people or find another conveyance. Political strategist Lee Atwater coined the phrase "perception is reality." And it's equally true in elections and marriages. Even if you're technically innocent, take the Bible's advice: *"Keep away from everything that even looks like sin"* (1 Thes. 5:22 NLV).

Online infidelity.

With social media being such a huge part of our lives, the minefield of romantic temptation is more complicated and treacherous than ever.

Let me ask you a question: *Does talking with an old flame on Facebook count as spending time alone with them?*

I'll answer that with another question: *Could someone see the two of you on a Facebook wall and think you're having an affair?*

So yes, it does count. It's a risky situation, and you need to consider removing yourself from the temptation. I realize that's not popular advice, but it's a slippery slope from public chatting to private messaging to arranging an in-person hookup.

The instant gratification of Facebook and other social networks stimulates reward centers in the brain. And it's way too easy to find yourself craving the quick rush of an opposite-sex connection. When you're online, the human brain goes into overdrive. As you click back and forth, there's a tendency to idealize a cyber-friend. With no negative traits to mar the image, they can seem like a smart, funny, articulate — and potentially romantic — companion.

That's according to psychotherapist Ian Kerner. In his CNN article, "How Facebook Leads to Infidelity," Dr. Kerner writes, "Soon, a person may feel like an online friend 'knows' him or her better than a partner does. People feel freer to explore other parts of themselves, while real life (and a real relationship) feels stifling. This artificial sense of intimacy begins to consume a person's thoughts, which becomes all the more exciting because it's a secret. Most people don't deliberately set out to have 'e-motional' affairs, and that's the danger of social networks ... "

For me as a wife, it boils down to: *Why would I invest my time and energy in a relationship with anyone of the opposite sex when I could spend that same time and energy on my marriage?*

If you insist "It's no big deal" (or can't shake your addiction to social media), I caution you. Chris and I know people who started off by innocently "catching up" online with an old friend they once dated and ended up having an affair.

Trust me, I get the appeal. I mean, the perks are obvious — you don't have to wear makeup or find a cute outfit or fix your hair. If you put on a few pounds, no problem. And best of all, you don't have to invent a plausible excuse for why you'll be coming home late or lie about having lunch with a "friend."

It's a silippery slope from public chatting to private messaging to hooking up.

It's the easiest way ever to cheat on your spouse. Dr. Kerner agrees. "A friendly relationship snowballs into something more meaningful. A common myth is that only people in unhappy relationships have emotional affairs. In fact, many who commit emotional infidelity report that they were happy when they became involved with their affair partners. Rather than seeking out love (or sex), unfaithful partners gradually blur the boundaries between friendship and intimacy over an extended period of time."

Think about it. When you have an argument with your spouse, you can shut the bedroom door, click a button, and there's your old high school sweetheart, telling you how special you always were. And how cute you were. And what a great kisser you were.

Who needs a grumpy spouse when you can chat with a cheerful someone who always takes your side?

Instead of working out problems, you can retreat to a fantasy.

Kerner gives this advice: "Whether you're a man or a woman, if you're thinking more and more about the past, and getting to the point where you're fantasizing about what it would be like to be with that person again, it's time to unplug your computer, and get back to 'face-timing' with your partner instead ... "

Unfriend some folks if you have to.

Unplug from the grid if you have to.

There's no shame in removing or shutting down any device or any person that puts your one true covenant relationship in jeopardy.

Of course, every couple is different. And I understand the boundaries that work for Chris and me may not work for you. But you *do* need some kind of guidelines in place for the protection of your marriage. The important thing is to sit down with your spouse and agree on the boundaries for your relationship.

Do it now, *in advance.* Be intentional about keeping your marriage safe.

Stay back from the edge.

Boundaries between friendship and intimacy gradually blur.

When I faced Melina at our wedding, I made a public vow to save myself exclusively for her. I promised to "forsake all others." But my hormones didn't shut down when I said "I do." We're all living, breathing sexual beings. And being attracted to members of the opposite sex doesn't end just because we're in a monogamous relationship. Even the most devoted husband or wife is going to feel the warm buzz of attraction when someone catches their eye at a party or compliments their outfit or laughs at their joke or brushes up against them. It's human physiology.

So how do we stay on safe ground? Mentally picture yourself hiking in the mountains. Imagine you're on a high precipice in treacherous weather. It's raining, the rocks are slippery, and you're worried about plunging over the edge. What's a good strategy for not falling off? Easy — staying as far away from the edge of the cliff as you can!

To use an investing term, it's always wise to have a "margin of safety." Even if you're sure-footed and confident, staying twenty yards from the edge of the cliff ensures you never have to worry about slipping or being blown off by a gust of wind. Of course, some say that's not as exciting as living on the brink of disaster; many like the thrill of taking risks. But it's deadly to marriages.

> Our hormones don't shut down when we say "I do."

The average person says, "It's crazy to stay that far back — after all, I'm not technically doing anything wrong." Unfortunately, average people have average marriages, and average marriages happen to end in divorce.

I can hear the pushback: "Aren't you being overly cautious?"

Exactly. And the bottom of the cliff is littered with broken bones.

I have a friend who enjoys tap-dancing on the edge of the cliff. When we're out, he flirts excessively with women who are not his wife. He scopes out the ladies and seems to mentally undress each attractive girl. It's like his head is on a swivel.

His rationale is, "It's okay to look at the menu as long as I'm eating at home."

Maybe he can handle it, maybe not.

Personally, I hope he never slips because he has three precious daughters and a loving wife. However, the odds say that playing on the edge usually leads to a fatal fall. My argument to him has always been, "What's the point? Why even put yourself in that position?"

My friend teases me. He probably feels sorry for me. But he is playing with fire. And if he gets burned, it's on him. The Apostle James wrote, "*The temptation to give in to evil comes from within us. We have no one to blame but the leering, seducing flare-up of our own lust"* (James 1:13-15 MSG).

James is saying that temptation starts when we indulge our cravings (and let's be honest, we all have some!). This leads to enticement, that feeling of being lured into something, like bait dangling in front of a fish. The trigger for my friend is seeing a woman. As he checks out the "menu," his craving boils under the surface — a repressed inclination to *do* something about the tension he feels.

At a certain point, just ogling girls on the sidewalk won't be enough. Almost inevitably, a person who toys with lust will eventually give in to his impulses and start looking at porn or engaging in some kind of illicit sexual behavior.

In the field of neuroscience this is called hypofrontality. In his article, "The Four Stages of Temptation," Dan Armstrong explains that the prefrontal cortex of our brain is meant to slam on the brakes — to control the impulses we feel and make sane decisions based on our values. But after we've fueled our fantasies over and over, this region grows weaker, like a muscle that atrophies. (Scientists can actually see this change on a brain scanner.)

So it's only a matter of time until bad *thoughts* lead to bad *actions*. And the misery that follows.

If my friend takes his lingering, lustful gaze to its logical conclusion, what does it get him? In his case, a broken family, emotional instability in his lovely daughters, and years of time invested in his family thrown out the window. And for what? For a momentary thrill that always comes up empty.

That's a sucker deal all the way.

But as P.T. Barnum said, there's a sucker born every minute. Countless men and women have thrown away their lives, ruined their reputations, and wrecked their beautiful families for a short-term thrill. Not long ago, a famous actor-turned-politician was found to have had a sordid affair with a housekeeper. The made-for-tabloids scandal resulted in the very messy undoing of his marriage.

A glance at the gossip mags reveals a fresh (and unending) crop of high-profile affairs each time we go through the supermarket checkout.

When it comes to adultery, the Bible tells us *"countless victims come under her spell"* (Prov. 7:26 MSG). Over 41 percent of married people admit to committing adultery, either physically or emotionally. From blue collar workers to heads of state, extramarital affairs have always been snares. Executives, doctors, lawyers, teachers, pastors, coaches, players — unfortunately the list goes on.

And once adultery is discovered, only 30 percent of marriages will survive it.

That's the reality of the world we live in. A reality which statistics say will hit the majority of us. That is, *unless* we decide to hedge our bet by making the choice to have a radical commitment to our marriage.

The only proven way I've found to make sure you don't fall off the adultery cliff is to never, ever go anywhere near the edge. That way, if you do stumble, you just skin your knee on a rock or bruise your shin — you don't fall to the death of your marriage and family.

Could it happen to you?

Very few adulterers actually *intend* to have an affair. In fact, everyone we know personally who's had an affair says, "I never planned this. It just happened."

But nothing ever "just happens."

The unbreakable law of causation says every change in nature is produced by some cause. In tracing any affair backwards, we usually find the root cause was a missed opportunity to make a radical choice.

> Don't assume it could never happen to you.

Whatever the reason — curiosity, flattery, boredom, loneliness, libido, whatever — far too many people end up in the wrong bed. Which is why you must avoid assuming, "It could never happen to me." Just within our own circle of friends, there have been at least nine affairs. Writing that figure down stuns me; it's a tragic number. And it could be higher by the time you read this.

Consider these two real-life examples:

• **Earlier, we mentioned Bill and Mary, the model couple.** They'd been married ten years and were caring, devoted parents. And yet Mary "found herself in bed" with a co-worker. She didn't set out to commit adultery. She simply liked the guy's company. And she had to eat with *someone*, right? No big deal. Soon, they began to confide about little irritations they had with their spouses. Instead of trying to work things out at home, they put their energy into this budding relationship. Until one day they were in each other's arms. The emotional and financial cost of their two divorces was staggering.

• **Darryl and April were young marrieds and definitely in love.** April was pregnant with their first child when Darryl decided to join a yoga class to help alleviate his stress from work. It just so happened that his co-worker, Savannah, also belonged to the same gym and enjoyed yoga. As fate would have it, Savannah's car broke down. Since finances were tight, it seemed to make perfect sense for Savannah and Darryl to drive to class together. When Savannah saved up enough money, she'd fix her car.

What harm could there be?

Needless to say, as the thrifty friends attended class they began to develop a chemistry. Recreational companionship can be a big deal for a man, and Savannah really enjoyed their conversations. From Darryl's perspective, his flexible friend looked especially attractive in her tight-fitting, body-revealing yoga outfits. As time went on, the attraction grew stronger and one thing led to another. Their relationship turned physical and ended up destroying both of their marriages.

Each day, thousands of potentially beautiful and fulfilling marriages are shattered on the rocks of infidelity. The boulders are in plain sight, but most people think it's "too radical" to steer clear of them. Some who read this chapter will say we've gone overboard. Others will think we're old-fashioned. No problem. Our marriage is far too important to take any chances with. If doing everything we can to keep it healthy provokes some laughter or jibes, we're totally fine with that.

As Chris and I have pointed out, it's so important to never put yourself in a position where you risk being tempted by an affair. Infidelity happens far too often for you or me to imagine we're immune.

May I switch to a *positive* note? I absolutely adore horses and have been riding and hanging around stables since I was a young girl. Not long ago, I was at the tack store picking up some items for my horse, Brandy. While shopping, I met the owner, a fascinating woman named Yolanda. Soon we started talking about relationships and commitment. She told me that early in her marriage she encountered what looked like insurmountable problems. Fortunately, a radical decision and a surprising commitment changed the trajectory of her relationship.

Her husband was in the Army and would often be deployed overseas for long stretches. After several years of having to manage the house and raise their kids completely on her own, Yolanda was frustrated and worn out.

After five years of marriage, the spouses were basically just roommates who didn't cross paths very often. Things could not go on this way. She decided to tell her husband as soon as he returned from his current deployment. When she expressed her concerns, he did something amazing, something radical, something very few people would choose. Instead of getting defensive or angry, he remained calm. Instead of yelling about how he was off working hard to protect our country, he responded by telling Yolanda that he loved her very much and was 100 percent committed to making their relationship work.

> We all fall short of God's perfect standards to some degree.

Then he backed up his bold words with even bolder actions.

He resigned from the job he loved in order to focus on their marriage full time and be present in ways he couldn't previously. To me, the most awesome part of the story is that they have now been happily married for over 30 years! Think about it — five years in, Yolanda was at the breaking point. Then her husband made a radical commitment that altered the course of their relationship, resulting in a fulfilling and vibrant marriage that's still going strong.

I'm guessing there were many other selfless choices over the decades that demonstrated this couple's unusually high commitment to each other. Yolanda and her husband give real hope that any marriage can succeed — *if* you're willing to go against prevailing norms and maintain a fierce loyalty to your relationship.

We don't throw stones.

Adultery is a terrible mistake.

And it's human nature to pat ourselves on the back and judge those who commit it. But none of us have the right to condemn others. Why? Because we've all fallen short of God's perfect standards to some degree or another.

Ever fantasized about being with someone other than your spouse? Perhaps you've fixated on a real person like a co-worker or neighbor. Or maybe you've daydreamed about a movie star or a swimsuit model in *Sports Illustrated*. Or maybe you've visited adult websites. If you've ever grabbed an eyeful of anyone you're not married to, you need to know two things: Number one, you're human. Number two, you are guilty of mental adultery. But before you toss this book out the window, let me first say *most of us are equally culpable.*

Including me (we'll dig into that later).

In his Sermon on the Mount, Jesus said we were all capable of committing sins like murder and adultery in our thought life. *"You have heard it said, 'You shall not commit adultery.' But I tell you that anyone who looks at a woman lustfully has already committed adultery with her in his heart"* (Matt. 5:27 NIV).

> If you've ever grabbed an eyeful, you're guilty of mental adultery.

We've all slipped mentally. We've all had impure thoughts.

That's why Melina and I don't condemn anyone. Even if we are technically, legally innocent, we are all morally guilty and need to ask God's forgiveness. One version puts it this way, *"Don't think you've preserved your virtue simply by staying out of bed. Your heart can be corrupted by lust even quicker than your body. Those leering looks you think nobody notices — they also corrupt"* (Matt. 5:27 MSG).

So adultery is a matter of intent, not just action. But before you poke your eyes out to avoid temptation, consider these two points:

• **We're not talking about a casual glance at a handsome man or a pretty woman**. We're talking about the purposeful act of staring, the kind of locking in on somebody that stirs up our passion and enflames our imagination. Uninvited thoughts can flash across our mind — that's not a sin — but we don't have to dwell on them. An old country preacher once said, "You can't stop a bird from flying over your head, but you can stop him from building a nest in your hair."

• **God is not against sexual pleasure!** God created our wonderful bodies and our five physical senses to enjoy sex within the context of marriage. Remember, God invented the covenant of marriage way back in Genesis. And as author Tim Keller says, "What God institutes, he regulates." That means there are rules in place for our protection and provision. God knew that *intimacy without commitment* would lead to broken homes, unplanned pregnancies, and a bewildering variety of sexually transmitted diseases.

In movies and television, couples jump in and out of the sack with anyone and everyone (with no negative consequences). Cool characters have casual sex with multiple partners. Those who don't are portrayed as boring and backward. But the Bible offers this guideline, *"Marriage should be honored by all, and the marriage bed kept pure"* (Heb. 13:4 NIV).

Don't fall for what passes for intimacy in today's society — it's shallow and destructive and unsatisfying. Worse yet, it makes for lousy sex! Research proves that people who are faithful to their spouses report far higher levels of sexual satisfaction and overall happiness than those who play the field.

As always, the Bible is correct and pop culture is wrong. *"Honor marriage, and guard the sacredness of sexual intimacy between wife and husband. God draws a firm line against casual and illicit sex"* (Heb. 13:4 MSG).

Can I get really serious for a minute? Some of you reading this book have already committed adultery. Others are on the verge of having an affair.

To the first group, God offers unconditional, unimaginable love and forgiveness. Healing is always available. The Bible says, *"If we confess our sins, he is faithful and just and will forgive us our sins and purify us from all unrighteousness"* (1 John 1:9 NIV).

So things are never hopeless. God can wipe the slate clean.

When Jesus came upon the woman caught in adultery, the religious leaders wanted to stone her to death. But Jesus said, *"Let the one who has never sinned throw the first stone."* Of course, that ruled out everybody, and the bullies all went home. When Jesus was alone with the woman, he did not condemn her, but simply admonished her, *"Go and sin no more"* (John 8:1-11 NLT).

To the second group, we offer a challenge. The Ten Commandments show that God takes sexual sins very seriously. The seventh commandment says, "*You must not commit adultery.*" That's the *physical* act. The tenth commandment says, "*You must not covet your neighbor's wife.*" That's the *mental* act.

So God covers all the bases. He's not winking at adultery just because *Sex and the City* or *Game of Thrones* glamorize it.

INSIGHT: If your marriage is unhealthy in any area (sex, communication, finances, whatever), you're far more susceptible to sexual temptation. An acquaintance of the opposite sex will look like an appealing alternative to the emotional messiness at home. And if you're out of fellowship with God, you are *definitely* in the danger zone. Restore things spiritually, work on the broken areas of your marriage relationship — and slam the door on adultery.

Willpower is not enough.

None of us can be faithful to our spouses on our own strength.

Not you, not me, not the holiest roller you know.

Temptation is too subtle, too pervasive. Every day, we get a million messages telling us to drink up, strip down, and grab the gusto. From every side, pop culture is telling us we're missing out on all the fun, and that a world of unlimited pleasure is passing us by.

Fortunately, we don't have to fight the battle alone.

We have the biggest, toughest, smartest ally in the universe. "*No temptation that comes your way is beyond what others have had to face. All you need to remember is that God will never let you down; he'll never let you be pushed past your limit; he'll always be there to help you come through it*" (1 Cor. 10:13 MSG).

What commitment IS.

Remember the Warrens? What a rocky start they had? In 2015, after 40 years of marriage, Rick and Kay renewed their vows publicly at Saddleback Church. Kay finished her portion by saying: "So to the love of my life, let others have the candy sweet love songs as 'their' song (nothing wrong with that!); ours will always be Huey Lewis' 'Happy to Be Stuck with You.' And stuck together we are — like the sturdiest, most industrial-strength super glue EVER. Two stubborn mules yoked together with bonds (commitments, vows, pledges, promises, oaths) that hold infinite sweetness."

What commitment is NOT.

Please note that we are not saying there is never a time for separation. Or that anyone should ever remain in a dangerous situation (for themselves or their children) solely for the sake of "staying committed." While we are in favor of couples fighting for their marriage and working through the difficult times (all relationships have some), we also recognize that in severe cases such as physical or verbal abuse, there are *absolutely legitimate* reasons for separation. Domestic violence is a serious matter not to be trivialized or ignored. Our paramount concern is always the safety of the abused spouse and children. Take action to create enough distance for safety, and to be able to properly evaluate what the next steps should be. Do not hesitate to get professional help — bring in therapists, counselors, or law enforcement as needed.

Over the top?

Melina and I sometimes make marriage decisions that the average person might consider extreme. Here are two real-life situations:

- **In college, I had a good friend who happened to be female**. We were quite close and spent lots of time together. We stayed in touch after we graduated, even after she moved across the country. When Melina and I got married, I naturally invited my friend (and her boyfriend at the time) to our wedding. Some months later, Melina opened up to me that she did not feel comfortable with me communicating regularly with my female friend.

At first, I was a bit upset. After all, this was my longtime confidante we were talking

> Every day, we get messages to drink up, strip down, and grab the gusto.

about. I asked why she felt this way. Her reply surprised me — she said my friend was romantically attracted to me!

"That's ridiculous," I snorted. "She has a steady boyfriend and we're just friends."

Melina explained her uneasiness. During our reception she had noticed the unusual way my old friend was staring at me. Worse yet, when my friend danced with me, Melina got the clear impression she wanted to be more than platonic. I was angry and frustrated. It felt like Melina was being paranoid and putting unreasonable demands on me. After all, this was someone I'd known for years before I even met Melina.

What business did she have telling *me* who I could or could not be friends with?

I stewed over this situation for several days. To her credit, Melina never actually demanded that I end the friendship, and she never gave me any ultimatums. She simply expressed (several times) that she didn't feel comfortable about my ongoing relationship with this individual.

Over time, I realized it didn't matter if Melina's feeling was real or perceived — the bottom line was that *she* was my wife and that made her the most important person on earth to me. I was faced with a radical choice: Stick up for my "rights" or protect my marriage. I chose to essentially let the friendship fade away.

By doing this, I publicly acknowledged that my wife and my marriage were more important than any outside relationship.

• **Another situation involved my former manager.** She was a dynamic leader, and we had developed a close working relationship. Together we'd won many hard-fought battles in the marketplace. We made a strong, capable, and successful duo. It was fun being on her team and chasing the deals. When l left that company, I made it a point to stay in touch. This was nothing new; I often stayed in touch with former employees or bosses.

The twist here was that she was the first *female* colleague I'd done this with. For several years, we talked back and forth. We even planned to have lunch sometime to catch up and encourage each other in our current positions.

It all seemed innocent to me. One day I casually mentioned to Melina that I had exchanged some emails with this former boss.

"I don't think it's a good idea for you to meet Margaret for lunch," Melina said gently. "You're putting yourself in a position that could lead to an affair."

"That's absurd," I retorted. "We're just friends and there has never been any romantic connection between us. I'm just keeping in touch with her the same way I have with many other colleagues."

Melina paused. "This is different. It might seem the same, but it's different."

I shot back angrily, "Just because she's a woman? Is that what it is?"

"Mostly. But it's also because you are energized when you interact with her, and I just don't think it's a good idea."

I'd like to say I agreed with her and made the radical choice right then and there. But I didn't. We continued the discussion for several years.

Please pick up on this — by not making the radical choice *for* my marriage, I was actually (by default) making a choice *against* my marriage. Of course, I never intended to harm our relationship. I loved Melina as much or more than ever. But by letting this linger, I was putting our relationship at risk and missing a chance to demonstrate to my wife just how strong my commitment to her was.

Truthfully? Deep in my heart I suspected she was right.

The secret I never really admitted — even to myself — was the sexual tension between this former manager and me. I'm not sure if *she* felt it, but *I* did. That should have set off flashing red lights and sirens blaring "DANGER! STAY AWAY." I think I ignored the warning signs because I enjoyed the experience of working together so much. I rationalized that I was okay because there had never been anything romantic between us, not even any teasing or flirting.

Bottom line? I finally, grudgingly, admitted there *was* sexual tension (at least for me) between us. To willfully put myself in that situation was exposing my marriage to tremendous risk. At that point I told Melina she was right and that her concerns might well have saved us from disaster.

INSIGHT: At the time, I was no longer working for that company. But what if I was? In my mind, the radical choice was clear — I would've left the firm (or at least transferred to a different department or division). Again, many might call that unnecessary or fanatical. After all, my job paid our bills and supported the family. To quit would impact us financially. But a radical commitment to the most important relationship (outside of our relationship with God) must always override other concerns.

An ounce of prevention.

What did we learn?

Any opportunity for an emotional or physical affair — no matter how harmless it appears — increases your risk. Experts say most infidelity is inadvertent! Spouses rarely intend to be unfaithful. They just ignore the danger signs (feelings of attraction, deep conversations, sexual curiosity) until it's too late. Prevention is the best medicine; be hyperaware around the opposite sex and even change your environment if necessary.

Above all, make your spouse your top priority.

TALK IT OVER.

Enough meddling. Now it's your turn. Discuss these topics with your spouse:

1) What do you think about having a radical commitment to your marriage? Think about the consequences of making — or *not* making — a bold commitment.

2) Do you enjoy being "close to the edge of the cliff?" Why? Think through the potential consequences to your relationship if you continue living on the edge.

3) Think about any potential situations in your life right now that pose a risk to your marriage. What do you need to do about them?

TAKE ACTION.

Let's get practical. These steps will move you along:

1) Make a radical commitment to "choose us." Vow to put your marriage first in your life. Resolve to stay far back from the edge of the adultery cliff.

2) Be intentional about making your marriage extraordinary, no matter what it takes. Prepare to cheerfully meet your spouse 100/0 if necessary.

3) Affair-proof your marriage. Sit down with your spouse and talk about setting agreed-upon boundaries and non-negotiable limits.

4) Promise each other to eliminate the "D-word" from your marriage vocabulary. Tell each other that divorce will never be an option.

CHAPTER 2

Sticks and Stones:
Harnessing the power of positive words and expectations

The pen is mightier than the sword.

But the spoken word trumps them both.

Think about the life-altering impact words can have: *Your child is safe … You're fired … I do … It's cancer … Not guilty … We regret to inform you …*

Words can make peace or declare war. Calm a crowd or incite a riot. Proclaim love or fuel hatred. And nowhere is the power of words more potentially volatile than in personal relationships.

As kids on the playground, we shouted, "Sticks and stones may break my bones, but words will never hurt me." That's a flat-out lie, and a dangerous one at that. People are deeply wounded by words, and the pain can be debilitating. A careless remark or malicious comment can warp someone's self-image for a lifetime.

A far more truthful cliché is, "What you say is what you get."

I've found that axiom to be true, especially in marriages. If what you say to your spouse is generally positive, uplifting, and encouraging, you'll end up with the person (and relationship) you're describing. Conversely, if your words are generally negative, condescending, and discouraging, you'll *also* get what you say.

Which would you prefer to have in your life?

For an outstanding marriage, be sure the language you use when speaking to (or about) your spouse is optimistic, nurturing, and complimentary. We should always strive to build up our marriage partner's self-image — not shaming, blaming, or picking them apart until they feel like a doormat.

Have you ever thought of your words as a deadly weapon? How about as a miraculous cure? Proverbs 18:21 tells us, *"Death and life are in the power of the tongue."*

That means you can virtually kill a good marriage with a stream of negative verbiage. Or *revive* a bad marriage with words of positive reinforcement. Neither scenario happens overnight, but eventually a person starts to believe what they hear and then act upon it — for better or worse.

> A careless remark can warp someone's self-image for a lifetime.

Our choice of words can alter a person's self-image by building them up (or tearing them down) in their own eyes. The tongue is so powerful that we'd be foolish to use it haphazardly: *"The words of the reckless pierce like swords, but the tongue of the wise brings healing"* (Prov. 12:18 NIV).

Maybe you've heard the expression, "Give a child a good name and they'll live up to it." That's certainly true. But it's equally important for Mom and Dad to give *each other* a "good name" by lavishly complimenting their spouse. Agree?

Now let's take a trip to the balmy South Seas ...

The great exchange.

Johnny Lingo is the wealthiest trader in all of Polynesia.

He is shrewd, honest, and badly in need of a wife.

One day, Johnny sails to a nearby island to bargain for a bride. In his native culture, it is customary for a young man to offer a dowry to the father of a prospective wife. Payment is made in cows — the more desirable the bride, the more cows required. An average woman commands two or three cows; an exceptionally desirable wife might bring four or five.

The woman Johnny Lingo has come for is named Sarita — a plain girl, lacking in self-confidence and charm. She walks with her shoulders hunched over and is considered by her neighbors (and her own father) to be of little value. She is described as "sullen, skinny, and undesirable."

When Johnny arrives at Sarita's hut to discuss the dowry, her father doesn't expect much for his unexceptional daughter. He feels the girl is worth only one cow, but since Johnny is known to be wealthy, he asks for three. This bluff is so disproportionate that the whole village breaks out in derisive laughter.

Surely, Johnny the expert negotiator will make a counteroffer of two cows and cut his losses on the mediocre bride-to-be.

As the bargaining is about to begin, the island women brag loudly about how many cows their husbands had given for each of them. In front of everyone, they snicker that Sarita's father will be lucky to see one cow from the deal.

Suddenly, Johnny signals for silence. In a loud voice, he announces that he will give *eight* cows for Sarita.

The villagers are stunned! No one has ever paid such an exorbitant sum for any wife. Everyone assumes Johnny will reconsider his decision and default on the lopsided deal. But the next day, Johnny shows up with eight cows, marries Sarita, and returns to his home island.

Sometime later, a visitor to the area hears about this unusual marriage arrangement and decides he must locate Johnny Lingo. He wants to ask why a brilliant trader would strike such a bad deal for a so-so wife.

When he arrives at Johnny's home, he is greeted at the door by the most beautiful woman he has ever seen. Her eyes sparkle and she moves with a grace and confidence that come from deep within.

Can this possibly be the same Sarita the villagers described?

When the visitor inquires, Johnny replies, "Many things can change a woman. Things that happen internally, things that happen externally. But the thing that matters most is what she thinks about herself."

Johnny explains that back in Sarita's hometown, she believed she was worthless. But now she knows she is more valuable than any woman in the islands. Johnny says he has made the best exchange of his life — eight cows for an entire lifetime with the strong, self-confident woman he loves.

The other villagers are amazed when they see the transformed Sarita standing proudly at the side of the great Johnny Lingo. She is dignified, resplendent, and seems to always be smiling — the perfect partner for the renowned trader.

Does that resonate with you?

Johnny recognized the potential in Sarita, but he wanted *her* to recognize it, too. By offering a veritable fortune for her dowry, he proved that her true worth wasn't based on what others saw, but in who she truly was. Johnny was looking for an "eight-cow wife," and by treating the woman he loved in that manner, she rose to the occasion, exceeding everyone's expectations.

> The value we place on people is reflected in our words.

How many marital problems could be eliminated if we followed the principles described in this story? Reading it made me reevaluate my own words and actions — both public and private — with Melina. Now, before speaking I ask myself, "Will my words make my wife feel worth one cow or eight cows?"

Male or female, the value we place on people is reflected in our words. And the hearer responds according to the value they *perceive* we're ascribing.

INSIGHT: The original story, "Johnny Lingo and the Eight-Cow Wife," was written by American crime novelist Patricia McGerr, and first appeared in *Woman's Day* in 1965 and later in the *Reader's Digest*. It's been adapted for movies and retold in countless lectures. Wherever it's shared, people get an eye-opening look at the impact of words and the power of spoken expectations.

The eye of the beholder.

Johnny Lingo was a brilliant man.

That's according to Dr. James Dobson. In his book *Night Light: A Devotional for Couples*, Dobson says Johnny knew that his negotiations with Sarita's father would forever seal the self-concept of the woman he loved. That's why the formerly unassuming Sarita exuded such confidence and beauty after her generous betrothal.

Dobson challenges all spouses, "You have the power to elevate or debase each other's self-esteem. Rather than tear down, don't miss a single opportunity to build up."

There's an old adage: "We are not what we think we are. We are not even what others think we are. We are what *we think others think we are.*" In other words, our self-worth is greatly influenced by what people say *to* us and *about* us.

Their words either show respect or disdain, and over time those verbal interactions shape our self-concepts and our personalities.

Oftentimes, our tendency is to be like the villagers in the story and focus on the negative — both in others and in ourselves. This negativity is deeply ingrained and requires a conscious and deliberate effort to change. Did you notice how intentional Johnny Lingo was in assigning positive value to his wife? His "eight-cow thinking" and words of affirmation brought out the absolute best in his bride by enabling her to see herself as valuable.

So much in life depends on how we feel about ourselves. If we *feel* good and have positive experiences, we're more willing to grow and take risks. Why? Because being rewarded for previous efforts makes us optimistic about future endeavors. Which in turn makes us more likely to gain even *more* good experiences. Some call this a positive feedback loop. I call it a virtuous, upward cycle — and it can result in stronger relationships, brighter careers, better health, and so on.

> Rather than tear down, don't miss a single opportunity to build up.

Unfortunately, the opposite is also true.

Negative feelings about ourselves lead to decreased self-esteem, more insecurity, and less risk-taking. Which results in even fewer positive, inspiring experiences. A spirit of pessimism can begin to take root. And if it's reinforced by injurious, demeaning words, the downward spiral accelerates.

Speech defect.

The consequences of how we speak to ourselves and others are astounding. It's hard to comprehend, but in one sense, our words have the capacity to alter or create our futures … and influence the lives of those around us.

For Johnny to have an eight-cow wife, he needed Sarita to fully believe she was *worth* the huge dowry. A person's belief about themselves is shaped by many influences. Many are beyond our control, like heredity, environment, and parenting. However, there is one influence that can be changed — the pattern of speech we use in daily interactions.

Consider the way you talk to your spouse. If your words tend to be positive and point out strengths, their self-image will be bolstered. If your words tend to be negative and focus on weaknesses, their self-image will be diminished.

Tell the negative committee inside your head to shut up.

Too often, negative speech from a spouse reinforces our own negative self-talk. Their words can echo the voice that's already in our head: "*I always mess things up ... I keep slipping back ... I'm such a loser.*" Sound familiar? If so, you need to take charge of that nagging voice.

Children's author Ann Bradford says, "Tell the negative committee that meets inside your head to sit down and shut up."

Prisoner of words.

What do a baseball star and a prison inmate have in common?

I discovered the surprising answer — based on the power of words — in a book called *Different Children, Different Needs* by Dr. Charles F. Boyd.

In it, Dr. Boyd shares how a major league baseball player was brought into a maximum-security prison to speak to a group of hardcore prisoners. Volunteering his time, the sports celebrity gave an encouraging message to the inmates. The ballplayer shared how as a kid he used to pitch to his dad every day after school. When he would throw a wild pitch over his dad's head, his father would say, "Son, someday you are going to be a major league pitcher."

Notice how the wise father *chose* to focus on the positive aspects. He could have easily belittled his son's lack of control. One day his son threw a wild pitch and smashed a window. Most parents would hit the roof. Vent their frustration. Ridicule the child for wasting hard-earned money to fix the glass. But instead of getting angry over the broken window, his father said, "Son, with an arm like that, for sure you'll be playing in the big leagues some day!"

When the ballplayer finished, a prisoner sheepishly approached him. After thanking him for the message, the inmate confided, "My father did the same thing as your father, but he constantly told me, 'Son, one day you're going to end up in prison.' I guess I fulfilled his expectations."

> Our words are especially powerful to those who love us.

Our words are especially powerful to those who love us and look up to us. Parents and spouses, take note.

The silver linings playbook.

Ever been caught with your hand in the cookie jar?

As a kid, it was always awkward to have a parent or teacher walk in while you were breaking a rule. I'm guessing you can recall a time when you were caught red-handed doing something wrong.

One of my personal heroes, Dale Carnegie, had a different spin on getting busted.

In 1936, Carnegie wrote a little book called *How to Win Friends and Influence People*. It became the second best-selling nonfiction book of all time. One of the book's main principles is to "catch people doing something right."

That means praising people for each and every improvement, even the slightest ones. He advised us to be quick in our encouragement and lavish in our praise. Let people know you've caught them, that you saw their growth. If you do, Carnegie said, people will do everything they can to support you in return.

Be quick in your encouragement and lavish in your praise.

I've always liked that word picture — instead of catching someone doing something *wrong*, try and catch them doing something *right*!

I had the good fortune to know and work for the late University of Michigan Honors Psychology Professor, James McConnell. He is the highly respected author of the classic psychology textbook, *Understanding Human Behavior*.

Professor McConnell was also one who accented the positive. He encouraged me to always look for something to compliment a person about when I first met them, "Even if it's just their shoelaces that you like." His point was that we can always find something positive about someone, even if it's a small detail.

Obviously, he was a big believer in using "positive reinforcement" to shape behavior. Simply put, that means encouraging a behavior by rewarding it, like giving your dog a treat for obedience. ("Negative reinforcement" refers to taking something away or using punishment and reprimand.)

> Be quick in your encouragement and lavish in your praise.

Here's how it works: Imagine a rat in a cage that has a lever rigged to release a food pellet when pressed. Now picture Mr. Rat scurrying around until he accidentally presses the bar and — like magic — a tasty treat appears. In no time, the rat is furiously pushing the lever, hoarding his pile of pellets.

Professor McConnell taught us to reinforce and reward any behaviors we want repeated. His underlying message for interpersonal relations was to focus on the positive as much as possible, and use our words to compliment others on the *things we like* and the *behaviors we desire more of.*

Let's tie that back to marriage. What are some positive things we can say to our spouse? It's easy to see flaws and react to the negative, but if we look carefully there is always a positive side we can focus on. If dinner is burned, look at the bright side — you get to dine out. If the fender's banged up, be glad that the car isn't totaled. Even if it's something small, find a silver lining and start there.

INSIGHT: If you emphasize catching people doing something *wrong* (instead of something right), their goal will become to avoid mistakes. They won't play to win; they'll play to not lose. They'll be afraid to go above and beyond or take risks. People who are criticized become timid, mediocre performers. For exceptional results (and marriages) we need to praise others whenever possible.

Bad news travels fast.

"Kind words can be short and easy to speak, but their echoes are truly endless."

That was Mother Teresa, a woman who spoke words of love and hope to the poorest of the poor. She knew we may never understand the profound impact words of affirmation can have on individuals.

Another woman who understands the power of words is Florence Littauer. The title of her book, *Silver Boxes: The Gift of Encouragement*, came from a little girl in a Sunday school class Florence was teaching. The child described encouraging words as "little silver boxes with bows on top." A beautiful thought indeed — our words should be like gifts we give to each other, silver boxes with bows on top.

After reading Littauer, we resolved as a couple to think twice before speaking to family, friends, or anyone else. Someone created the acronym T.H.I.N.K. as a cool reminder: *Is it True? Is it Helpful? Is it Inspiring? Is it Necessary? Is it Kind?*

> If dinner is burned, look at the bright side — you can dine out.

That grid filters out a lot of negative chit-chat. An old proverb cautions us not to speak too hastily, "Speak only when your words are more beautiful than silence."

How we view the world is up to us.

The glass is half-empty *and* half-full at the same time — we have the choice of which one to call it! We can focus on positive words and hand out "silver boxes" to our spouses. Or we can injure their self-image with a snarky comment or sarcastic remark (or even a silent eye roll).

The power to build up or tear down with our tongue is immeasurable. It's important to recognize that it may take dozens of compliments or affirming statements to build up a "wall of trust" in somebody, but only one negative remark to knock that wall down.

Ever wonder how we can remember — in great detail — all the negative things our spouse has ever uttered from the day we met until today? *("Don't be so cheap … You could afford to lose a few pounds … Maybe you should earn a little more.")*

Most of us have had far more happy experiences and conversations than ones that were unhappy. Yet we tend to zero in on the *bad* memories.

Why?

"Almost everyone remembers negative things more strongly and in more detail," says Clifford Nass of Stanford University. The psychology professor adds, "We tend to ruminate more about unpleasant events than happy ones."

Which is another reason to choose our words carefully — it's virtually impossible to forget them or retract them effectively.

In her article "Positive and Negative Words," Peggy Bert asks, "Why can't a big bouquet of roses or a coveted ticket to a sporting event make up for hurt feelings? Why do we remember critical remarks more than positive ones? You can blame it on the brain."

Published in *Today's Christian Woman*, Bert says our brain has a "negativity bias" built in. "Our brains are actually more sensitive and responsive to unpleasant news. That's why personal insults or criticism hit us harder and stay with us longer. It's why negative ads are more effective than positive ones."

Humans have an inherent partiality toward negative information. Bad news chokes out good news. Unkind words drown out — or even erase — kind words.

Bert says, "Our brain needs a higher number of positive entries to counterbalance this built-in negativity bias. And several small, frequent, positive acts pack more punch than one giant-size positive. The size of the positive doesn't count; quantity does. It's strictly a numbers game."

> Unkind words drown out or erase kind words.

So speak positive words *often*. Though it can be difficult at first, building each other up with the positive power of words is critical to the survival and success of your marriage. It's that simple.

> **INSIGHT**: Pay it forward. Practice random acts of kindness and spontaneous words of affirmation. Make it a goal to surprise someone — especially your spouse — each day with at least one unexpected compliment. Make hefty deposits of praise into your partner's emotional bank and enjoy big dividends later.

I grew up in a positive family. We were upbeat. We got along. No cuss words. No put-downs. I was never told to shut up or be quiet. I was never ridiculed, belittled, or spoken to in a critical way.

I was the epitome of positive — or so I thought.

Meeting my husband opened a door into a whole new level of positive thinking and speaking I had never imagined. I remember walking across some ice and casually remarking, "I better watch out or I'll slip and fall."

Chris quickly replied, "You just planted a picture of falling down into your mind. Now you have a higher likelihood of doing just that! It's better to tell yourself, 'I need to walk carefully so I stay on my feet.' Keep an image in your mind of the result you want."

Wow. Such a little twist on words, but what a totally different picture it created!

I distinctly remember bringing Chris home with me for a family holiday. I recall my relatives saying things like, "Melina is always late. In fact, Melina will be late to her own wedding!" and having them all burst out laughing. They warned Chris, "Tell Melina at least a half-hour before she really needs to be somewhere if you want her there on time!"

I can still hear them saying, "She'll be late to her own funeral."

When we got home that night, Chris and I talked about it. I said, "Well, they're right, I am always late to everything." Chris responded, "Of course you are — you and your family are always saying that's who you are. But now that we're together and we recognize this tendency, let's change it!"

Did Chris badger me? Did he set my watch a half-hour ahead? No. He made the effort to *catch me doing something right* — like being on time — and then verbally affirming me. Sometimes I would slip and say things like, "Well, you know I'm always late." Chris would gently correct me, "That's not true. You weren't late to your hair appointment and you were on time to pick up your friends."

Even if I was only punctual two times out of ten, he always made me feel positive. I began to find myself saying, "He's right. I'm *not* always late." When we were around my family, conversations would still shift to making fun of me for being late. But Chris would speak up, "No, that's the old Melina. She's changed; she's on time now more often than not."

> Surprise your spouse with unexpected compliments. Daily.

The more he pointed out when I *was* on time, the more I focused on those examples. I even started changing my self-talk. Instead of telling myself, "I better hurry or I'll be late," I started saying, "I better hurry because I'm always on time."

And guess what? Today I am known for being timely and prompt for appointments — and my overall self-image is better as a result!

———

At a recent women's conference, I heard a speaker say, "Our words have the power to bring life or death to situations. God *spoke* the world into existence. He *said* 'Let there be light' and there was light."

Then she described how Jesus was tempted by Satan in the desert for 40 days. Did he fight his enemy with a fist, a knife, or a lightning bolt? Did he call down angels to help him? Nope. Jesus responded by quoting passages from Hebrew scripture. Since we are created in God's image, shouldn't his words be our weapon, too? Doesn't it make sense there would be power in the words we choose?

Perhaps you're wondering: *What does this have to do with marriage?*

Everything! Chris and I are always telling people how much we love being married. When we meet someone new, we tell them we're newlyweds at heart and best friends forever. And our kids? Yep, we've brainwashed them for sure! They tell everyone, "Our parents are so in love. They're always going on date nights and hugging and kissing in front of our friends."

And they say all this on their own initiative. When they do, we like to lean in close and start smooching and cooing, "You mean like this? Speaking of date nights, how about Friday? Samantha, would you please watch the puppy?"

(Followed by squirming, squealing, and giggles all around.)

> What we think and say becomes what we do.

Bottom line? What we *think* becomes what we *say*, and what we *say* becomes what we *do*. Sometimes folks tell me, "But you don't know how awful and negative my thoughts are." Actually, I do. If that's you, I understand your pain and your darkness because I was once right where you are in many areas of my life.

But the good news is that you're reading this and you *can* change. Just like I did.

Slaying the negativity dragon.

Positive talk makes us feel safe, loved, and valued.

Negative talk makes us feel insecure, wounded, and angry.

So it's a no-brainer to choose the former.

But what does positive communication look like in the daily grind? Let's look at two ways to change our negative speech patterns:

1) **Begin by changing your words — especially your self-talk — and your actions will change as a result**. Actress Naomi Judd said, "Your body hears everything your mind says." How true. And science backs this up. Brainwave tests prove that when we use positive, life-affirming words, our "feel good" hormones start flowing. Positive self-talk releases endorphins and serotonin in our brain, which then flow through our body, making us feel good. The flip side? These same neurotransmitters shut down when we use or hear negative words.

2) **Start hanging out with couples who speak highly of each other**. Find husbands and wives (of any age) who are obviously still in love and value their marriage. It's important to socialize with couples who build each other up with good-hearted, uplifting conversations and life-affirming compliments. Call it osmosis, the power of suggestion, or even peer pressure, but when you hang around positive people it's hard to be negative. And that's our point entirely.

> **INSIGHT**: Surround yourself with people who look for the best in themselves and their spouses. Being around couples who pledge to support each other under any circumstance is like a spiritual booster shot for your marriage. Likewise, avoid the grumblers. Hanging out in the wrong place with the wrong people opens the door to the three deadly Cs — *competing, comparing, and complaining*.

———

Changing your speech may feel awkward at first.

It may even feel like you're stretching the truth to say you're madly in love with each other. But say it often enough and it will tend to become reality. Incidentally, doing this is copying our Heavenly Father who *"speaks of future events with as much certainty as though they were already past"* (Rom. 4:17 TLB).

Like anything, the more you practice positive speaking, the easier and more natural it will feel. Trust me, if *we* can make the change so can you!

Speak no evil, hear no evil.

Another powerful lesson from Johnny Lingo is the importance of helping those around us — especially our spouses — rewrite the destructive internal story they may be telling themselves daily. How? By shifting their focus off their own negative traits to their most positive attributes.

When we help our spouses uncover and maximize their best traits, they start seeing themselves in a new, positive light. Transformation doesn't happen instantly, but we can build them up day by day, one conversation at a time.

Remember Sarita's dowry? The villagers naturally expected Johnny Lingo to negotiate down to the absolute minimum rock-bottom price. Instead, Johnny placed his future wife's self-esteem *above* his own reputation for driving a hard bargain. He considered her happiness and honor more important than the ego gratification of "winning" the negotiation with her father.

In much the same way, we need to intentionally lift our spouse's needs above our own. Many of us have the need to always be right or the need to feel superior or the need to call the shots. If you want an extraordinary marriage, you need to make a 180-degree reversal in those areas.

It won't be easy, but God can help us swap priorities.

The Bible says "*honor one another above yourselves*" (Rom. 12:10 NIV). The original language implies we are to outdo each other with honor. That doesn't mean we don't see each other's faults. But we are to act and speak lovingly *despite* our mutual flaws. Author John Piper says, "The tenderness of our relations is rooted in the tenderness of God in Christ. When we elevate someone by becoming their servant, we're painting a picture of Christ."

I don't know about you, but I tend to look out for Number One. Far too often, the man in the mirror is my top priority (and that's an understatement). That's why Piper says, "Pray earnestly and regularly that God would do whatever he has to do to make you more and more into this kind of affectionate and honoring person."

> When you hang around positive people it's hard to be negative.

Put away the clippers.

When we lived in the Detroit area we attended Kensington Church (a very welcoming place, if you're looking). One of the founding pastors is Dave Wilson. When he's not preaching, Dave and his wife, Ann, speak at marriage conferences around the country. (Dave and Ann Wilson also host the daily radio program *FamilyLife Today*, heard nationwide.) At one service, Ann gave an unforgettable visual of how damaging a wife's harsh words can be to a husband's self-image.

Ann stood onstage next to a tall potted shrub, holding a pair of pruning shears. She began describing how she (lovingly) wanted to improve her husband Dave by (lovingly) pointing out his weaknesses to him. One by one, she began listing all of his shortcomings and any habits that annoyed her. Each time she berated him, she took a big whack with her clippers.

The audience gasped as chunk after chunk of the beautiful plant began hitting the floor. She would scold him (*chop*), put him down (*chop*), and correct him (*chop*) — all the while declaring how much she loved her husband and wanted to help him.

After a few minutes, the lush, healthy plant that represented Dave was bare. It was leafless, forlorn, and ready for the trash. The visual of how words can strip a man of dignity and purpose was clear. Instead of building his confidence, she had reduced him to a mere "stump" of himself.

Instead of giving him silver boxes with bows (eight-cow thinking), she was undermining him. Ann was demonstrating one-cow thinking by pointing out her spouse's weaknesses instead of his strengths. Her intent was good, but cutting words (pun intended) will hurt any relationship.

INSIGHT: We are *not* suggesting you ignore difficult situations or fail to discuss bad behaviors. Quite the opposite; tough love is often necessary. As we'll see in later chapters, candid communication and conflict resolution are necessary components of a healthy relationship. Our point here is that the overarching tone of our speech and actions should be *positive, optimistic,* and *affirming*.

———

Johnny Lingo teaches us that to have a vibrant, successful marriage we need to understand how the words we choose can help our spouses (and ourselves) to change the inner stories that may be holding us back.

Even if you're lactose intolerant, an "eight-cow marriage" is worth striving for!

Did this occur to you? Chris and I picture Johnny Lingo representing Jesus, and Sarita representing mankind. God loved us so much, that even in our ugly, fallen state he paid a shockingly high price for our salvation. Beyond its obvious application to marriage, Patricia McGerr's story suggests the incredible "dowry" Christ paid for us on the cross. Our hope is that you will feel like an eight-cow person, a precious child of God with divine potential.

TALK IT OVER.

Time to put on your thinking cap. Discuss these topics with your spouse:

1) Do you feel like a one-cow spouse or an eight-cow spouse? Be honest. What can you do to help each other change your self-image for the better with a Johnny Lingo focus on positivity?

2) Think back to your childhood. Were there any significant people in your life who impacted how you see yourself — positively or negatively — with their words? If negative, what can you do to change that?

3) How do you talk about your marriage and your spouse around others? Is it usually in a positive or negative light? If your current language is not helping your relationship, how can you change it?

TAKE ACTION.

Let's practice what we preach. These fun steps will get you started:

1) For 30 days, commit to only using positive speech. Put a "Negative Jar" in the kitchen. When either spouse says something negative, toss $1 in the jar. At the end of the month, use the money to go on a date and discuss the experience of focusing on the positive power of words.

2) Make a game out of "catching each other doing something right" with your spouse for a month. Decide on a prize for the winner — jot down 5 points for every time you catch your spouse doing something right and complimenting them about it! The most points in 30 days wins.

CHAPTER 3

Can You Hear Me Now?
Keys to effective communication

It's a foggy night in the North Atlantic. A tired Navy captain is standing on the bridge of his ship after a long week at sea.

Radar hasn't been invented yet, and because of the fog, the captain has sailors stationed as lookouts. Suddenly, one of the men runs up to him, "Sir, we've spotted a light coming right at us. We're going to collide!"

The captain orders his radioman to send a message. "Tell them, 'You are on a collision course. Advise you change your heading by 20 degrees!'"

They get an immediate response, "I suggest you change *your* heading by 20 degrees."

The captain is offended. He snaps out an order, "Tell them 'I am a U.S. Navy *captain* and I advise you to change your course.'"

A response comes across, "I am a *second-class seaman* and I advise you to change your course."

By now the captain is furious. He growls, "Tell them 'I am a 40,000-ton *battleship* and I advise YOU change course now.'"

The reply comes back, "I am a *lighthouse*. Advise YOU change course now."

What a difference a few words can make!

Without clear communication, we all run the risk of crashing our marriage into the rocks. We're surrounded by shipwrecks and it's often because couples don't *understand the message* their spouse is sending.

I have to admit that I can identify with the captain. Sometimes my pride gets the better of me. Can you relate? Being stubborn or pulling rank on our spouse makes it even harder to hear the important warnings they're sending.

And the resulting confusion is a stone-cold marriage killer.

"Lack of communication is the *leading cause* of divorce in couples I've worked with." That's what Minneapolis-based therapist Eva Kraus-Turowski told Melina and me. After 38 years of working with couples, Eva found the most serious communication failures occur "in the areas of finances, sex, and raising children."

It's no surprise that open communication is critical to a thriving marriage. Yet most of us take it for granted. In this chapter we'll explore the important differences in communication styles and how to adjust for our blind spots.

The art of conversation.

Communication is defined as "using words, signs, or behaviors to express your ideas, thoughts, and feelings to someone else."

In a marriage, that "someone else" is our spouse. And we must learn how to express our "ideas, thoughts, and feelings" to them in ways they can understand and embrace. If not, we're doomed to a subpar relationship.

Many people assume their spouse automatically knows what they're feeling or thinking. But why? When we go to lunch, we don't assume the waiter knows what we want — we *tell* them. And then we make them *repeat it back*. How much more important to make sure we're on the "same page" with our spouse!

No matter how much we love each other, we are two separate beings. Two brains, two personalities. And no matter how well we know each other, we will inevitably miss some distress signals and emotional symptoms. If we cannot effectively verbalize our thoughts and feelings, our marriage won't last.

Bottom line? We can be truly, deeply, madly in love, but to go the distance, we all need to upgrade our interpersonal communication skills.

First, we need to step back and look at a key difference between men and women. In his classic book, *His Needs, Her Needs: Building an Affair-Proof*

Marriage, Dr. Willard Harley drops a bombshell. He says the number one need for a woman in a relationship is (drumroll, please) *communication*.

Can you guess what it is for men? That's right, sex.

Communication is as important for a woman as sex is for a man! (By important, I mean "urgent, essential, gotta have it.") I was honestly surprised to learn this, and I'm guessing most guys do not understand this dichotomy. That's not to say sex and other needs aren't important to a woman; it's just that communication tends to be the most important.

> If we can't verbalize our feelings, our marriage won't last.

Melina has pointed this out to me many times. If she doesn't feel connected to me *emotionally* by our communication, she won't be very eager to connect with me *sexually*. Guys, here's a tip between brothers — you'll find your wife to be more open and responsive to you about making love when you keep her "communication tank" filled. If you want better (and more frequent) sex, don't let your spouse's communication gauge read empty.

I'm a slow learner, but I know this from *experience*.

One night I was really in the mood for what prisoners call a "conjugal visit." We were in bed, the candles were lit, and I was anticipating fireworks. Suddenly, Melina started chattering away about something! Needless to say, this unexpected verbal interruption totally killed my mojo. I was tempted to be frustrated and angry and just roll over (a very mature response, don't you think?). Thankfully, I decided to sit up and pay attention instead of pouting. Considering the awkward timing, I figured that whatever she had to say must be important for her to get out. Here's the kicker: While I was respectfully and enthusiastically listening, Melina began to feel highly connected to me emotionally.

The result? Let's just say the rest of the night was rated "R" for remarkable.

It may sound oversimplified, but good sex depends on good communication. Dr. Kevin Leman says "Sexual intimacy is an expression of the care a couple shows each other in communicating their thoughts, sharing their feelings, and even doing chores around the house." Which explains the title of his book, *Sex Begins in the Kitchen: Creating Intimacy to Make Your Marriage Sizzle*.

> **True intimacy is cultivated outside the bedroom.**

Leman's main point is that true intimacy is cultivated *outside* of the bedroom and not the moment you light the scented candles. Couples have to be intentional about carving out time for regular, in-depth conversations. Life is way too crazy to expect opportunities to just pop up.

Dating is easy. Marriage is hard.

After the honeymoon, keeping emotional intimacy alive and well depends on how much talking and listening we're doing.

INSIGHT: The happiest couples we know — regardless of age — are the ones who don't relegate communication to the back burner. They schedule "alone time" with each other to share their needs and feelings away from the deadlines and demands of kids and careers. That oasis may be as basic as taking a daily stroll together or sharing coffee before the rest of family wakes up.

The sounds of silence.

If you're a parent, you know the joy of hearing your child's early attempts at talking. At first, it's unintelligible. But around six months or so, those sweet sounds start to become real words. You may even recognize "Mama" and "Daddy." If you're like me, you will cry over this miracle and grab your video camera. At some magical time between 18 and 24 months, our kids began forming little two-word and three-word sentences. Then they started stringing more words together. Before long we were having conversations with them!

So if *toddlers* can do it, why is this communication thing so hard for us adults?

The answer is partly in our DNA and partly in our attitudes.

Remember how easy it was when you were first dating? Chris and I jabbered around the clock! We never ran out of subjects to discuss. But over time, things can happen in a marriage that constrict the verbal connection. We've all seen those sad, muted couples sitting in a restaurant with nothing to say, staring at their food, surrounded by happy diners shooting the breeze.

Don't get me wrong. Not all silence is bad.

Chris and I often enjoy the priceless experience of sharing time and space together without the need for spoken words. It could be hiking a trail, watching a sunset, or just riding beside each other in the car. Infused with love, connection, and our own brand of ESP, these are the positive sounds of silence.

But there's a *negative* side, too.

Many married couples endure the kind of silence that reflects disconnection, boredom, tension, exhaustion, or conflict. I have married friends who confide this frustrating descent into silence, "Melina, we just don't talk anymore."

Is this conversational dead zone inevitable?

Great question! For most couples, it's an uphill battle as the years roll by. But there is real hope for change once you understand the problem — and the *causes*.

In her article, "When Couples Stop Talking: Reasons and Remedies," psychologist Suzanne Phillips targets some of the reasons people clam up:

• **The Monologue.** Sometimes a spouse is so needy for attention or affirmation that they never stop talking. Interested only in their own words, they leave no space for a response. Like a bored audience, the listening partner dutifully complies, but eventually sees no reason to continue.

• **The Critique.** Speaking has become "unsafe." If a partner implies by criticism or obvious disinterest that what the other is saying is unimportant, the speaker shuts down. Some are embarrassed into silence. Some give up. Some find outside confidantes eager to listen (can you say *affair*?).

• **The Interrogation**. This happens when a spouse demands their partner report the day's events or demands a reaction to their remarks. They turn the natural wish to share into an obligation. The result is an emotional shutdown. Events may be reported, but no one is really communicating.

Sometimes an uncomfortable silence occurs because one partner is holding back important info from the other. This "secret" can be a moral failure, financial problem, marital infidelity, self-doubts, or even a new personal goal. At this point, authenticity is impossible and real communication is compromised.

A tragedy or traumatic event can also drive a couple into silence. Whether it's the death of a loved one, a job loss, or a serious illness, they avoid discussing it as a way to avoid the bad feelings attached. Until some degree of healing occurs, talking about the event (or anything else) feels impossible.

Most of us have experienced some or all of these conversational roadblocks, either with spouses or friends. Negative emotions and events can disrupt any relationship — and create a wide gulf of silence.

In a *Psychology Today* article, Dr. Barton Goldsmith lists additional reasons couples don't communicate:

• **Laziness**. No deep mystery here. Some spouses are just too lazy to want to engage in conversation. They'd rather hang out and stare at a TV instead of using their heads and hearts to connect with someone they claim to love.

• **Exhaustion**. Sometimes even the best conversationalist will be too tired to talk. Sooner or later, we all get physically or mentally drained. When it happens, lovingly tell your spouse you'd like to chat with them — at a later time.

• **Bitterness**. Unhealed anger will make almost anyone withhold conversation. If you're mad at someone you love, tell them and get it out in the open, so you can get back to normal. The "silent treatment" never solves a problem.

Complacency is the enemy here. We must be proactive.

It's not about *having* time to talk. It's about *making* time.

Dr. Goldsmith says, "If you're a busy person, you might not think about taking time out to talk with those you care for. Make sure your life doesn't take away from your love. The conversations don't have to take long; they just have to take place."

Doing nothing is not an option. Creating opportunities to communicate at a deep level with our spouse is mandatory. I can almost hear you asking, "But what if that door has been slammed shut on me?"

That's a fair question. *Can* wounded couples find a way to speak again?

Professor Phillips thinks so. "If partners want to reset their relationship, almost anything is possible." She adds, "It is always valuable to start with self, as we have more capacity to change self than anyone else."

With that in mind, ask yourself:

- *Am I speaking in a way that makes my partner want to listen?*
- *Am I listening in a way that makes my partner want to speak?*
- *Are my nonverbal cues shutting down communication and closeness?*

Sometimes, life feels like a treadmill. We get stagnant. Stuck in a rut. If that's you, a change of pace (or place) can stimulate conversation.

A quick way for partners to reset a pattern of talking together is by sharing something *new*. When you jump into a fresh activity, conversation just naturally flows. Things like planning a trip, taking dance lessons, or starting a business are awesome conversation starters.

Professor Phillips adds, "Couples research tells us that what is novel stimulates interest, neurochemistry, and even sexual arousal."

(Maybe *now* Chris will take that ballroom dancing class with me.)

INSIGHT: A great jump starter is doing a project. When two people share a mutual goal, they naturally talk about it. And when they speak, their common interest makes them feel valued. If you've ever worked on a charity event or taken a mission trip, you've experienced that warm shift from stranger to friend. Bonds are formed, emotions are stoked. Sometimes, pursuing a goal even ignites physical desire (which explains why affairs often begin at the workplace!).

Communication breakdown.

Melina's right. When we were courting, we communicated like crazy.

Late nights on the phone, long talks, love notes, the whole bit. And I'm sure it was the same for you. You couldn't wait to unload about your day or how you felt about each other. You never ran out of things to say. Unfortunately, it gets harder as we face the daily stresses inherent with a long-term relationship.

Remember the story of the ship and the lighthouse? The safety of the sailors depended on a two-way transmission. In communication, you always have a *sender* and a *receiver*. That's true for any message, verbal or nonverbal.

In a marriage, we alternate our roles as sender and receiver. And each position has its own risks, rewards, and responsibilities.

It's not about having time to talk. It's about *making* time.

When I am the sender, I want my spouse to understand something. It's my responsibility as initiator to communicate in a way Melina will clearly understand.

If someone doesn't speak Spanish, but you address them in that language can you really blame them for not understanding? *Es una locura y una injusticia!* (Translation: "That's really too crazy for words and very unfair.")

Nothing you're trying to convey — romantic desire, vital information, whatever — will get across unless the sender speaks in the receiver's language.

Likewise, the receiver has a responsibility. It's important that we really "listen" to what our mate is saying, not just "hear" their words. *Hearing* is simply the act of perceiving vibrations through the eardrum. It's involuntary and unfocused. *Listening* is something you consciously do. It means your brain is processing the meaning of the words bouncing around the room.

Someone said, "listening leads to learning." True enough. But only if it's the kind of listening that focuses on what's behind the words, not just hearing the syllables. Active, attentive listening is what your spouse desires.

I learned this the hard way — like most guys.

Sometimes when Melina is speaking, she can tell I'm not tuned in. So she calls me out on it, "Hey, you're not hearing a thing I'm saying." Usually, I can smugly repeat what she said word for word, like a trained parrot. But when she presses me, I have to confess to missing the *heart and soul* of what she was trying to convey (I hate it when she busts me ... and she's usually right!).

Clear as mud.

It's a noisy world. We're bombarded with messages.

To keep our sanity, Chris and I have learned to block out lots of nonessential input. But we realize it can be tough for couples to zero in and pay attention to each other. Real listening requires grasping the intellectual premise, the emotional context, and above all, the speaker's intent.

Motivational trainer Zig Ziglar brilliantly demonstrated that *how* you say something can dramatically alter its meaning. Ziglar designed a little game around the simple phrase, "I didn't say she stole the money."

At first glance, it seems basic and clear. Now try reading it out loud and putting emphasis on a different highlighted word each time:

1) "*I* didn't say she stole the money."
2) "I *DIDN'T* say she stole the money."
3) "I didn't *SAY* she stole the money."
4) "I didn't say *SHE* stole the money."
5) "I didn't say she *STOLE* the money."
6) "I didn't say she stole the *MONEY*."

The same words can have decidedly different meanings. Version 4 implies that somebody stole the money but doesn't say who. Version 5 suggests that maybe she just borrowed the money. And in Version 6, the implication is she stole something, but not necessarily the money.

This humorous exercise shows the risks of casual listening.

It also shows the overwhelming superiority of a face-to-face exchange versus relying on social media, email, or texting, where context and intent is often lost. Somebody wisely said, "Texting is a brilliant way to miscommunicate what you feel and misinterpret what other people mean."

Active listening.

Popular radio host Dennis Prager says, "I prefer clarity over agreement."

That goal is especially helpful in a marriage. One way to boost clarity and understanding is to employ "active listening."

This term simply means you're trying to *concentrate, understand,* and *respond* to what's being said. An active listener asks for clarification during the conversation by paraphrasing snippets of it back to the speaker.

For instance, I often interject questions to Melina as she's talking: "So what I hear you saying is such-and-such. Is that correct?"

This interaction accomplishes two things:

1) **Clarification**. It confirms what you think your spouse is saying — on the spot. It clears up misunderstandings and keeps both parties engaged and alert. If something is missing, each side can quickly correct the error and move on.

2) **Affirmation**. Active listening validates your spouse. It says you really care about the conversation, that it's important to you (because it should be!). This kind of approval builds up good feelings about you and

the relationship.

To be an active listener, eliminate distractions (turn the TV off, don't check Instagram), keep your emotions in check (don't overreact, don't argue), and refrain from judging (don't insert your opinions, don't shut down the speaker).

In his book, *Devotions for a Sacred Marriage,* Gary Thomas says marriage is a call to listen. But instead of listening patiently, human nature wants the instant gratification of getting our licks in first! Thomas says, "Our natural, arrogant selves are eager to speak, to be heard, and to be understood. We can't wait to express our opinion, state our outrage, or make clear our intentions."

(Does this man have a camera inside my home?)

I often find myself half-listening, just waiting for a pause in the conversation so I can interject my pearls of wisdom. Business author Stephen Covey nailed it, "Most people do not listen with the intent to understand; they listen with the intent to reply."

> God gave us two ears and just one mouth for a reason.

I'm beginning to see a pattern here. Maybe God gave us two ears and just one mouth for a reason. What does the Bible say about our tendency to speak instead of listen? *"Don't talk so much. You keep putting your foot in your mouth. Be sensible and turn off the flow!"* (Prov. 10:19 TLB).

I'm not a theologian, but I get it. Gary Thomas puts it this way, "The pause button on my tongue's remote control should get much more use than the play button."

German author Paul Tillich agrees, "The first duty of love is to listen."

You've probably heard, "90 percent of all communication is nonverbal."

This concept comes from research done by Dr. Albert Mehrabian of UCLA back in the '60s. His pioneering work revealed that 55 percent of communication is body language, 38 percent is our tone of voice, and only

7 percent is the actual words spoken. The exact ratio depends on context, but it's basically true.

Mehrabian found that our gestures, posture, and expressions convey a host of subtle (and not-so-subtle) signals. These nonverbal elements present a listener with important clues to the speaker's inner thoughts and true feelings. They can *reinforce* what you're saying or *contradict* your words. To be effective in communicating to our spouse, it's essential we complement our words with the appropriate body language and the right tone of voice.

Your words mean little when your nonverbals are saying the opposite.

The ancient Chinese philosopher Lau Tzu said, "The soul has no secret that the behavior does not reveal." In other words, your words mean little or nothing when your nonverbal language is saying the opposite.

The reverse is also true! To *listen* better, watch your spouse for facial expressions, eye contact, gestures, posture, and tone of voice.

Remember, nonverbal signals can increase trust, clarity, and rapport. Or generate tension and mistrust. Unspoken physical clues will tell your spouse if you care, if you're being truthful, and if you're listening closely.

The Fix-It Guy.

Remember *Home Improvement*? There wasn't anything Tim the Tool Man couldn't fix with the right tools and just a little more power!

Guys especially loved Tim Allen's role as a typical male who loved working with his hands (but hated reading the instructions). If something broke, Tim could always repair it, even if it cost more than buying a new one.

Tim set the bar for every husband who is called to fix a leaky faucet or repair a broken appliance. That's cool; we're up to the task. But guys, when it comes to communicating with your spouse, being the Fix-It Guy is a bad move.

Fix-It Guy is always ready to save the day with his utility belt of ready answers and quick solutions. When his wife speaks, his immediate reaction is not to listen and reflect, but to grab a hammer and solve it for her right then and there by saying, "Well, *here's* what you *should* do ..."

Gentlemen, unless your wife is specifically asking for help, avoid jumping to a solution right away. Most of the time, she just wants you to listen so she can bounce ideas off you or get something out of her system.

That trait touches on another key difference between men and women.

Men tend to compartmentalize things. When we deal with something, we check a box. We close that door in our minds. We are then immediately free to move on to the next compartment. Women, on the other hand, tend to have numerous things symbiotically connected in their minds and emotions. One thing flows to the next and to the next, like an intricately woven jumble of string.

When her husband jumps to a solution too quickly, a wife can feel frustrated, unimportant, even trivialized. While the husband is racing toward a quick fix, the wife is still inching along the zillions of interconnected strands in her brain, trying to figure out what she's feeling at that particular time.

This disparity was a hard lesson for me to learn because Melina and I are on the extreme opposites of the scale. I'm very quick to jump to a solution; she is very thoughtful and reflective. I'm like a hunter who wants to "kill that task" and move on to the next target. Melina, however, is very verbal and can talk for long stretches of time (unwinding that knot of emotional string) before she even arrives at what she's feeling or trying to communicate.

Sometimes there's a rational progression, sometimes not. A typical *non sequitur* from her might prompt me to ask, "Honey, how did we get from your friend Patti and her sick horse to the space shuttle to our kids' math grades?"

> When it comes to communicating, being the Fix-It-Guy is a bad move.

Sometimes she just needs (or wants) to talk; there's no particular purpose or point she's trying to make. She's just communicating freely, like a musician strumming a guitar in a jam session. This was hard for me to grasp. Eventually I learned to ask in advance if there was ever going to be a point or not, so I could skip the frustration of digging around for one.

Nowadays, she signals me in advance, "Honey, there's no point here. I'm just talking." That caveat lets me know I can relax and enjoy listening to her and not feel exasperated by trying to find a focus when there isn't one.

Another thing women do well is effortlessly switch from one topic to another.

Men avoid touchy subjects until they can't be ignored.

To help me keep up, Melina devised another cue. When she's discussing one subject and flows into another, she announces, "I'm shifting gears on you." If she's talking about the kids' homework, then segues into the price of tomatoes, I'm prepared! Instead of waiting to see *if* and *when* and *how* the "grocery store" will ever connect back to the "homework," I just enjoy the ride.

These nuggets worked wonders to improve our communication.

When a groom carries his bride across the threshold, he's toting baggage from two distinctly separate worlds. Each newlywed brings along their own past experiences, value system, and personality quirks. Each brings their expectations of what love and respect are, based on their family environment growing up.

Even the way we show and receive affection tags along with us. All these disparate elements come crashing together into the "oneness" of marriage.

This mash-up can be rough.

Feelings get hurt. Hopes get dashed. Egos get bruised.

Early in your relationship (and throughout the marriage), it's critical you communicate openly about your needs. Men often make the mistake of avoiding touchy subjects until they can't be ignored. They compartmentalize issues and *pretend* things are okay until a situation escalates or certain critical needs are not being met. Then their bottled-up, stuffed-down lack of fulfillment starts to bubble out or, in some cases, explodes in a messy argument.

Women, on the other hand, tend to assume husbands are mind readers and will automatically pick up on their wife's unspoken needs. At some fairy-tale level they imagine: *If he really loves me, he'll know exactly what I'm needing.*

Uh, excuse me, but he won't! Unless you happened to marry a psychic (I didn't), you will have to say it, sing it, write it, mime it, and maybe tattoo it on his forehead to make an impression on his male brain!

> Women tend to assume husbands are mind readers.

As the *sender*, it's important to be really truthful here, even if it's embarrassing or uncomfortable at first. As the *receiver*, it's important to be accepting, nonjudgmental, and utterly respectful about your spouse's needs.

Both parties must learn how to honestly share what they need, in a language their spouse will understand.

The language of love.

Want to know what makes your partner tick?

Try speaking their "love language."

That term was coined by longtime relationship counselor Gary Chapman. His bestseller, *Five Love Languages: The Secret to Love That Lasts*, makes a lot of sense. The basic idea is that we all express and feel love differently — and understanding those differences can help our relationships.

Truth is, it's one of the simplest ways to improve communication.

Chapman says, "There are basically five emotional love languages. Within the five basic languages are many dialects."

Why does it matter? Learning the right "language" is a way to *understand* each other. For example, suppose a wife expresses love by giving her spouse special, carefully chosen gifts. She's hurt and frustrated when he brushes them off with a lukewarm reaction. But once she realizes that "Receiving Gifts" isn't his love language, the ho-hum response makes sense. She finds that a better way to reach him is "Words of Affirmation," telling him how special he is. Both spouses will be far happier.

With a little effort, couples can learn each other's language and then incorporate it in their communication style (to access Gary Chapman's free online survey, check our Take Action section at the end of this chapter). Find out what your partner needs, then try to meet it — in the appropriate language.

In case you're wondering, Melina and I asked ourselves these questions a long time ago and the results were spot on:

• For Melina, "Quality Time" turned out to be her primary language, followed by "Physical Touch" as number two. I prioritize time with her by going on long walks, driving trips, and date nights. Sometimes it's just sitting side by side in the backyard. From a coffee shop to a weekend getaway, the key is we're *alone together*.

• For me, "Words of Affirmation" is my primary language, also followed by "Physical Touch." My wife is very encouraging! She puts love letters under my windshield wipers and sticks Post-it notes on the bathroom mirror. Just when I need a boost, she texts me with the affirming words I crave. The key is she pumps me up.

> Learning the right "language" helps us understand each other.

To meet our mutual need for touchy-feely stuff, we're romantic, creative, and playful with each other. We're constantly hugging, kissing, and holding hands (yeah, it embarrasses our kids). Meaningful touch can be a peck on the cheek or a full massage.

Maybe you're thinking, *Sounds good, but who's got the time?*

"Being busy is no excuse," Chapman says. "If we understand the importance of keeping love alive in a relationship, then we need to make time to do it." How? Like all your important appointments, lock it into your schedule. In writing if you have to!

No matter what a couple's love language is, it takes intentionality to communicate on an emotional level. And that means making it a priority.

For example, I know that Melina craves time with me. So I'm careful to set aside chunks of my life — big or small — when I can give her my undivided attention. One day we might spend time wandering around a local flea market. Or we might take a drive along the coast. Other times, we meet for lunch or just lie in the backyard looking up at the stars. When the kids were small, we made sure to hire a babysitter on a regular basis so we could reconnect and talk for hours at our favorite date night bistro.

Incidentally, just because we recognize and utilize our primary languages doesn't mean that the runners-up aren't relevant or important to us. They are. It's just that the others matter more.

"You can receive love in all five languages," Chapman says. "If you speak the primary language adequately, then when you sprinkle in the others, it's like icing on the cake."

Love languages aren't a magic cure for every problem, of course. They can't make your pile of bills shrink or stop your spouse from snoring. But they go a long way in communicating better, and we believe that is Job One in a marriage.

> **INSIGHT**: Improving communication will improve virtually any relationship, not just marriage. In a work environment or social situation, it's enormously useful to understand what matters most to people you deal with. Think how it can help you better understand friends, co-workers, and family — especially children. Learning how our kids were "wired" allowed us to adjust our parenting style for each.

Melina here. Failure to communicate allows molehills to become mountains.

Here's an example. When our children were toddlers, I would stay home and run the house while Chris worked. As all parents know, even the best kids can wear you down, and my days were exhausting.

When Chris stepped into the house after work, my expectation was that he would immediately engage with the kids and play with them. Surely, he missed his family after being gone all day! Instead, he would walk right by them to check voice messages and read the mail. That ticked me off. I reacted angrily and even compared him unfavorably to other dads we knew. Bad idea. Instead of feeling motivated to change, he felt attacked and defended himself. Loudly. Later on, I tried a wiser approach. I shared how I was feeling disappointed and a little hurt.

When I opened up the lines of communication, he was able to explain that it wasn't that he didn't *love* the kids or want to *engage* with them, but that he just needed a little time to decompress and separate himself from his day at work.

Chris needed to move from the "work" compartment to the "dad" compartment. By communicating with him, I was able to understand *his* need to unwind and detach from work. And he was able to understand *my* need to have him be a loving, active father with our kids. It was a win-win deal.

But what if I hadn't told him how I was feeling?

What if I had naively assumed "he should just know" what I was upset about? Over time, my resentment might have turned into bitterness. And that attitude could've seeped into how I spoke and interacted. By the time Chris and I finally addressed the cause of my anger, he might've already withdrawn by burying himself in his job or hobbies. Or maybe by confiding in a member of the opposite sex at work or at the gym — anywhere he could find release from the tension of our unresolved situation.

> Failure to communicate allows molehills to become mountains.

It's easy to see how so many marriages end up on the rocks because couples neglect communicating openly and honestly. If we don't talk about our feelings and needs, problems only get worse. (In the next chapter, we'll address ground rules for talking through particularly thorny issues.)

Keeping it real.

Over the years, I've developed three communication "coaching points." They're simple but have proved effective for us. Ready?

1) **Guys, when you get home, don't ask your wife, "What did you do today?"** It seems harmless, but to me it felt like an interrogation. It made me defensive — as if I needed to justify everything I did (or did not do) that day. I knew it wasn't Chris' desire to put me on the spot, but it was annoying. I explained it would be better to ask me something open-ended like, "How was your day today?" That simple rephrasing invited me to freely express my feelings and emotions.

2) **Guys, we girls think and talk differently than you!** When two women talk, we interrupt each other all the time, flowing easily from one topic into the next. It's just how we do it, so try not to get upset when your wife does it to you. And ladies, please understand your husband will likely take it as you not respecting what he's trying to say or that you're not listening. Which could result in him shutting down.

3) **Couples, there are certain deadly trigger words we never allow in our vocabulary.** They are *always* ("You always spend too much … You always side with your mother"), and *never* ("You never listen to me … You never want to have sex"). Of course, we also took the word *divorce* off the table long ago. Ban it from your home, too. We'll do a deep dive into this trio in the next chapter on conflict resolution.

Don't you hate glib answers?

When I asked our teenage son Alex how his day was, he used to reply with the universal "Fine." In the Hann family, that doesn't cut it.

I crave more details. I want to hear specifics like, "Football practice was really good. I made some great catches that the coaches noticed." If I don't get them, Mama Bear comes back strong with more questions for him!

Why is that important at his age? One day I picked Alex up from school and got the usual one-syllable answers to my usual questions. Then I imagined him as a grown man — as a husband. If he didn't learn the value of open communication now, he might give his future wife the same annoying default. ("How was work? *Fine.* Drive home? *Fine.* Our marriage? *Fine.*")

> There are certain deadly trigger words we never allow in our vocabulary.

Right there, I described how critical communication is to a woman, and how it would serve him well as a future spouse to learn it now. While I was sharing, I remembered how Chris had helped me understand his need for decompression time after work. Driving home, I asked Alex to think about "downtime" and to let me know how long he needed to decompress. We drove along in silence. Then, out of the blue, Alex blurted, "Five minutes. That's what I need to decompress, Mom. After I get separated from the day, I can get into more details with you."

It's amazing he grasped that concept at age 15. I am thrilled he will be so much further ahead in his relationship skills than we were as newlyweds!

INSIGHT: In general, women want the *fine print* ("How did that make you feel?"), while men want the *headlines* ("What's the bottom line?"). So, ladies, give your husband the main point up front! Or at least get there quickly and *then* ask if he's up for hearing more of the collateral. Conversely, men should be prepared to expound on their topic *du jour* with gentlemanly patience ... and juicy details.

TALK IT OVER.

Discuss these topics and (actively) listen to your spouse's answers:

1) On a scale of 1-to-10, how do you rate your effectiveness as a communicator in your marriage? Discuss what each of you can do to improve.

2) Are there unmet needs or expectations that cause friction in your marriage because you haven't openly communicated? If so, what are they? How can you work together to make sure those needs are met?

3) What is one thing you need to improve as a communication *sender* to your spouse? As a *receiver* from your spouse?

TAKE ACTION.

Action speaks louder than words. These steps will get you moving:

1) Discover your love language — online for free. Each of you will take a fun 10-minute analysis to determine your emotional communication preference. The results are emailed back to you. Click on *5LoveLanguages.com/profile*.

2) Practice being an "active listener." Each of you will listen carefully and intentionally to your spouse on any subject of their choice for 10 to 20 minutes. Then reverse roles.

CHAPTER 4

Conflict Resolution:
I love you, but I want to strangle you

Ken Jennings holds the record for the longest winning streak on *Jeopardy!* In 2004, Jennings won an amazing 74 games in a row. He netted $3,196,300.

That's a person who wants to be right. All the time.

All … the … time.

Does that sound familiar? A major cause of conflict in marriages is when one or both spouses have to be right all the time.

News flash: Marriage is not like *Jeopardy!* The burning desire to be right won't make you rich and famous. And it won't make Alex Trebek shake your hand.

> Let's quit being obsessed with proving we're right.

But it can make your spouse miserable.

I saw a poster: *Would you rather be right or be happy?* Perhaps a better question is: *Would you rather be right or have a happy home?*

For the sake of domestic tranquility, I suggest we quit being obsessed with proving we're right. For many of us, our competitive spirit drives us to be right about every subject that comes up. I know, because I love to win. If there's a squabble, I say *bring it.* A quarrel? I say *game on.* But there's a downside. Sometimes we win the battle (the argument) and lose the war (the relationship).

If you're stubborn like me, it's hard to concede. Hard to give in. We pride ourselves on being right. But here's an inconvenient truth that can save your marriage: It's better to be *kind* than to be *right*. Better to be gentle than overbearing. Better to yield than to insist on victory.

If we want to stay married, we don't need a razor-sharp mind that speaks well and wins debates. We need a gentle spirit that *listens* well and wins hearts.

I'm not talking about compromising your ethics or ignoring your moral compass. I'm saying be humble and flexible on issues that aren't deal breakers. Keep your insanely high brainpower to yourself and see the bigger picture. Keep your quick wit and snarky comebacks under control.

Vince Lombardi famously said, "Winning isn't everything; it's the only thing." That's good for football, *horrible* for marriage. In a loving relationship, there's no place for fist-pumping, gloating, or trash talk.

> In a loving relationship, there's no place for gloating or trash talk.

In fact, the Bible calls for just the opposite: *"A gentle response defuses anger"* (Prov. 15:1 NLT). I've found this to be true, haven't you? In every potential conflict, you have the option to pour gasoline on a fire or douse it with water. *The Message* translates the same passage as, *"A gentle answer deflects anger, but harsh words make tempers flare."*

Be the spouse with the fire extinguisher.

And yes, I know you're wondering — what finally stumped Ken Jennings?

After winning 74 games, his Final Jeopardy category was Business & Industry, and the clue was: "Most of this firm's 70,000 white-collar employees work only four months a year." Jennings responded with "What is FedEx?"

The right response was "What is H&R Block?"

I'll take anger for $200, please.

Conflict is hard. It's messy. And it can flare up when you least expect it.

A while back, Melina and I had a pretty intense fight outside a local Starbucks. It wasn't about latte versus cappuccino. It was about how to deal with an incident involving one of our kids. By then, our babies were teenagers (how'd *that* happen?) and expressing their growing independence a bit faster than we'd prefer. This young adult thing was new for us and full of potential hotspots.

In the heat of the discussion I said something insensitive. Melina got very upset and left the table in a huff. She grabbed our dog and walked to her car, angry and hurt. Reflecting back, she recalls feeling numb. "I remember thinking, *I'm done ... I don't want to talk about this anymore ... I'm out of here.*"

But as my wife got into her car, she realized that leaving would not help the situation. Despite my harsh words, she decided to come back and discuss it further and work toward resolution. When she walked up, I apologized sincerely and asked forgiveness for what I'd said that hurt her.

Happy ending, right? *Wrong.*

She sat down without saying a word. Internally, she was still angry and wounded by the sting of my hurtful comments. I waited. I tried to make small talk. Nothing worked. After five full minutes with no response, I was frustrated. My attempt to reconcile was being rebuffed. In public. I decided to give her time to cool down by heading to the gym and working off some of my own anger. That was the plan. That's what I intended to say. But what came out was an abrupt, nasty-sounding "If you're not even going to respond, I'm going to the gym."

I stood up, took my gym bag and headed to my car with every intention of leaving. As I put my key in the ignition, I had a flash of insight. Just like Melina, I realized that driving away was only going to pound a wedge deeper between us and push our relationship the wrong way.

I locked the car and walked back. I sat down and looked at her for what seemed like forever before she thanked me for coming back.

It took us over an hour to work through the issue. It was hard, but we both took the time to express what we were feeling, and to listen without stifling the other person with criticism and judgment. Oddly, the argument wasn't about a major issue, but it had escalated into a major fight with embarrassing behavior.

Of course, how we raise our kids is of utmost importance to us. That's a given. But it wasn't the *topic* that was the issue, it was our disproportionate anger. Like two volcanoes.

If either of us had actually walked out and *stayed* out, it could've raised the emotional stakes to a damaging level. The pain and insult of such drastic behavior could've grown into a deeper divide. As time passed, it would have become increasingly difficult to put behind us. My point?

Knowing how to handle conflict without capitulating or escalating is essential.

Conflict is ugly and painful, but it is possible to navigate through it to a win-win outcome — *if* you refuse to take your ball and go home when things get uncomfortable.

Knowing how to handle conflict without throwing in the towel (capitulating) or overreacting (escalating) is essential to a thriving, extraordinary marriage.

Pretend about nothing.

Ever meet a couple who seems too good to be true? A husband and wife who never argue, complain, or toss the occasional dish?

Some couples see conflict (or even the *appearance* of it) as something to be avoided at all costs. Like a root canal or a tax audit. They choose to avoid tough issues rather than face the scary challenge of working through them. So they either live in a make-believe fantasy world (deceiving themselves), or pretend to get along perfectly (deceiving others).

Both are terrible strategies.

As any counselor will tell you, the question is not *if* a marriage will experience conflict, but *when* and how often. All relationships have issues at some point. It's the human condition. What matters most is how well we resolve them.

When a couple tells us they "never fight," Chris and I grimace.

Assuming they're not outright lying, we figure they either don't communicate at all or simply hide from tough issues. Either way is a ticking time bomb. Sweeping emotional junk under the rug is deadly to relationships. Ignoring problems or stuffing them down only delays and intensifies the bad outcome.

Recently, I was challenged by three words of advice by author Larry Crabb: "Pretend about nothing." At first glance, you might think the most successful couples are the ones who never seem to disagree. But the opposite is true. Couples who admit and discuss their conflicts have a huge advantage. They not only help themselves, they inspire others with a dose of reality. Mature, going-the-distance couples don't hide behind masks. They don't fake it. They don't cover up their struggles. And when things go sideways and life goes off the rails, they face their conflicts head-on and find a resolution together.

The title of Crabb's book says it all: *The Pressure's Off.* Conflict can be stressful, but pretending it doesn't exist is even more stressful. It takes tremendous energy to pretend everything is all right when it's not. Once you admit to conflict, healing can begin. You can share the burden and fix the underlying problems.

> The question is not *if* a marriage will experience conflict, but *when*.

Remember the movie *Apollo 13*? Think about the immortal line, "Houston, we have a problem." After hearing a sharp bang and seeing warning lights, astronaut Jim Lovell radioed Mission Control. Notice he did *not* say, "Houston, everything is fine and dandy." He didn't sugarcoat the situation. Lovell recalls, "Oxygen tank number two blew up, causing number one to fail. Our normal supply of electricity, light, and water was lost, and we were stranded 200,000 miles from Earth."

By facing the issue head-on, the astronauts and ground crew devised heroic measures to save the ill-fated mission from disaster.

Whether you're orbiting the Earth or just circling your kitchen table, being authentic about problems is step one.

Try a little tenderness.

Couples who survive conflict develop healthy strategies for moving toward resolution instead of trying to "beat their opponent."

Their goal is not to win some kind of one-sided victory, but to resolve the issue. In my case, this took a huge change in attitude. Psychologist

William James said, "When you're in conflict, there's one factor that makes the difference between *damaging* your relationship and *deepening* it. That factor is attitude."

Over time, my attitude shifted from "winning at all costs" to putting the long-term success of my marriage ahead of my short-term ego boost.

Ever play *Mortal Kombat?* The popular fighting video game is known for its unique "fatalities," finishing moves that allow characters to end a match by destroying their defeated opponents in a violent manner.

> The goal is not a one-sided victory but to *resolve* the issue.

Sadly, some couples approach real-life conflict the same way — they destroy their adversary with a finishing move that crushes their spirit. They use a verbal knockout punch to flatten their opponent. That's fine in a video game. But the goal of conflict resolution in marriage is not to vanquish your foe — it's to find a mutually agreeable, mutually beneficial outcome.

Fresh advice from 2,000 years ago.

In Ephesians, the Apostle Paul tells us to *"speak the truth in love."* Most of us live by half of that verse — *which* half depends on our personality.

Some of us are very good at "the truth" part. We're quick to notice and point out anything wrong in our spouse. We state facts, we confront, we judge. Case closed.

Others of us lean toward the "in love" half. We'd rather do anything than risk hurting someone's feelings or making a fuss. So, we stand by in passivity and silence, tolerating almost any behavior.

Success in communication depends on balancing *both* of these concepts. We should address wrong behaviors, but always with tenderness and sensitivity. We should stand up for what's right, but in a gentle way that honors our spouse.

INSIGHT: It takes balance to ride a unicycle. And it takes balance to keep a conversation from crashing, too. Author and teacher Chuck Swindoll said, "When telling the truth in love, the sole motivation is the good of the other person, which means your speech will be laced (balanced) with patience and kindness."

When conflict arises in our marriage, our aim is threefold: To achieve a joint resolution, to move past the issue at hand, and to grow closer as a couple in the process. We know that if one of us insists on "winning," we both lose something extremely valuable to us.

There's a great scene from the movie *Road House* that sums this up. Patrick Swayze plays a rough-and-tumble bouncer for hire. In one scene, he's getting a cut stitched up by an ER doctor. After checking his lengthy chart and seeing the dozens of scars on his body, she asks glibly, "Have you ever *won* a fight?"

> If one of us insists on "winning," we both lose.

With a serious look on his face, Swayze responds, "*Nobody* ever wins a fight."

That's the point — even if you "win" a fight with your spouse, your marriage loses. There are no winners. And the emotional scars and bruises keep adding up. In his song "Tender Is the Night," Jackson Browne penned an insightful lyric about mutually destructive conflict: "You win, I win, we lose."

Take a moment to reflect on this point; it's a big one.

Rules of engagement.

How do you hold back when your blood pressure's through the roof and every nerve in your body is screaming to protect your turf and wreck your opponent?

When tempers flare, it helps to rely on *predetermined* rules about what is fair and unfair to do and say when a fight breaks out.

When the U.S. military goes overseas, it does not use its massive fighting capabilities indiscriminately. Soldiers follow what's known as "rules of engagement" — written directives that define the circumstances and manner in which deadly force may be applied. For instance, we don't intentionally target civilians, we don't use poison gas, and so on. Certain tactics and responses are off limits.

Same for marriages.

Every couple needs to agree on limits and boundaries for "fighting fair" — well in advance! During peacetime, you both need to predetermine and agree to play the game of conflict by ironclad guidelines for the protection of your marriage.

> Every couple needs to agree on boundaries for "fighting fair."

Melina came up with the metaphor of two boxers entering the ring. Before the first punch is thrown, the referee reminds the fighters of the rules. For example, you cannot hit below the belt. You cannot kick, head-butt, wrestle, bite, spit on, or shove your opponent. Violating any of these rules is considered a foul and results in a warning, point deduction, or even a disqualification.

Without agreed-upon rules, boxers could be severely injured, maimed, or even killed. The goal of a boxing match is to win the decision — without permanently harming your opponent. Likewise, the goal of a marital conflict is to reach resolution without harming your spouse or your relationship.

INSIGHT: Having a plan in place before a conflict starts is essential. But it's no guarantee you'll follow it. In the heat of battle, we can all slip back into destructive patterns. Heavyweight champ Mike Tyson famously said, "Everyone has a plan until they get punched in the mouth." If you cross the line, apologize and start over. If you're normal, you'll have plenty more chances to get it right.

House rules rule.

I don't drive without a seat belt. Or water ski without a life vest. Or bike without a helmet. So why would I ignore basic safety within my marriage?

"Rules give us safety when addressing a threatening subject," says Julie Nelson, a professor at Utah Valley University. And of course, we fully agree with that.

But we didn't *always* have safe boundaries in place ...

We discovered the glaring need for a set of "house rules" early in our marriage. We had just moved into our very first home back in Michigan when it happened. One day we were well into a heated argument about something absolutely important. (It was *so* important that neither of us can remember what it was about. Isn't that the way it often is with conflicts?)

As our fight escalated, my voice got louder and my face got redder. Suddenly, for the first time ever, I blurted out, "You are being such a b***h!"

Melina immediately shut down.

She felt so violated by my outburst that she determined the fight was over and had to leave our apartment that instant. Seeing her walk out so abruptly shook me out of my anger and rage. I had the distinct impression that if she drove off it could begin the unraveling of our young marriage.

I told her, "Don't leave — I'll sleep on the couch if you prefer, but we need to work through this." She relented.

Looking back, we see how critical this event was in setting the first set of ground rules for our marriage. We had both thrown significant bombs at each other. We were both guilty of going over the top. Our negative behavior could easily have set a destructive tone for our marriage. Instead, our hurtful words and actions motivated us to establish healthy boundaries for handling future conflicts.

Thankfully, Melina unselfishly "chose us" that day instead of storming off. As we discussed the episode later, she explained that in her family she had never heard any cussing or personal attacks. No one even used harsh words like *shut up*!

This was a revelation. I grew up surrounded by high-intensity family conflicts that included plenty of swearing and verbal attacks. This penchant for screaming matches and altercations seemed like a normal part of my Polish heritage, tilted to the negative. Unfortunately, as an adult my passionate personality amplified this family trait.

Melina explained that when I attacked her verbally, she was no longer in conflict mode but literally went cold and shut down. For her, resolution was not possible because the fight was *over*. She was done with it and out the door.

For my part, I explained that her quick readiness to withdraw and retreat worried me. I said that shutting down and closing off could undermine our marriage if it became a pattern. As we both cooled off and talked it through, we agreed right then and there on our first two boundaries — rules of engagement that would frame our conflicts for the rest of our marriage:

1) **There would be no cussing or personal attacks.**

2) **We would not walk out or tune out.** We would not leave the scene of any conflict without reaching resolution. (Unless we mutually agreed to a cooling off period. A boxing referee often separates fighters if things get too rough.)

Later, we added a third rule:

3) **We would not go to bed angry.**

I shudder to think what would've happened to our relationship if we'd taken the easier route of pursuing our own self-protective, self-defensive actions.

Both Chris and I have intense personalities.

And we're both natural born "fighters." Without developing those early rules for conflict, I'm fairly certain we would've split up like our families had. Remember, our parents on both sides are all on their second or third marriages. We could have easily followed suit.

Going back to our boxing metaphor, we pictured ourselves as fighters preparing for battle, having the *ropes* (boundaries), the *referee* (rules), and the *mat* (the firm foundation beneath us) in place. These three elements protected our unwavering commitment to the relationship. They gave us the security and freedom to enter into conflict without fear or shame.

INSIGHT: This cannot be a one-way street. To ensure *fairness*, we decided to set the guidelines together, based on open discussions and mutual agreement. To ensure *clarity*, the reasons behind the rules would be totally understood by both of us. If one spouse is not onboard, any rules you make are virtually useless.

Don't sleep on it.

Ever hop in the sack boiling mad?

All that pent-up emotion and stomach acid make for a rotten night. But unresolved anger can cause even bigger problems than sleeplessness.

Our third rule of engagement was "We won't go to bed angry." This wisdom comes direct from the Owner's Manual. In Ephesians 4:26, Paul advises, *"Do not let the sun go down while you are still angry"* (NIV).

Early on we determined not to say goodnight with unresolved issues hanging in the air. This isn't always easy. One night we'd been struggling with a conflict for several hours (unsuccessfully) and were both dead tired. Frankly, we just wanted to go to sleep. It was 4 a.m. before we were finally able to work through the issues, feelings, and emotions to reach a solid resolution.

Next day we were completely exhausted. But we both felt good about it. Being tired was proof we had "chosen us" and stuck to our commitment to obey our own rules. Our relationship grows stronger with each late-night resolution. Even if we're sleep-deprived zombies the next day.

Why not just douse the lights and deal with it tomorrow?

Because it's human nature to take the easy way out. We'd find a dozen excuses by breakfast to drop the subject and go on with our busy schedules. Conflicts that aren't handled promptly can keep growing like an infection festering under the skin, until marital gangrene sets in and requires drastic measures.

Do we ever bend the rule? There are rare times when Chris and I agree to set a conflict aside (temporarily) to rest up for a fresh perspective in the morning. But it's only with the mutual understanding that we'll take up the discussion at the first opportunity on the following day.

Going to bed angry not only causes hard feelings in the short term, it erects a relational wall that gets higher each time you fight. The negative consequences are cumulative, and over time they create an atmosphere of hopelessness and resignation. If the bedroom becomes a place of simmering resentment, two things are going to suffer — your sex life and your sleep patterns. Protecting both is vital for physical health, emotional stability, and a happy marriage.

> Conflicts that aren't handled promptly keep growing like an infection.

Family First founder Mark Merrill says, "How you handle end of day conflicts either builds up or tears down your marriage. The message you send to your spouse when you have a pattern of going to bed angry is that your marriage and your spouse's well-being are less important to you than winning in conflict."

Science agrees with this biblical advice. A recent study in *The Journal of Neuroscience* published evidence that indicates going to sleep after experiencing negative emotions reinforces or "preserves" the icky feelings.

That means if you go to bed angry, you wake up just as upset. You don't cool off or mellow out by sleeping — unless you settle the issue *before* nodding off.

INSIGHT: Our friends Gerry and Marilyn have a unique spin on how to patch things up before going to sleep. Their rule is if it's approaching bedtime and they still have unresolved conflict, they must completely undress and face each other in the nude to have the discussion. The openness and vulnerability created by seeing each other in the buff puts the conflict in perspective and helps move them beyond superficialities to resolution. And that's the naked truth.

Don't shoot your mouth off.

All of us say things out of frustration and anger.

But using our tongue as a weapon is the kiss of death for marriage. Unleashing a verbal blast of profanities may feel good for a moment. I get that. But long after the rush of adrenaline subsides, your nasty words are still at work, undermining and eating away at the foundations of your precious relationship.

Depending on your background and where you're at on your spiritual journey, cleaning up your vocabulary may be tough. But do it anyway. Someone said that cursing doesn't add strength to an argument, merely violence. And any kind of violence — verbal or physical — has absolutely no place in a marriage.

Using off-color language against your spouse is awful. And it shows lack of respect. But there are other deadly speech patterns that are equally (if not more) destructive. These threatening or manipulative attacks don't always use curse words, but they contain intimidation, bluffs, and ultimatums:

- *"This isn't what I signed up for."*
- *"Sometimes I wish I never met you."*
- *"If you don't like it, hit the road."*

We vowed to never attack each other with belligerent hyperbole, like taunting the other to "Pack your bags," or "Go back to your parents." (This rule acknowledges the power of words as discussed in Chapter 2.)

It's easy to let hurtful words fly during a fight. But once you say something harsh or vindictive, you can't take it back. There's no rewind button on life. Once uttered, words fly to their target — your spouse's heart — like a poison dart. They embed themselves, seeping poison long after the incident.

I have two friends who suffered the consequences of firing off hurtful barbs at their husbands. They had no "fair fighting" rules in place and no filter on their speech. Both women were very strong fighters with intense personalities. When they got into conflict, they sought to dominate and control. In the heat of anger, they often blurted out things like, "Why don't you just get the blankety-blank out of here? I really don't care and I want you gone."

This kind of bold in-your-face statement would typically end the fight. In an attempt to make peace, the husbands would back down and say something like, "You don't really mean that … I don't want to leave … I'm sorry, you're right."

> Once you say something, you can't take it back. There's no rewind button.

Unfortunately, after years of this unhealthy rhetoric, both husbands decided to take their wife's suggestion and acted on their invitation to leave!

I can imagine their thoughts: *She obviously doesn't want me around. She keeps telling me to leave. I'm sick and tired of all of the fighting. I'm out of here.*

So they packed up and left.

I later found out that neither wife actually wanted their husband to leave — they were "only fighting." They had no clue. And yet their harsh, careless words came true nonetheless. Both women told me sincerely that they never wanted a broken relationship, and their unexpected divorces left them with huge regrets.

Chris and I agreed we would never play that dangerous game.

Things never to say to your spouse.

Over the years, we've asked couples what kinds of speech they find most hurtful. Here's a partial list of things never to say to your spouse:

• *"This is all your fault!"* Ever since Adam blamed Eve, men and women have been ducking responsibility for their own mistakes. In marriage, one partner is rarely (if ever) 100 percent at fault. Share the blame and move on.

• *"Why can't you be more like so-and-so?"* Never make comparisons to other people's husbands or wives. The grass only *seems* greener on the other side of the fence. This insulting question undermines your spouse's confidence.

• *"You're just like your mother!"* Nothing makes a spouse more defensive than an unfair comparison. Plus, by inferring that your in-laws are defective in some way, you're insulting both your spouse *and* their parents.

• *"If you really loved me, you'd do this."* Seriously? Don't be a drama queen (or king). Playing the victim card or coercing your spouse by making them feel guilty is tacky. And it's disrespectful to minimize their true feelings.

• *"My father warned me about you."* Dragging others (parents, siblings, etc.) into a fight only makes matters worse. And telling your spouse they're not liked by their in-laws is devastating. Imagine the vibe at your next holiday dinner.

• *"I don't care."* This blunt phrase is a downer, the ultimate dead end to any discussion. You might think "being neutral" is magnanimous, but it sounds like you're disinterested. Opting out of a decision is seldom good.

• *"Don't be ridiculous."* How can your spouse feel safe sharing their honest opinions if you dismiss their ideas as absurd or silly? Try seeing things from your partner's perspective and don't claim they're overreacting.

• *"Where I go is not your business."* Nobody wants a snoopy spouse. But there should be no reason for concealment, either. Secrecy kills intimacy, arouses suspicion, and shows disrespect. Being open and transparent erases doubt.

• *"I wish we'd never met."* Really? Nothing good has *ever* come from the relationship? This childish fantasy is as foolish as it is harmful. Blaming your partner for every single bad thing since you met can devastate self-confidence.

> **INSIGHT**: Choosing your words is important. But so is the tone of your voice. Speak respectfully and *gently* to each other (remember Mr. Rogers?). There's an old saying, "Nothing is as strong as gentleness, nothing is as gentle as real strength." That notion's almost forgotten in our noisy world. But it's true. India's great leader Gandhi said, "In a gentle way, you can shake the world."

Conversational land mines.

If I make a mistake in golf, I can ask for a mulligan. But in speech, there are no "do-overs." Once a word rolls off my tongue, it's out of my control.

I can try and make amends. I can ask for forgiveness. But the kind of words that weaken confidence in each other are hard to erase. To avoid this, Melina and I agreed that certain derogatory words and concepts were *verboten*.

Even in the blaze of a red-hot debate, these are simply off limits:

• *"I hate you."* The nuclear bomb. Total annihilation. So it's off the table. The rule applies to any declarations that rob your spouse of their self-worth. It includes jabs like "loser" and "pathetic." No eraser can undo these barbs.

• *"Shut up."* This hostile command is rude and disrespectful to anyone, let alone your spouse! Even if you're upset, cutting off the person you love ends the possibility of resolving anything. It's never appropriate.

• *"I want a divorce."* Using the D-word to scare or punish your spouse erodes your relational foundation. It cuts the deepest and it's the hardest to take back. Since splitting up is not even an option for us, why toy with the word?

• *"You always/never do this."* Using absolutes and exaggerations doesn't bring about the desired change — it removes incentives to improve.

These words get tossed out during conflicts as a character attack, angrily pointing out an area where our spouse is lacking ("You *always* quit too soon ... You *never* listen to me"). They escalate the problem by immediately putting the other person on the defensive. Making generalizations takes our focus off the real issue ("We *never* have sex anymore … You *always* watch sports … You *never* give me enough cash") and derails the resolution process.

Not to mention that statements with *always* and *never* are illogical. No husband or wife *always* or *never* does anything!

> **INSIGHT**: We're not saying controlling our words is easy. In fact, just the opposite. The Bible says, *"No human being can tame the tongue. It is a restless evil, full of deadly poison"* (James 3:8 NIV). It takes God's help to use it wisely.

Silence is (not always) golden.

Perhaps the most frustrating tactic in a conflict is the "silent treatment."

Shutting off communication is part of what researchers call the "demand-withdraw" pattern. According to a *Wall Street Journal* story by Elizabeth Bernstein, it occurs when one partner approaches the other with a request (asking for attention or change) and is met with avoidance or deafening silence.

Bernstein writes, "Frustrated by the lack of response, the person who made the demands makes more. The person who withdrew retreats further."

And the problem gets worse. "It becomes a vicious cycle," says Sean Horan, assistant professor of communication at Texas State. "Soon you're no longer addressing the issue at hand. You start arguing about arguing."

(Been there, done that. Yuck.)

Bernstein cites work from *Communication Monographs* that finds the demand-withdraw pattern to be "one of the most damaging types of relationship conflict and one of the hardest patterns to break. It often is a predictor of divorce."

Take that very seriously, readers.

Each partner has a hand in the silent treatment, yet each blames the other. "The demander feels her partner won't open up and her emotional needs aren't being met, while the withdrawer feels he is being hounded."

Analysts say the partner making the demand is typically female (women love to talk things out) while the one withdrawing is typically male (men prefer to process feelings alone). Sometimes the roles are reversed, but both get hurt.

And the resulting damage is both emotional *and* physical.

> Perhaps the most frustrating tactic in a conflict is the "silent treatment."

Researchers found the silent treatment causes "lower relationship satisfaction, less intimacy and poorer communication." Couples showed personality changes, physiological problems, even impaired immune systems.

Ways to beat the silent treatment? Bernstein says, "Agree to take a timeout. It helps to decide on a signal ahead of time." We totally concur — establish rules for resolution *before* conflicts arise ... and before your spouse clams up.

There are 107,601 seats in the Big House.

Two of them belong to me. Every year, my son and I fly back to Ann Arbor to watch the University of Michigan play. It's my alma mater. But it's more than that. Melina says I bleed maize and blue. I watch every game. If I miss one, I record it. I have U of M license plates. In a sea of UCLA and USC flags, I proudly fly the big M.

So I know a bit about football.

And one thing I know is that *whoever's ahead when the clock runs out wins.* But what if one team just kept playing?

That used to be me in a conflict. As long as I was angry, I wouldn't let go — even *after* Melina apologized! Because of my ego, I continued a one-sided discussion despite my spouse being fully ready to resolve the issue.

To avoid this "conflict overtime," we ruled that when either of us is ready to take the first step, the other person has to accept their apology and offer forgiveness upon request. No gloating. No singing "Hail to the Victors."

'Nuff said. Did I mention I'm a Michigan fan?

Finally, a Top Ten list worth reading.

Ladies, is it just me, or is this whole Top Ten thing getting out of control?

One website claims to have 128,569 different Top Ten lists. (Top Ten celebrity stalkers. Top Ten worst Halloween candies. Top Ten people named Rodney, etc.) Their motto is "Top Ten lists for everything under (and including) the sun."

However, they do not have *our* list!

For your marital conflict convenience, we humbly present the official **Hann Family Top Ten Rules of Engagement:**

1) No profanity or personal attacks

2) No storming off and leaving

3) Don't go to bed angry

4) No threatening or manipulative attacks

5) Don't use the words *divorce, shut up, I hate you, always,* or *never*

6) No "silent treatment" or avoidance

7) No hanging up in anger during a phone call

8) No bringing up past issues — stick to the conflict at hand

9) When an apology is made, it's to be accepted without hesitation; when forgiveness is requested, it must be given on the spot

10) Once it's done, it's *done* — conflicts can't be recycled

Got a whistle? Violating any of these rules gives either party full authority to "throw the penalty flag" for ignoring the guidelines.

Without our trusty house rules, we probably wouldn't have made it this far. We'd be toast. And we humbly think they can help any couple. Of course, no set of rules can strengthen your marriage if you don't *apply* what you're learning!

You can adopt our "Top Ten" as they are or tweak 'em to fit. Or even create your own version. Then ask God for strength to implement them.

If you're in the habit of breaking the house rules, don't feel super guilty or beat yourself up. Now's a great time to make a 180-degree change. Ask your spouse for forgiveness, then begin turning away from negative behavior or speech. It will be worth the effort. Except for your relationship with God, marriage is the most important and sacred covenant of your life.

INSIGHT: Not everything in a marriage is worth arguing about. Ask yourself, "Will this matter a month from now? A year from now?" If not, get over it. Don't waste your emotional and intellectual energy on trivial stuff. If you don't pick your battles wisely, you may be too tired to fight fair on the bigger issues.

Five Steps to Conflict Resolution.

We originally titled this section: "Divorce lawyers hate this plan." And they do!

Melina and I utilize a problem-solving framework to deal with tough issues. I can't remember where we first heard it, but I guarantee it will guide you toward resolution while avoiding intense fights, escalating conflicts — or worse yet, attorney fees.

We use these five basic steps in our own marriage to navigate particularly thorny issues (almost always with good outcomes!). I can't overemphasize how helpful they can be in moving even contentious issues to resolution.

Warning: Most people let things simmer until they can't take it anymore, then explode in a burst of anger at their spouse. They delay confrontation until things pass the tipping point, then snap and lash out.

Don't be that couple. Don't wait for the proverbial "straw that breaks the camel's back." Be proactive. Be the initiator. Make these five steps a habit. You'll avoid unnecessary difficulty and pain.

Let's unpack each step and explain its importance:

1) **Pray for God's wisdom.** This seems self-explanatory, yet many people balk at the idea of seeking God's help. All I can say is that God loves you — just as you are —and promises to give you guidance if you ask sincerely. Scripture clearly promises, *"If any of you lacks wisdom, you should ask God, who gives generously to all without finding fault, and it will be given to you"* (James 1:5 NIV).

> Ask yourself: "Will this matter a month from now? A year?"

Let's say you had car problems. Wouldn't it be great to speak directly to the engineer who designed it? What a privilege to ask the Creator of the Universe and Inventor of Marriage for his ultimate knowledge, wisdom, and guidance in your difficult conflicts.

2) **Pick the right place and time.** This is critical. If a wife approaches her husband while he's juggling two sick kids and a backed-up toilet, she's practically asking for a ruckus. He's not in a good place to discuss *any* issue (other than asking for a plumber). Similarly, if a man phones his wife about a conflict while she's making a presentation to her boss at work, he's asking for failure. The key point here is to pick a time when your spouse is not stressed out, physically exhausted, or focused on another task while you try to bring up the issue.

We've found it helpful to get out of the house and go for a walk when we have tough issues to work through. Others talk most freely when they're out driving. Anywhere without interruptions or distractions will work. Just remember that picking the wrong time or place will doom any efforts at resolution.

3) **Affirm the relationship.** The goal of conflict resolution is moving the relationship forward, *not* winning the fight. Tell your spouse how important they are to you; how important your marriage is to you. Tell them what you value most about the relationship. Tell them what you want to preserve, protect, and build upon. This lets them know you want resolution instead of just trying to beat them down. It shows you are "choosing us" instead of "choosing me."

By focusing on what is right and valuable about the relationship, you frame the conversation in a positive light. You also remind *yourself* about the value of the relationship. This avoids our natural tendency to gravitate toward negativity.

4) **State your case in a non-accusatory manner.** This is where most people mess up. The Latin phrase *argumentum ad hominem* means "against the person," attacking a person's character rather than addressing the issues. Used by politicians (and couples), this logical fallacy uses insults instead of evidence to make a point.

Instead of making a negative statement about the person ("You are a total slob — you don't pick up after yourself"), state how their behavior makes you feel ("When you leave the kitchen messy, it makes me feel taken for granted"). This gets us away from a personal attack on our spouse and avoids the typical defensive response. Instead, it moves us into a side-by-side situation with our spouse, rationally evaluating how a specific behavior affects us.

> Conflict resolution is about moving forward, *not* winning the fight.

Unfortunately, most people do the opposite — they go right for the jugular.

It may feel cathartic and empowering to "give them a piece of my mind" and "tell them off." But it's destructive. Marriages often end in divorce because couples do what comes naturally! Instead, let's take Einstein's advice. He said, "Insanity is doing the same thing over and over again and expecting different results." Let's do things *differently* in our conflicts … and get radically different outcomes.

5) **Shut up and listen.** Once you've said what you need to say about an issue, stop talking and let your spouse think it over and respond at their own pace. Be sure your mannerism, body language, and sealed lips give them full permission to speak. Let them take all the time they need.

People in conflict typically get all wound up and present their argument — and then *keep blabbing*. In their agitated condition, they rehash the same issue over and over again. Maybe the emotional release makes us feel better, but it usually shuts our spouse down or (worse) pushes them into a defensive posture.

If you won't quiet down and listen to their response, you are launching what feels like a verbal attack. Needless to say, this usually doesn't end well. And the result is a fight — with each side intent on "winning" instead of discussing options. Shutting up and listening allows your spouse to participate in the cooperative effort of two equals working toward a mutually agreeable resolution.

Picture with me a pair of imaginary couples ...

The first couple has a "fight to win" approach. They direct their anger and frustration directly at their spouse. They would be pictured as a husband and wife standing on opposite corners of a boxing ring, like opponents facing off against each other and ready to rumble.

The second couple has a "resolution and growth" approach. They are standing side by side, shoulder to shoulder. They're both facing their mutual "opponent" — the conflict. They discuss the issue and how to resolve it as a team and then move beyond it. They respectfully address the *issue* instead of attacking each other.

Which word picture describes your marriage?

No piling on, please.

Extending our boxing analogy, imagine a referee at a big Las Vegas title match. What if he were related to one of the fighters? What if he bet money on the outcome? Would that be fair? Of course not.

A good referee must be totally impartial and not favor either boxer. They must have no stake in the outcome.

In the same way, it's important for us to avoid going up into the grandstands to ask our "fans" to help "referee" our match.

I've seen too many people get in a conflict with their spouse and then go to their fan base (friends, family members, etc.) for support! Worse yet, they particularly seek aid and comfort from those who don't have the best opinion about the spouse. The reason they seek outside help is not to work toward resolution, but to gather ammo to strengthen their argument: "Can you *believe* what he did?"

Recruiting reinforcements only drives a deeper wedge into the issue and takes it *farther* away from resolution. Although it's tempting, it's critical that you do not bring in feedback or input from someone who favors you over your spouse. It's hard enough to work through conflict without introducing others who will drag the situation down into the muck of negativity and pandering.

That doesn't mean you should never seek guidance or counsel beyond the two of you. Just be sure it's an *impartial* observer who only has the marriage's best interest in mind. An independent "referee" will help you both work toward resolution and be willing to use tough love if they think either of you is in the wrong. Having someone arbitrate the disagreement can be a good route as long as you're both comfortable with the choice of counselors.

Two things we desperately need.

The Beatles sang, "All you need is *love*."

Aretha sang, "All I'm asking for is a little *respect*."

Turns out they were both right!

These two little words made a big difference in our lives. Here's how: Every couple has their own set of hot-button issues. Certain topics just seem to ignite conflict and cause friction whenever they come up. For Chris and me, it was our finances.

> Every couple has their own set of hot-button issues.

Seemed like anytime we discussed money we ended up in a brawl. Finances are a critical part of a marriage, and as we saw in Chapter 3 on communication, financial disagreements are one of the *top three causes* for divorce.

For years, I tried to bring up finances in different non-accusatory ways. But no matter how diplomatic I was, it always ended badly. Although I believed Chris was a confident man in most areas, I concluded he must be very insecure about finances. Why else would he react so negatively to my attempts to discuss them?

Fortunately, a friend suggested reading *Love and Respect: The Love She Most Desires; The Respect He Desperately Needs* by Dr. Emerson Eggerichs. As I read it, I began to wonder if my husband's angry reaction wasn't because he was insecure, but because he felt *disrespected* by the way I approached the subject.

Finally, I asked Chris if that could possibly be the case. He replied that it definitely was! I was totally floored: *All these years he wasn't feeling respected. He didn't think I trusted his ability to provide for our family.*

We've since made significant strides, but in all honesty, it's still an area we struggle with. However, the key concept from Dr. Eggerichs' book was a huge help in shaping our overall approach to conflict resolution.

In short, it proposes that a wife's deepest desire is to feel *loved*, while the husband's biggest desire is to feel *respected*. If husbands and wives don't speak these gender-specific languages to each other, neither can feel fully satisfied.

Eggerichs bases his premise on a teaching by the Apostle Paul, *"Each man must love his wife as he loves himself, and the wife must respect her husband"* (Eph. 5:33 NLT). Paul is not saying that husbands don't need to feel loved or that wives don't need to feel respected; but certain needs resonate more with each gender.

> Wives desire
> to feel *loved*.
> Husbands desire
> to feel *respected*.

Paul challenges both spouses: Husbands are called to love their wives sacrificially, *"Husbands, love your wives, just as Christ loved the church and gave himself up for her"* (Eph. 5:25 NLT). Equally important, wives are called to respect their husbands. If either doesn't happen, Eggerichs says it's a downward spiral. "When a husband feels disrespected, it is especially hard to love his wife. When a wife feels unloved, it is especially hard to respect her husband."

(In case you're wondering, the "love and respect" issue is absolutely not an excuse for bad behavior by either gender.)

It looked good on paper. Could it be true? We decided to test it out.

If Chris did or said something that provoked an unexpectedly negative reaction from me, he would ask: "Did I do or say something you felt wasn't *loving*?"

Similarly, if he had a strong negative reaction to me, I would ask: "Did I do or say something you felt wasn't *respectful*?"

The questions were not magic bullets that worked 100 percent of the time, but we were both surprised by how often they got to the root of issues. We began to appreciate each other as being *different*, not necessarily *wrong*.

It hasn't been easy. In fact, it's hard work. That's where God comes in.

Accentuate the positive.

Do you ever assume the worst?

I know *I* do. It's a cognitive distortion that psychiatrists call

Even if you're not a pessimist, it's normal to "catastrophize."

"awfulization." Even if you're not a born pessimist, it's normal to occasionally "catastrophize."

Experts say these "snowball thoughts" (where bad things keep getting bigger) occur even in healthy relationships — despite lack of any evidence that they're *valid*. It's the human condition to self-talk ourselves into negative possibilities, but we need to consciously reframe our thoughts when it occurs.

Here's what I mean: Sometimes when we get upset with our spouse, it's not because of what they actually *say* to us, but because of an unintended *meaning* we read into it. So much conflict could be avoided if we learned to stop and assume a *positive* intent instead of a *negative* one.

Sometimes we ascribe dubious intent to a perfectly innocuous statement ("Aren't you overdue for a raise?" or "Looks like she's been working out"). When you wonder if your spouse is implying something negative, give them the benefit of the doubt. Ask yourself: "What is the most positive interpretation of what I just heard?" Again, not foolproof, but it can keep us from immediately jumping to dire conclusions (something I tend to do much more than Melina).

Negative thinking can pop up anytime. It's how we're wired. But when it becomes a pattern, it's problematic. Assuming the worst about our spouse can feed suspicion and distrust. When they phone you, "I'll be late tonight," you have a choice — you can *worry* they're having an affair or *trust* they're just working overtime.

When it comes to conflict resolution, Melina and I believe in the "power of positive expectation." Next time your mind drifts to a negative scenario, try curbing your tendency to think the worst of people — *especially* your spouse.

The power of forgiveness.

Perhaps you've been to a funeral or special event and heard a prayer that sounded familiar. Chances are it was what's called the Lord's Prayer. No portion of the Bible is more frequently quoted. It goes something like this:

"Our Father in heaven, hallowed be your name. Your kingdom come, your will be done, on earth as it is in heaven. Give us this day our daily bread. And forgive us our debts, as we forgive our debtors. Lead us not into temptation, but deliver us from evil. Amen."

Millions have memorized it. Every Christian denomination in the world recites it. But are we willing to *follow* what it says?

Archbishop of Canterbury Rowan Williams warns it won't be easy. "It's radical … It's praying for the most revolutionary change you can imagine in the world."

What's so radical? Right in the middle, the prayer asks God to *"forgive us our debts* (our sins) *as we forgive our debtors* (those who sin against us)."

In other words, my forgiveness by God is linked to *me* forgiving *others*. That's a really scary thought!

The Archbishop agrees, "Praying 'forgive us our debts' is the hardest bit because it tells us straight away that to pray is also to be *willing to change.*"

Husbands and wives, we must be willing to change — willing to forgive our spouses and to ask their forgiveness. It's the essence of conflict resolution. If we technically reach a settlement but harbor animosity and bitterness in our hearts, it defeats the purpose. If we pretend to accept an apology, but inwardly refuse to forgive, we will be miserable and angry.

Psychologists agree. "Forgiveness is a paradigm-shifting solution for transforming anger." That's according to Dr. Judith Orloff. "It liberates you from the trap of endless revenge so you can experience more joy and connection."

> Assuming the worst feeds suspicion and distrust.

There's an old saying that holding a grudge is like drinking poison and waiting for the other person to die. It's totally self-defeating. In an article for *Psychology Today,* Dr. Orloff agrees, "Forgiveness does more for you than anyone else because it liberates you from negativity and lets you move forward."

Amen to that. Forgiveness functions as "oil" to lubricate and smooth out the rough spots in relationships. But asking for it is not *always* from the heart.

For example, many people simply say "I'm sorry" without identifying what it is they're sorry for. Worse yet, they'll offer a weak non-apology ("I'm sorry you feel that way"). The apologizer is not at all sorry for their behavior or speech, but only that silly old you are offended by it! Their non-apology insinuates the person taking offense is irrational or thin-skinned for being upset in the first place.

> Holding a grudge is like drinking poison and waiting for the other person to die.

The key difference between fake apologies and truly seeking forgiveness is specifically calling out *what* action, behavior, or offense we are sorry for ("I'm sorry I lost my temper and yelled at you in the car. I didn't assume positive intent and blew it by calling you names. Will you forgive me?"). Being specific puts the issue clearly in the spotlight so your spouse can see that you understand exactly what caused the hurt … and that you are indeed remorseful.

Sometimes couples do need to "agree to disagree" on minor issues. But for a major conflict, issuing a non-apology is a cop-out that ignores reality. It keeps the relationship stuck, unable to move forward. Brushing off conflict without genuine regret communicates that you don't care. It takes no ownership or accountability for the wrongdoing and basically puts the onus on your spouse: "It's your fault you feel that way (hurt, angry, disrespected, etc.), and I'm sorry for that."

That's *not* a good strategy for resolving conflict. Or for staying married.

———

Forgiving from the heart is difficult work.

Author Nancy Leigh DeMoss targets the problem, "Most people can think of at least one person they struggle to forgive. The pain is too deep, and the hurt is too tender. Christians are no exception. It's the fabric of our fallen world."

As I scan the TV and movies, it seems like revenge and payback are far more popular themes than forgiveness. Retribution and vengeance dominate the news. In her book *Choosing Forgiveness*, DeMoss says, "The mindset of our culture gives us permission to cling to our resentment, broken relationships, and unresolved conflicts, but the Word of God gives us a higher standard ... to forgive even as we have been forgiven."

We can choose to respond to offenses biblically. It's up to us. Forgiving is a choice which frees us from the burdens of bitterness, anger, and isolation.

DeMoss says we can't do it on our own. And we don't have to. "Jesus has already paid the price. He wants us to follow in his steps and walk the road of forgiveness that leads to blessing. He will give you the strength and courage you need."

INSIGHT: Remembering how much *we've* been forgiven will make us more compassionate when our spouses offend us. Picturing Jesus Christ on the cross, asking the Father to forgive his enemies (including us!) will help us respond to hurtful people and unwelcome circumstances with grace and patience.

Getting things unstuck.

Ever go running with a buddy?

Usually one jogger wants to call it quits before the other guy runs out of steam.

It's like that in marital conflicts, too.

Usually one spouse is ready to stop fighting before the other. An effective technique for getting things unstuck is for whoever reaches that point first to take ownership for their part in the issue (big or small) and seek forgiveness from the other. Even if their part's only a fraction of the issue, apologizing for it sends a clear message that they value the relationship, truly want resolution, and (correctly) understand they had a role in the conflict.

Very rarely is one person totally at fault for any conflict!

Admitting your role in the conflict (even if it was only 10 percent) and offering an olive branch of peace helps cool the other guilty party down. You taking the first step helps your (relieved) spouse refocus on the issue at hand. Remember, it's all about *resolution* and *growth* — not "winning."

Don't wait. Don't be stubborn. Be the first to reach out.

Progress, not perfection.

The road to divorce is paved with eye rolls, poor communication, and lots of small, unresolved conflicts. There will always be issues in any relationship — and without resolution, the cost is simply too high. If conflict is ignored, it eventually affects every area, causing emotional turmoil and even physical illness.

Following the "Five Steps" doesn't guarantee life will be easy. Sometimes resolving conflict is like pouring antiseptic on a wound — it can sting. *Oh, man, can it sting.* But left untreated, even a small injury can weaken or kill the relationship.

Maybe you're discouraged because your marriage is less than perfect. Welcome to the human race! English theologian, Nicky Gumbel, offers this perspective: "I am far from perfect. I sometimes find it hard to believe that God really loves me -- especially when I mess up, fail, or make bad decisions."

Can you relate? Gumbel says you're not alone. "Actually, no one is perfect — apart from Jesus. But God so loved the world that he gave his one and only son to die for us (John 3:16). *Therefore, God must love imperfect people.*"

Isn't that a relief?

Gumbel concludes, "God knows perfect people do not exist. We all fail. God's love for you is bigger than your mistakes … Everyone knows that their marriage partner's not perfect, their children aren't perfect, their parents aren't perfect. But if we can love imperfect people, it shouldn't surprise us that God loves them even more!"

INSIGHT: I'm not perfect. Melina's not perfect. And I'm guessing you're not, either. But God says we're fixable. And that's good because in the biblical marriage plan, there is no escape clause or exit strategy. As relationship blogger Dave Willis says, "A perfect marriage is just two imperfect people who refuse to give up on each other." Let's vow to love our imperfect spouses — till death do us part.

TALK IT OVER.

Discuss these topics and try not to get into an argument doing it:

1) What are the "trigger" areas you tend to have the most conflict around? Objectively discuss why they're hot buttons. Reach an agreement on several things that you could do together to lessen the conflict.

2) Compare how your families resolved conflict growing up. Are there any unhealthy patterns being repeated in your own marriage? If so, decide to work on changing them. Inversely, were there any good models you can apply?

TAKE ACTION.

Applying what we learn is how we grow. Jump in while it's fresh:

1) Commit together to using the "Five Steps to Conflict Resolution" (page 92) from now on in your marriage. Keep a cheat sheet handy until you memorize them:
   • Pray for God's wisdom
   • Pick the right place and the right time
   • Affirm the relationship
   • Say what you have to say in a non-accusatory manner
   • Shut up and listen

2) Go on a date (just the two of you, out of the house), and discuss your own "Rules of Engagement" for conflict. Write them down as a preliminary list and then work together to play by the rules you've set up together.

3) Examine your heart and ask God to reveal any areas where you've been unwilling to forgive your spouse. Then make the conscious choice to forgive them as an act of your will (even if you don't feel like it emotionally). Pray for help to move past the hurt and see your spouse through God's eyes.

CHAPTER 5

Understanding Each Other's Needs:
What makes your spouse tick

Felix Unger is an uptight, compulsive germophobe.

His best friend, Oscar Madison, is an easygoing bohemian.

When Felix (the fussy one) is thrown out by his wife, he moves in with Oscar (the messy one). A cigar-chomping sportswriter, Oscar enjoys a casual lifestyle of sloppy clothes, poker parties, and negligible housekeeping. But Felix is incapable of relaxing and spends his time cleaning and complaining.

Although Felix means well, his suggestions are annoying. In just a few days, the mismatched pair is on the verge of a breakup (or murder). Felix can't stand Oscar's incorrigible grunginess; Oscar can't handle Felix's obsessive cleanliness.

Played by Jack Lemmon and Walter Matthau, these polar opposites made history in Neil Simon's movie *The Odd Couple*.

In one scene, the usually mellow Oscar blows his top: "I can't take it anymore, Felix, I'm cracking up. Everything you do irritates me. And when you're not here, the things I know you're gonna do when you get back here irritate me!"

Ever feel like that? These two best buds really did care for each other, but their needs were so different they drove each other insane.

Do opposites attract?

When I first met Melina in Mexico, I was drawn to her because she was *different* — different from the other girls I knew and different from me. Ironically, after a few months of marriage, the differences that were once so charming and appealing began to get under my skin. Things she did started to tick me off.

I wondered, "Why can't she be more like me? Isn't it obvious that my way of thinking and doing things is superior?" So naturally, I tried to change her. I tried to reshape and remake her in my image. And she returned the favor! As years went by, this mutual remodeling project led to frustration and conflict.

> Men and women are intrinsically "mismatched." And that's a good thing.

As we tried to "fix" each other, we were forgetting one universal truth — living with someone who's different is good for us! It's how we grow, how we learn, how we improve. In *The Odd Couple*, Oscar and Felix eventually rub off on each other in positive ways. Oscar gets more organized; Felix learns to loosen up.

In our case, I learned to be less rigid; Melina learned to be more disciplined.

In this chapter, we'll look at how *all* married couples are "odd" couples. None of us are mirror images of each other. In fact, men and women are intrinsically "mismatched." And that's a good thing — if you're aware of the ramifications.

Apples and oranges.

Ever notice that men and women are different?

The answer seems obvious, given the clear physical and emotional disparities. However, many people seem unaware there's another important way we are different — in our basic needs. Understanding and accommodating the deepest needs of your spouse is a key ingredient to having an extraordinary marriage.

Let's define terms. There are lots of things I *want* in life — new skis, six-pack abs, a bigger man cave, etc. But a "want" is not necessarily a "need."

So what exactly *is* a need?

According to the dictionary, it's "a physical or mental requirement needed for well-being; something a person must have in order to live or succeed or be happy."

> If a spouse can't get their needs met in a marriage, they fulfill them elsewhere.

In short, needs are the "must haves," the non-negotiable things our spouse requires to succeed and be happy. Warning! If a spouse can't get their needs met within a marriage, they may attempt to fulfill them somewhere else.

Did that sink in? Getting our key needs met outside our primary relationship can be hazardous — if not deadly — to the health of a marriage. Don't play with fire. It's critically important you fully understand what your spouse's needs are (as well as your own) so you can discuss them honestly ... and before it's too late.

Martians and Venusians.

In 1976, NASA successfully soft-landed an unmanned spacecraft on the surface of Mars. This Viking lander relayed the first panoramic photos of the red planet.

Sadly, not a single Martian has ever been spotted.

This lack of life on Mars didn't keep author John Gray from titling his book *Men Are from Mars, Women Are from Venus*. Published in 1992, it sold 50 million copies and spent 121 weeks on the bestseller list. A relationship counselor, Gray asserted that fundamental psychological differences between the sexes are so profound that men and women might as well be from totally different planets.

Gray's central metaphor became an icon of pop culture because it humorously sums up an underlying truth we all instinctively knew: "Not only do men and women communicate differently but they think, feel, perceive, react, respond, love, need, and appreciate differently."

Chris and I have found this to be surprisingly true. Like inhabitants of two very different worlds, each sex has its own language, customs, habits, and expectations ... especially when it comes to what we need most from each other!

Embracing our differences.

Want a great marriage?

Want better sex, fewer arguments, and less tension?

If you just answered, "Sign me up!" here's the secret sauce: The core of any great relationship is understanding and meeting each other's deepest needs.

Often, we *want* to make our spouse happy; we just don't know *how*.

As we mentioned in Chapter 3, a book that helped us in this area was *His Needs, Her Needs: Building an Affair-Proof Marriage* by Dr. Willard Harley. After years of counseling, Harley discovered a repeating pattern of unmet needs behind marital unhappiness.

As Melina and I read his list of top needs for men and women, we were surprised by how we both had assumed that the other's needs were the *same* as our own!

For example, I had no clue that sex didn't appear on Melina's list of top needs. It's such a huge need for me (and most men), that I naturally assumed it was the same for her. Wrong. That's not to say sex isn't something women need and desire, but it's not nearly as important as it is for men.

Melina was equally surprised to see how important hanging out together was to me. Learning previously unknown things about each other kicked our relationship into overdrive — strengthening the bond between us.

Harley's book challenged us to analyze our own marital needs and craft an original list that reflects *our personal experience*. See if it resonates with you!

We suggest that a WOMAN'S highest needs in marriage are:
1) Romance
2) Verbal Communication
3) Transparency & Truthfulness
4) Security

We propose that a MAN'S highest needs in marriage are:
1) Sex, Sex, and More Sex
2) Being a Dynamic Duo
3) Home Sweet Home
4) Cheerleading

Keep in mind our Hann categories don't apply equally to everyone. Some will look at their gender's list and disagree with the selection or ranking. Great! Others will see needs listed for the opposite sex that seem applicable to themselves. Cool. That's to be expected and may even change from year to year.

In this next section, we'll unpack some of the distinct (and wonderful) differences we've discovered. We'll bounce back and forth between each sex — with a practical take on each need. Buckle up!

#1 Need for WOMEN: Romance

Did you know that romance novels outsell science fiction, mystery, and literary novels combined?

When most men hear the word "romance" they think "foreplay." They equate kissing and hugging with a warm-up for sexual relations. And of course, there's definitely a time and place for sex. But what many women crave most is *nonsexual* romantic affection — in fact, it's their primary way of feeling loved, cherished, and emotionally connected within a relationship.

What does this kind of romantic affection look like? It's when a (smart) man spends time embracing, kissing, and caressing his wife — but without making her feel obligated to have sex in return. He engages in playful physical touch like back rubs, holding hands, and spontaneous hugs with no implied expectation of sex. Think "tenderness and fun" versus "passion and heat."

This is a tough concept for guys to wrap their heads around, but it's crucial to understand. Melina told me she *wanted* to feel close and connected to me. She *wanted* to feel like a woman who is valued and cherished, and nonsexual affection was the answer. When a man is fondling his wife and salivating and dropping not-so-subtle hints, it can be frustrating for the woman. The typical male's one-track pursuit of sex can make women feel devalued and objectified. Melina remembers thinking, "Can't we just chill out and talk for a bit?" While she wanted conversation, all I was thinking was, "Let's jump in bed right now!"

The key to meeting her need was the absence of sexual pressure. Over time, I learned to express my affection with no agenda, coupled with affirming verbal communication. This shift from the traditional formula of physical touch automatically (and inevitably) leading to the bedroom was a breath of fresh air. She explained how romantic it felt for me to walk by while she was cooking and just run my fingers across her bare shoulders. To give her a big hug, whisper "I love you," and then walk away left her feeling wonderful.

In fact, it freed her up to possibly want sex later on.

Ironically, when men give women nonsexual affection with "no strings attached," it may stimulate a hot night between the sheets! When a man meets a woman's *emotional* needs, she is often more inclined to meet his *physical* needs. On the contrary, if she doesn't feel emotionally connected, she won't be responsive to her husband's overtures. Can you blame her? Nobody wants to feel used.

> The male's one-track pursuit of sex can make women feel devalued.

In a nutshell? Show love to your wife because she's valuable and precious — not because you want an all-access pass to her body.

The big plus for Melina was in knowing my affection was not a covert method of seduction, but a genuine, heartfelt way of showing that I loved, respected, and cherished her. Melina has many friends who complain that the only time their husbands touch them is when they want sex. One of her friends actually had an affair because her husband hadn't kissed her passionately — kissing for the sake of kissing — since they were dating. All she wanted was to innocently hug and kiss, but her unromantic husband only complied when he wanted sex.

Guys, remember dating? Remember how romantic and exciting it felt just to go for walks, hold each other tight, and simply hang out together?

When I dated Chris, he couldn't keep from stroking my hair, squeezing my hands, and cuddling whenever possible. Sadly, this playful, romantic courtship gets lost as marriages get "older" and the busyness of life (jobs, kids, money pressures, fatigue, etc.) wear on a couple. But that original tenderness and physical touch were part of what established a bond between you in the first place. Treating your future wife as a person (not an object) was part of the reason she said "yes" when you proposed! She agreed to marry you because you were meeting one of her most important needs — most likely without either of you realizing it.

Men, I challenge you to bring that unabashed romance back into your marriage. For the next month, I dare you to intentionally show affection to your wife several times a day without any expectation of things moving beyond it to sex. You'll be pleasantly surprised with the results. Trust me; your wife will be more eager for bedroom fun when you demonstrate self-control and nonsexual touch.

Appropriate signs of affection include warm caresses, playful pats on the rear, and light kisses on the neck as you're passing by. If she's willing (don't force it), this can also include passionate kissing — the kind of "making out" you both craved while dating. Why not take her for a drive, find a romantic place to park, and have some great conversation? Make sure you are actively listening to her, then spend unhurried time just kissing and cuddling. You can steam up the windows, but use restraint and chivalry — showing you want to meet *her* need, not yours!

Romance can also include your words; tell your wife you love her, that you appreciate and value her. You can also use gifts, flowers, and love notes — especially if her love language is gift giving. Marriage therapist Dr. Corey Allan adds this important tip: "Make a habit of looking your spouse in the eye. Whether you're talking or just in the same room throughout the day, make a connection with their eyes. Respect them by giving your attention in conversations. Close the laptop, pause the TV, put the paper down and look them in the eye."

Amen to that. The key is expressing romantic behavior in multiple ways without the expectation that it has to lead to something sexual. Free your wife to feel your love straight from the heart — it's (probably) her number one need!

#1 Need for MEN: Sex, Sex, and More Sex.

According to a Gallup poll, men eat more fast food than women do.

No surprise there; men are always in a hurry.

Especially when it comes to sex.

I'm guessing you've heard the analogy that men are like "microwaves" and women are like "Crock-Pots." There's a lot of truth to it. Ladies take a while to warm up, simmering and cooking the meal for most of the day. Gents on the other hand, want a meal zapped and ready in 30 seconds. It's a humorous way to remind husbands and wives about how differently we view this vital area of intimacy in marriage — and how hard it can be to get on the same page.

> Wives, don't be offended your husband has only "one thing on his mind."

Wives, please don't be offended that your husband has only "one thing on his mind." Men, please don't be frustrated that your wife isn't like the hot-and-ready women on TV. Ladies, understand that he is not just pawing at you to irritate you or because he "has a problem." Men, please be sensitive that your spouse is your beloved life partner, not a Stepford Wife programmed for your pleasure.

I had an eye-opener on this when I read *For Women Only: What You Need to Know About the Inner Lives of Men* by Shaunti Feldhahn. I learned that men are primarily visual; that even happily married men struggle with being pulled toward staring at other women — both in person and on websites.

Ladies, if you're shocked, don't be. If you're angry, blame the male DNA. Then ask God for ways to love the man in your life. Despite his Cro-Magnon tendencies.

Because wives don't share their mate's built-in craving for sex, we can vastly underestimate how powerful and pervasive this need is. Notice I didn't say "desire" or "want." Sex is a *need* — a man's number one basic need. Chris and I know a couple who got divorced because the husband had an affair to satisfy his unmet sexual needs. The wife talked candidly with me after the divorce. She expressed frustration that she never knew how important sex was for her spouse. Up until his affair, she felt "If he's getting sex once a month, that's okay."

Her ignorance was a leading contributor to the erosion of their marriage and the ensuing pain she and her children went through in the years that followed.

We understand there *are* women with sex drives comparable to the men in their lives (or even more so), but the vast majority are simply not as highly sexed as men. Although each individual is different, I know very few women with a sex drive similar to a typical male. But you'd never get that impression from books, movies, and TV. In fact, modern media portrays just the opposite — that women *crave* sex (desperate housewives, desperate career women, desperate soccer moms, etc.) and can't wait to get it on, baby!

> Men are like "microwaves." Women are like "Crock-Pots."

In the fantasy world of Hollywood, two strangers can meet in a bar or a cab, and within the hour, they're making red-hot love somewhere. Over and over, women are shown hopping in the sack with a neighbor or a co-worker — and often shown as the initiator.

The implication is that smart, hip, sophisticated women everywhere are sexually aggressive — and if you're not, you're the under-sexed oddball.

We'll explore this falsehood in Chapter 6, but you can see how this exaggerated depiction of the female sex drive confuses us men!

The big lie of the always-ready, seductive playmate creates false expectations, disappointment, and even guilt in real-life relationships.

> **INSIGHT**: For a man, sex is a physical and emotional necessity. If the woman in his life isn't meeting it, I guarantee he'll be tempted to get it fulfilled elsewhere. Of course, this biological imperative is never a valid excuse to have an affair — infidelity is wrong under any circumstance. We're simply pointing out the risk it poses to a marriage if the wife isn't meeting her husband's need.

Hey ladies, time for a little girl talk. We women need to understand that when a man says "I do" to us in marriage, he has literally taken the number one need in his life and put it in our hands. Are you up to the challenge?

It's interesting how the world and our spiritual enemy work against God's plan for marriage from two sides. When you're single, the pressure and push is to have the *most* sex possible before marriage. It's glorified in music, movies, and advertisements. However, after a couple is married, the push is to keep them so busy and distracted that they have the *least* sex possible.

When's the last time you saw a movie that showed or implied a married couple having great sex? An article in *Sexuality & Culture* analyzed how sexuality between married couples is depicted in popular films. "Of the occurrences of sexual behavior, married partners represented 15 percent of the total compared to 85 percent for unmarried couples. The most common sexual behavior among husbands and wives was kissing ... by comparison, intercourse was the most common sexual behavior among unmarried partners."

What would a viewer conclude from this lopsided portrayal? "This and other findings suggest that sexual behavior among married characters is rare and rather mundane compared to those having unmarried sex."

(Note to Chris — not in *our* house!)

It gets worse. When a married person *does* have sex in a movie, it's usually not with their spouse — it's in the context of adultery or prostitution. But even with this societal disdain for keeping sex in the confines of marriage, a woman needs to realize she has a responsibility to be a gracious, willing partner with her husband in this area. Your husband has forsaken all others for you alone, and he has no legitimate way to address his need for sex if you're not attentive.

Girls, if you forget everything else, remember two things: First, that sex is your man's number one need, and second, that you don't view it the same way he does! It's how guys feel connected, significant, affirmed ... and manly.

Why is it such a big deal? As author Shaunti Feldhahn says, sex is the primary way a man feels desired by his wife. It fills a powerful emotional need. It makes him feel loved. In fact, he can't truly feel loved and respected without it; frequent, fulfilling sex is what gives him confidence.

> Biological imperative is never a valid excuse to have an affair.

Chew on this for a moment: It's just as devastating to a husband if his wife denies him sexually as it is to a wife if her husband stops talking to her.

The solution? Get into each other's head and align your priorities. Feldhahn says, "The more we understand the men in our lives, the better we can support and love them in the way they need to be loved."

———

Sometimes Chris and I are separated for an extended period, due to a business trip or other obligation. Lots of men (and women) make really bad choices "on the road" and hook up with someone for quick sex. We came up with a practical way to reduce this unhealthy temptation. Before we part ways, we make sure we both have our needs met here, together!

For him it's the physical connection of a sexual union; for me it's the emotional connection of making sure my "affection tank" is full. What good is it for me to make sure Chris has clean laundry for a trip if I miss his most important need as a man? We do this intentionally to protect our marriage.

We are *individually* responsible for our own actions, but we are *jointly* responsible for keeping our marriage healthy.

INSIGHT: If we expect our spouse to remain faithful, we need to help by doing our part to meet their physical and psychological needs. Not just to lessen the temptation of affairs, but to make their lives more satisfying and rewarding. *"Value others above yourselves, not looking to your own interests but to the interests of the others"* (Phil. 2:3,4 NIV).

#2 Need for WOMEN: Verbal Communication.

Women use three times more words a day than men.

That's what I've always heard. But is it true?

It's quoted in countless self-help books by so-called experts, and it bolsters the stereotype that women spend their days gossiping while men keep it zipped.

The original claim dates back to a controversial 2006 book called *The Female Brain*. Its author, Louann Brizendine, stated that a woman uses about 20,000 words per day while a man uses about 7,000.

Baloney.

Science magazine published a major study blasting the popular myth that women are the more talkative sex. Researchers found that in reality, women speak a little over 16,000 words a day.

And the men? A little under 16,000.

The difference between the genders is "not statistically significant."

Even the scientists were surprised (speechless?). They had bought into the pervasive meme.

Psychologist Matthias Mehl of the University of Arizona says the myth needs debunking, not just because women are demeaned by the "female chatterbox" stigma, but men are harmed by the equally erroneous "silent male" stigma.

So, the "prattle of the sexes" turns out to be a draw.

Women and men have equal verbal output.

Why is that important? Because men have been hiding behind this false dichotomy to avoid talking to their wives! Guys, you have just lost your last excuse for not satisfying your wife's need for conversation.

We covered verbal communication in Chapter 3, but it's important to note that along with conversation being integral to a good marriage, it's also one of a woman's most important needs. It's crucial that a husband recognizes this and works to fulfill this need — even if he's "not in the mood" (just like *she* might not be in the mood when he's hankering for some bedroom Olympics).

Although both sexes utter the same number of words, studies *do* show they use them differently. For instance, women tend to talk more about people, while men tend to focus on inanimate objects. Since women stress relationships, their everyday conversation is studded with pronouns and emotions. Since men talk more about concrete objects, their conversation is sprinkled with numbers and factoids. Another difference is that women often form friendships while talking and sharing; activity is *not* needed. Men however, form bonds while working or playing; activity *is* required as a backdrop for conversation.

These differences in style and subject matter do *not* absolve a husband of his obligation to work hard to meet his wife's need. How to get started? Listen intently when she speaks. Remember to use "active listening." Instead of just hearing her words, pursue her meaning like a detective — or a talk show host.

Krista Tippett, host of public radio's *On Being* show, says, "Listening is not just about being quiet while the other person talks. It is about being present and willing to be surprised and curious."

When your wife talks to you, ask her follow-up questions like: "So how did that make you feel? What happened next? Can you tell me more about that?" A husband must address his spouse's deepest needs, whether it comes naturally or not. Practice will make this easier over time.

When you were dating, verbal communication was easy and exciting.

The "prattle of the sexes" is a draw.

What about now as a married man? Think back to spending late nights on the phone, just enjoying the sound of each other's voices, never wanting to hang up. If you're like me, you couldn't wait to talk with her — about anything and everything. It was effortless to send texts, scribble notes, and chat for hours on dates. That high level of communication was part of why she fell in love with you! Too many guys make the fatal mistake of neglecting the art of conversation once they say "I do."

It's a top need of hers, gentlemen. If you're not meeting it, somebody else eventually will be.

INSIGHT: The myth that women are hyper-talkative may have come from observing the "demand-withdraw" pattern we spoke about in Chapter 4. That's the scenario where a woman typically wants to talk through problems and her male partner typically wants to withdraw emotionally. If that's you, beware of the "gender box," and realize that silence is usually *not* golden to a wife.

Men are experts at avoiding conversations. We can work late. We can over-schedule our time. Or if we do come home, we can retreat into projects, internet, and television. In some cases, men even escape into alcohol. Time slips away, and before you know it, another day goes by without verbally connecting with our wives. Consciously or unconsciously, we sabotage our chances to meet our wives' vital need for meaningful conversation.

To break that pattern, I offer a two-word solution: *Be intentional.*

Men, as a woman, I guarantee that when you prioritize your wife's need above Monday Night Football, you're headed for a happier marriage. When you deliberately plan a date night, a long walk, or even a coffee break to include lots of verbal communication, you're going to impress the person you married!

To calm your nerves (and to avoid awkward pauses), it's helpful to have a few hot topics ready in advance. Here are some conversation starters from authors Robert and Pamela Crosby:

- *What's the best book you've read recently? Why did you like it?*
- *If you could possess extraordinary talent in any of the arts, what would you choose?*
- *If you could have witnessed any biblical event, what would you choose?*
- *What goals would you like us to accomplish in our marriage in the next year? Five years? Ten years?*

Now let's stir in a batch of our personal Hann favorites. Hopefully, these ideas will grease the wheels for smooth, revealing communication:

- *If you didn't have to worry about making a living, what would you most like to do for the rest of your life?*
- *If you could live in any era in history, past or future, what would you choose? Why?*
- *What five things are you most thankful for right now?*
- *If money's no object, what's your idea of a perfect dream vacation?*
- *Is there some hobby or sport you did before we got married that you'd like to start doing again?*
- *Imagine our house is on fire. We're all safely outside. What is the one item you most want to get out?*
- *Let's say you have to tell your life story in 60 seconds. Ready, set, go!*
- *Before we got married, what was our best date? Why was it so fun?*

It's important that we talk. But it's equally important that we keep our words predominantly positive. Dr. John Gottman says, "What really separates contented couples from those in deep marital misery is a healthy balance between their positive and negative feelings and actions."

Gottman says, "I carefully charted the amount of time couples spent fighting versus interacting positively — touching, smiling, paying compliments, laughing, etc. Across the board I found a very specific ratio exists between the amount of positivity and negativity in a stable marriage ... That magic ratio is 5-to-1. As long as there is five times as much positive feeling and interaction between husband and wife as there is negative, the marriage was likely to be stable over time."

Guys, make sure you have at least five positive conversations for every negative one!

Couples headed for divorce tend to have a 1-to-1 ratio. Avoid discussions when you're exhausted (at the end of the day) or upset (work conflicts, budget problems, disobedient kids, etc.). Instead, schedule chats when you're at your best and brightest. Because you're human, any given conversation may drift in a negative direction. If things get crunchy, hit the pause button and start again.

To sum up: Don't be defensive, don't be confrontational, and always be respectful of your spouse's feelings. Remember that 5-to-1 ratio and fill your wife's need for verbal communication with lots of praise, validation, and affirmation.

#2 Need for MEN: Being a Dynamic Duo

Starsky & Hutch ... Batman & Robin ... Kirk & Spock.

Noticing a trend? *Bert & Ernie ... Penn & Teller.*

Men often work in pairs. And there's a reason. From *Woody & Buzz* to *Holmes & Watson*, dudes connect best in the process of doing something together.

As guys, we build relationships organically just by "hanging out" together. Given the chance, we'll watch sports, play cards, go fishing, hit the gym, meet for a run, or play golf — *together* with a buddy.

Without even trying, men often form tight bonds of friendship simply by *experiencing something together.* Ask any former high school jock and he can probably still name the guys on his team. Men often form lifelong friendships from playing sports, working a job, or serving as volunteers.

It's no wonder doing fun things together with their spouse is a top need for a man!

For example, fitness has always been important to me; it's an essential part of my daily life. And it's a habit we wanted our children to develop. But it was *not* something that Melina was accustomed to doing. Her physical activity came from being around the stables and out on the trails with her horse.

We started working out together — as a dynamic duo — when Melina read that resistance training is necessary to prevent a woman's bones from weakening and becoming prone to osteoporosis. On top of that, we were both feeling the effects of age. Noticing our bodies were getting a bit flabbier (not a fun discovery), we vowed to maintain a healthy muscle tone by working out together at the gym.

What surprised us both was how much I *absolutely loved* having her with me. Just "hanging out" together while exercising was my idea of a really great date.

Truth? Melina was not 100 percent on board at the beginning ...

At first, I was hesitant to go to the gym with Chris. I mean, who wants to have their husband see them all sweaty with no makeup on? I wasn't a basket case, but I knew my body didn't look quite the same after having two kids. And in general, I didn't feel very attractive in my gym clothes. Maybe you can relate.

One day, Chris suggested we go for a family bike ride with our young kids. I really did not want to go (for the reasons mentioned above). But during the ride I was pleasantly surprised to find Chris especially attentive. In fact, he was actually flirting with me! For some reason he was unable to keep his eyes off my body. I looked down to see if maybe I had a lot of cleavage showing, but noticed I was wearing a crew neck tee. I finally asked lover boy what was going on and why he was being so affectionate. He replied, "I don't know ... you're out on a ride with me ... I just love it!"

Suddenly, I realized Chris was thrilled to be doing something he loved — but as a duet instead of a solo! It was like a bell went off in my head: *"Ding, ding, ding! This is a top four need for a man."* I had mistakenly thought that for Chris to find me attractive I had to look perfect. I thought he wanted me to look like a movie star — perfect makeup, perfect hair, and a tight little bike outfit showing off some curves ... all the stuff that television, movies and media portray a man wanting. But actually, it was the simple act of spending time with him in activities he enjoyed that attracted him the most!

Wives, don't worry about being perfectly groomed. Just get out there.

With that revelation, I thought: *How many times did I miss out on a wonderful connection and a big dose of affection just because I didn't think I looked good enough and declined to do something with Chris?*

I know some of you guys might be saying, "A tight bike jersey with some cleavage does sound good, actually." And I also know Chris completely agrees! My point is that a man's need for recreational comradery is so strong that ladies should never worry about being perfectly groomed or coiffed — just get out there and join in.

Sometimes a wife isn't comfortable with the activity ("What if he makes me bait a hook?"), or worries she won't be good at it ("What if I look silly on skates?"). Believe me; your husband is not expecting you to be an expert out of the box!

Whether you're a natural or a klutz, your husband will love it, and you'll love his reaction. As we said earlier, men connect through *activity* and women connect through *conversation*. This can be a chance to do both! Incidentally, there's an added benefit to working out or doing physical activities together — getting in shape also hits a man's need for physical beauty, so it's a triple win.

———

Just what *is* being a dynamic duo? It's simply spending time with your husband doing things he likes. It could be morning walks or evening runs.

It could be going to the lake or going to the library. It could be attending sports events in person or watching at home on TV. It could be anything from bicycling to rock climbing — whatever he enjoys doing that you can do with him.

My friend has a husband who spends his spare time tinkering around in the garage. She confided that she often felt frustrated when he would "disappear into his man cave" and leave her alone. One day she decided to go out there and see what he was doing. She quietly sat down near him while he was working. For quite some time he didn't realize she was there. When he finally looked up, she just smiled her biggest smile. He was surprised to see her, but went back to his tinkering. Five minutes later, he looked up again to see if she was still there. Again, she just gave him a big smile. And again, he went back to work. Third time he looked up, he saw her smiling ear to ear at him. He blurted out, "I don't really know what you're doing, but I *love* it!"

For him, having her join him while he tinkered on projects was a satisfying form of leisure time companionship, as simple as that sounds.

We know another couple whose story didn't end as well. Tamara was a good friend of mine. When she was dating her future husband, they used to go running together all the time. Physical activity and staying fit were important to him. He was obviously attracted by her similar desire to stay in shape, and the shared experiences they enjoyed as a *couple* met his need.

However, once they got married, Tamara stopped running. She rationalized that she didn't have time anymore. She felt he should understand how busy she was with the kids and her job and helping make ends meet.

Knowingly or not, she had been meeting a top need of his, both while they were dating and early in their marriage. Her decision to stop running left that need unfulfilled.

Sadly, he found somebody else to fill it.

A wife can get angry and frustrated and say it shouldn't matter. But a wife abdicating her husband's need for companionship is as hurtful as him abdicating her need for conversation. If he clammed up, she would seek out somebody else to meet that need. When that "somebody" happens to be of the opposite sex, bad things happen to marriages. Tamara and her husband found that out the hard way. Unfortunately, they became a divorce statistic. Their painful breakup left huge emotional scars for themselves and their children.

————

You met our friends April and Darryl in Chapter 1. Darryl's affair resulted from having his need for "dynamic duo" companionship met by another woman. If you recall, the couple's mutual pal Savannah rode with him to yoga class when her car needed repair. It resulted in a pair of messy divorces. Experiencing recreational activities with their spouse is a powerful male need that many wives take for granted. Don't ignore it.

> Experiencing recreational activities with their spouse is a powerful male need.

INSIGHT: In America, there is one divorce every 36 seconds. That's nearly 2,400 divorces per day, or 16,800 divorces per week. Each of those numbers represents real people experiencing real consequences. These numbers from the national Centers for Disease Control and Prevention (CDC) are all too real. Try to imagine the human tragedy caused by this shocking statistic of 876,000 divorces a year.

#3 Need for WOMEN: Transparency & Truthfulness.

Imagine being marooned on a deserted island.

In the movie *Cast Away*, Tom Hanks plays a FedEx executive — Chuck Noland — on an international flight. During a storm, his plane goes down somewhere in the South Pacific. Everyone else is killed in the crash, and Chuck finds himself alone on an uncharted island. Fortunately, FedEx packages also wash up on the beach, allowing him to meet his basic needs for food, water, shelter, and fire.

But he soon finds out that survival has an *emotional* component, too.

Chuck becomes so lonely, so desperate to talk to someone, that he paints a face on a volleyball and names it Wilson. For the next four years, he communicates his deepest hopes and dreams and fears to a white ball named Wilson. Ironically, his chats with Wilson are surprisingly open and honest — in fact, more so than the superficial chats he used to have with his fiancée.

Without someone to talk to (even an inanimate object), Chuck would have gone insane, given up, or committed suicide. Do you see the parallel to marriage? In a powerful way, communication at a deeper level is essential to the life of a marriage, just as it was essential to the life of Chuck Noland.

As Dennis Rainey says, "If you don't communicate, your marriage will die."

In his book, *Staying Close*, Rainey says, "Good, open communication is the top need in marriage. Using words correctly and skillfully is an important part of communication, but even more important is that both husband and wife have a willingness to communicate in ways that result in deeper honesty and openness."

That's the tricky part. It's easy to gab about the weather or the neighbor's noisy dog, but it's much tougher to be transparent and bare your soul. Especially for men. And yet that's exactly what a wife needs from her husband!

Guys, she wants you to talk with her, in an open and truthful way. She needs you to be vulnerable and share how you're feeling, what's going on in your head. I remember Melina explaining to me, "Women *talk*. I mean, we *really* talk!" About anything. And it can occur anywhere, apparently. She explained how she could be in a public restroom, ask a woman in the next stall to share some toilet paper and end up in a deep conversation! That's impossible for guys to understand (in fact, every man who just read that is cringing). When we walk into a restroom full of guys at the urinals, there's a code of silence that you do not break. We don't say *anything* to *anybody*; it's all about taking care of business and moving on.

Unlike my "can-you-spare-a-square" wife, it is *not* natural or easy for us guys to open up and be vulnerable with others. Even when it's our own wife. Nevertheless, it's a top need of hers to have this type of intimate communication with you — so put on your man-pants and get busy.

Practice being an open book until you get better at it.

To be honest, it's not rocket science; it's just opening up some of the containers in our "waffle-ized" heads and letting our wives know what's in there. Don't be afraid or reluctant to give them a glimpse of what you're feeling, what you're scared of, what you're excited about — you get the idea.

Recently, Melina complimented me for my openness while mentoring our teenage kids about finances. Swallowing my pride, I candidly shared many of the financial mistakes I had made in my life and in our marriage.

Wives need husbands to be vulnerable and share their feelings.

Melina was so appreciative that I was willing to be vulnerable and expose my failures. In fact, she said it made me look *stronger* in her eyes. That's important because most guys are petrified to admit their mistakes to their wife, incorrectly fearing she will laugh or think less of him. Actually, the exact opposite is true — your openness and honesty will only increase your standing and stature in her eyes.

Men, it's time to drop the mask.

Dennis Rainey says, "Many people spend tremendous time and energy building facades to hide their insecurities. They are afraid if someone finds out who they really are, they will be rejected. For men in particular, deep and honest communication can be very threatening. Too many wives and husbands are afraid to be honest with each other."

Being transparent can be daunting. Intimidating. That's why many husbands stick to surface issues — menu items, household chores, the superficial stuff. But your wife craves (and deserves) to get an inside look at the real you, to have the deep, meaningful conversations of life. It's a little scary, and honestly, a little risky. But as you build up trust and commitment, it becomes second nature.

INSIGHT: Men, if you don't learn to fill this need, somebody else may slip in behind your back. And nothing leads to a sexual affair faster than intimate, emotional conversations. Women are starved for it. Also, the Bible says *"don't throw your pearls before swine."* Don't be reckless and open up to just anyone — reserve your transparency for your one and only spouse.

#3 Need for MEN: Home Sweet Home

"I hate housework. You make the beds, you wash the dishes, and six months later you have to start all over again."

That was Joan Rivers. Another lady who disliked chores was Roseanne Barr, "I'm not going to vacuum until Sears makes one you can ride on."

Truthfully, I see their point. After a hard day, I'd rather take a nap on our couch than sweep under it. And there are days I'd rather eat out than wash dishes.

I'm not alone in this.

Supposedly a newlywed saw his young wife scrubbing their bathroom. He asked her, "Are we moving?" In his world, you only cleaned the apartment to get your security deposit back. Guys are pretty messy in their bachelor days. We can be knee deep in pizza boxes and dirty socks and not be flustered.

But when most men get married, something shifts in their brain and they want to live in a clean, orderly space. They want an environment they can be proud of, a home that's tidy and presentable to friends and family. They want their abode to be well run, well organized, and well cared for.

The old saying "a man's home is his castle" still rings true!

Disclaimer: Unlike the majority of men, this is not a huge need for me personally (hopefully, I can substitute a double-dose of sex or cheerleading).

Up until the 1960s, the household pattern was basically: *Dad goes to work and mom stays home. Repeat five days a week for 40 years, then retire.*

That *Happy Days* model is now just one of many hybrid situations. In today's world, both spouses are often working full or part-time. Other variations reverse the traditional role with the wife being the primary income producer and the husband staying home as caregiver. New trends involve working from home or having multiple jobs on flex-time schedules. In these cases, duties like shopping, cleaning, and chauffeuring the kids are split up in a myriad of ways.

Bottom line? No matter who does what, a man's need for "home sweet home" means he wants the household well-managed and as free from stress and anxiety as possible. This brings us back to the critical importance of communication — in this case, regarding how the work of running the home will be taken care of.

> Married men want a home environment they can be proud of.

Let's define reality. Unless you can afford maids and butlers, tasks like scrubbing the toilet, feeding the family, and ironing the clothes need to be done by someone in the relationship, whether it's both parties chipping in equally or some agreed-upon division of labor. If one stays home while the other is off working, they would likely have the major share of these tasks. If both are working outside the home, then there will need to be even *more* communication due to your time demands. The first step in a wife meeting her husband's need for domestic support is deciding with him what your respective roles and jobs will be.

INSIGHT: Whether or not both spouses work, they both face stress and fatigue. Which means they both need time for rest and relaxation. As you schedule repetitive chores like cooking, cleaning, banking, laundry and other tasks, be respectful of each other's time and energy.

We realize traditional roles are changing. Radically.

But a wise wife still creates a home that becomes a refuge from the pressures and stress of life. A wise wife still balances domestic responsibilities so expertly that her husband would rather spend time at home with his family than be anywhere else. A man may not verbally complain about the condition of the house (they're a tight-lipped bunch), but if he's finding excuses to avoid being home, that's a red flag!

In his mind, he's working crazy hard to provide a good quality of life. He's draining his physical and mental strength battling dragons in the business world. On top of that, the shifting economy means many are worried about job security. Men internalize this tension and put their game face on, but it takes a toll. They long to "recharge their batteries" at home so they can face challenges the next day. To do that, home cannot be chaotic, disorganized, or low on essential supplies.

This doesn't mean a house needs to be perfect and ready for a white-glove inspection by a drill sergeant. It just needs to be peaceful and inviting. And that can be achieved in a variety of ways. Somebody once said, "My house isn't messy. I just have everything on display. Like a museum." Creating a warm, casual feeling of comfort and tranquility is more important than having a candlelight dinner on the table the minute the spouse walks in.

No two homes are alike, and no two will have the same solution. Factors like workloads and career paths are infinitely variable. And when children are added to the equation, everything changes! Young marrieds usually enjoy sharing domestic tasks, but with pregnancy, you'll need a better plan than "good intentions." Kids demand (and deserve) unimaginable amounts of time and attention. Your previous support schedule will be upended. Responsibilities will increase exponentially (along with expenses) and must be handled bilaterally in a loving, rational way that strengthens your growing family.

It's important to negotiate a plan that's fair to both and flexible enough to accommodate changes in health, employment, family size, etc. Incidentally, this is a two-way street. Career women also gain enormous benefit from living in a well-managed home.

> **INSIGHT**: Wives, a clean, well-stocked house is not a substitute for your husband's other needs. Most men would gladly trade a few dust bunnies for some recreational teamwork or romantic companionship. If you need to sacrifice mopping or shopping, so be it. Just hang a sign on your door: "Our house was clean yesterday. Sorry you missed it."

#4 Need for WOMEN: Security

Of all the Super Bowl memorabilia, a victor's ring is the most prized. (Which explains why a 1991 Super Bowl ring recently sold at auction for $230,401!)

A man I greatly admire has *two* Super Bowl rings. That remarkable man is Tony Dungy.

As a player, Dungy helped the Pittsburgh Steelers win the Super Bowl in 1978. As a coach, he led the Indianapolis Colts to a Super Bowl victory in 2007. The first African American coach to win a Super Bowl, he made the Pro Football Hall of Fame in 2016.

But the most important thing in Coach Dungy's life is not fame or fortune — it's being a dedicated family man. He challenges parents, "Our kids need us. Spend as much time with your kids as you can. Enjoy them. Be with them. Hug your children …"

And that goes double for us men. "There's no substitute for a full-time dad. Dads who are fully engaged with their kids overwhelmingly tend to produce children who believe in themselves and lead full lives."

Unfortunately, like many well-intentioned fathers, I haven't always lived up to Coach Dungy's example. And my excuse was … you guessed it, my *job*.

Men tend to be very task-oriented, moving from one challenge to the next. So we think the best way to love our family is by working harder and longer. Unfortunately, being a workaholic will not meet your wife's need for family security. Women are far more relationship-oriented than task-oriented. They want their men to be engaged with the family and physically present. There's no substitute for this.

That's not to say that earning a nice living isn't admirable; of course it is. But many good providers miss the point of all their hard work. Women crave security — and your physical presence is reassurance to your wife that you're rock-solid reliable!

Men, your wife needs security across the board. She needs to feel secure in your love for her ("Do you still love me?"), in your physical attraction to her ("Do you still think I'm pretty?"), and in your family commitment ("Will you always be here for us?").

Additionally, your wife needs a sense of security regarding *finances.*

This has led to friction between Melina and me. In general, men are more prone to risk taking than women. My wife is excellent with money, but her conservative views about finances often clash with my aggressive investing and business pursuits.

More than a few heated arguments began when *I* felt she didn't trust me, or when *she* felt I was being too risky (she was frequently right).

We eventually understood that her concerns were not a distrust of me personally, but an outgrowth of her top-four need for security. For example, when I wanted to use a line of credit to buy rental homes at below-market rates, a red flag went up in her brain. When I talked about changing jobs, it made her nervous.

Even when I pushed to relocate to California (where she's from), her "financial security sensors" went off. Since learning her need, I approach financial discussions in a new light.

Money is a great tool. And I'm all for getting more. But if a man willingly exchanges overtime pay for some additional time with family, his wife will appreciate it. She'll feel valued and loved. When a man is around his wife and kids, they feel *secure* and *happy.*

Isn't that the point?

In Chapter 3, I explained how I used to get frustrated with Chris for not engaging with the kids the instant he came home from work. From *his* perspective, he needed a little "me time" to unwind from the day before shifting into "dad mode." From *my* perspective, he was not prioritizing family time. As we discussed this, he adjusted *his* level of engagement with the kids, and *I* adjusted my level of respect for him as the exhausted provider.

Over time, he began to understand how much I craved security — with a daily demonstration of his commitment to the family.

Nowadays, Chris balances my need for both family and financial security. You may think that "secure finances" is a curious need for wives in this day and age. After all, women now comprise over 60 percent of all college graduates. And millions of women have achieved a level of economic success unknown to previous generations.

> Women by nature are nurturers. Men are providers and protectors.

So what's up? Despite gains in income equality, studies suggest most women *still* expect traditional gender roles in the breadwinner department. While I appreciate and respect women who are high achievers outside the home, women by nature are the *nurturers*; men by nature are the *providers* and *protectors*.

That might sound old-fashioned. But it's a biological fact.

As a wife, I can tell you most women gravitate to ambitious, hardworking men with a goal to improve their lot in life. As a mother, I want financial security — bills paid, food in the fridge, a decent home, and extra cash left over for savings and emergencies.

———

Does that represent every woman? No. Is it politically correct? Perhaps not. But these top needs are not going away; let's learn to deal with them graciously.

INSIGHT: Men, every husband and father *is* a role model, whether he wants to be or not. Your family craves security, and they're always watching to see your level of commitment. Make sure that you don't inadvertently put work and status and income above your family — even with good intentions.

#4 Need for MEN: Cheerleading

Ever watch little kids at play?

The young boys are always looking for people to watch them do something: "Hey lady, look how high I can jump!" "Mom, did you see that awesome kick-flip?" "Mister, watch how fast I can run!"

Little boys love an audience to watch them and (more importantly) praise them. That's relevant because, as someone has said, men are just little boys with bigger bodies and hairier legs. There's a reason sports teams have cheerleaders — guys love to have a squad of girls rooting us on and telling us we're doing a great job.

And it's something we never grow out of.

This top-four need of a man feeds his hunger for approval — a husband wants and needs his wife to admire him, respect him, and yes, even cheer him on.

Sound silly? A bit egotistical? Maybe. But a wife who ignores this need for positive reinforcement risks hurting her husband's feelings and leaving him vulnerable to flattery from outside sources. Perhaps it seems childish that a full-grown man still wants accolades, but trust me, an affirming wife is an incredible motivator.

If a wife wants her husband to be responsive and confident, she'll acknowledge his need for admiration and bring out her "inner cheerleader." Ladies, you don't need pom-poms — just a smile, a hug, and a pat on the back. Tell your husband that you love his big muscles and ask him to flex. Tell him you admire how hard he works for the family, or that you think it's cool that he was able to fix the sink. Tell him it's awesome that he's willing to be open and transparent with the kids.

Let him know that in your eyes, he's a total stud!

In Chapter 2, we looked at the power of positive words. Here's a great opportunity to leverage "eight-cow thinking." Wives, you can meet his need for admiration, and at the same time *speak into existence* the ideal man you want him to be. Your spoken words can literally build him up or tear him down.

As a wife, I know every husband craves his spouse's respect and admiration.

But what does that mean? Being a cheerleader is mostly about showing respect for his opinions, his character, and his actions — in private and in public. As we said earlier, women have the drive to feel loved and cherished, while men have the drive to feel admired and respected.

> A husband needs his wife to admire him, respect him, and cheer him on.

In his book, *Hidden Keys of a Loving, Lasting Marriage*, Dr. Gary Smalley provides practical ways for wives to cheer their husbands on:

• **Seek his advice.** Involving your husband in decisions (big and small) shows him you respect his opinions and decision-making skills.

• **Brag about him.** Look for opportunities to tastefully draw attention to your husband's positive qualities when you're out with others.

• **Express admiration verbally.** Talk about his achievements to your friends. Tell him face-to-face you're proud of him.

Wives, ask your husband what he wants to accomplish and help him reach those dreams — advancing his career, pursuing education, or enjoying a hobby or sport. Encourage him when he feels like giving up and praise him when he hits a goal.

Bottom line? No husband is perfect. When your husband annoys you, disappoints you, or exasperates you, praise him anyway. Smalley says, "Admiration looks beyond what he does to who he is. It's unconditional."

Ladies (cheerleaders), this won't surprise many of you, but an important part of meeting a man's need for affirmation is simply taking care of yourself — like you did when you were dating.

I bet you knew that. We all know that. What is surprising is that a wife who optimizes her appearance improves a couple's overall odds for a happy marriage! A study in the *Journal of Personality and Social Psychology* found that making an effort to look good actually led to a more satisfying marriage for both spouses.

Maybe you're thinking: *Do I have to spend my life in the beauty salon and the gym?*

No! A man's need for a cheerleader doesn't mean he expects the proverbial "Barbie." It means he needs his wife to at least put some effort into taking care of herself. He needs to see that she wants to look her best for him; that she's at least trying.

Men are visual creatures, so the idea is to keep his eyes *on* you and *off* the attractive damsel he meets in the workplace or shopping mall. Ladies, let me be blunt — if you're not capturing his eyes, somebody else is.

Regardless of your looks or age, the key is to do the best you can with what you have. You obviously cared while you were dating, so don't let it slide in the humdrum of daily life. Taking time to spruce up demonstrates that he's still important enough that you care about how you look. And that's really encouraging to any man!

> **INSIGHT**: Wives, don't let 24 hours pass without expressing admiration for at least one thing your husband has said or done. If you can't think of anything to cheer about, remind him of a character trait that you admire. From time to time, send him a thank-you card or a surprise gift to commemorate something he's achieved. Being a cheerleader boils down to making him feel like he's important to you.

Change – it starts with you.

There's an old saying, "You can't change other people; you can only change yourself." It's one of those life lessons I've had to learn the hard way.

There are certain difficult relationships (like marriage) that we don't want to terminate, we just want them to improve. But it seems like things will only improve if the *other* person (like our spouse) starts behaving differently. We think, "If only they'd be kinder or more attentive, I'd be less irritable and snippy."

I can tell you from experience, that's never going to happen. Whether it's something major or minor (is any problem ever "small" in a marriage?), the answer is always the same: All you can change is you.

Don't wait for them to meet *your* need before you meet *theirs*.

Don't sit back and think, "I'd be more affectionate if she took better care of herself," or "I'd show him respect if he handled our finances better." Instead, move forward with what you *can* control — your reactions, responses, and behaviors. Work on being the finest husband or wife you can be, strive to meet your mate's needs, and believe the best about them — even if they are not yet meeting *your* needs.

Be like Johnny Lingo. See them today as the improved person they can become in the *future*. As your words and actions show admiration and respect, you will be amazed at the positive change your "eight-cow thinking" brings about!

When your spouse meets your needs, be sure to thank them. Affirming feedback will reinforce their actions. Knowing they're "hitting the mark" will make them feel rewarded and motivated. On the flipside, if you have needs that are *not* being addressed, bring these up, but do it gently. Utilize the "Five Steps to Conflict Resolution" from Chapter 4. They'll help you achieve the desired result without your spouse feeling attacked or belittled. If they get defensive, you won't get your needs met *and* you'll have an additional conflict to work through.

Again, clear communication is crucial; any extraordinary relationship is all about two people understanding and meeting each other's deepest needs.

TALK IT OVER.

No blaming, no shaming. Discuss these topics with an open mind:

1) Turn to page 109. How well do the Hann "Top 4 Needs" match each of you?

2) Do you have other needs that are *not* on the list? What are they?

3) Choose the area (sex, security, housekeeping, etc.) where you tend to have the most marital conflict. Is there a top need being unmet by one or both of you that is causing the recurring conflict?

TAKE ACTION.

Don't dodge this subject. We *all* need to get out of our comfort zone:

1) Block off an hour or so of distraction-free time and review each of your top needs with each other. Talk openly and honestly about which are important to you, and why. Are they being met?

2) Read and discuss this quote: "A great marriage is not when the 'perfect couple' comes together. It is when an imperfect couple learns to enjoy their differences." In what ways are the two of you most different? Have either of you changed significantly during the course of your marriage?

CHAPTER 6

Sex:
The truth, the naked truth, and nothing but

Guys, be honest. Did you jump ahead to this chapter?

I know that I would have.

And I'm guessing I'm not alone among my gender. After all, men are from Mars. Which means we're pretty much hot to trot at all times. Or *does* it?

British writer Tom Chivers quips, "Venus is a warm and hospitable place of social interaction and empathy, but not a great deal of sex … Mars is a place of carnal obsession; a planet where inhabitants think about sex every seven seconds."

Like Chivers, I grew up hearing that men think about sex every seven seconds.

If you do the math, that's 8,000 times a day during our 16 waking hours! That statistic has been refuted — not only by common sense, but in a trial published in the *Journal of Sex Research*. It found that men think about sex 34 times a day. Another study says it's more like 100. Both sound a bit low to me. But regardless of numbers, all the surveys agree men are more sex-obsessed than women.

Tom Chivers concurs. "It seems that the 'sex-mad man' and 'cuddle-hungry woman' stereotypes are broadly accurate."

But is that a fair statement?

Psychologist Nicholas Epley thinks so: "The stereotypes are about things that make men and women different. One is more interdependent, one is more independent. One is more sociable, the other more competitive. And one is more sexually rapacious than the other."

Rapacious? That's a pretty good description of the male appetite for sex. It means we're "ravenous, with excessive hunger."

It's like this: If I'm hungry, I can eat in my car, at my desk, or even standing up.

But Melina prefers to sit down at a properly set table with fresh flowers. Same for sex. I don't need a fancy setting, but Melina likes scented candles, clean sheets, and just the right music. She wants romantic conversation and compliments.

And it helps a ton if I've just done the dishes!

Am I alone in this?

Or do men really have an "anytime-anywhere" sex drive?

"Study after study shows men's sex drives are not only stronger than women's, but much more straightforward." Writing for *WebMD*, Richard Sine says, "The sources of women's libidos, by contrast, are much harder to pin down."

Do men really have an "anytime-anywhere" sex drive?

Amen to that. Sine says mood makes all the difference. "It's common wisdom that women place more value on emotional connection as a spark of sexual desire." But women also appear to be heavily influenced by social and cultural factors as well.

Sine quotes University of Chicago professor Edward Laumann, "Sexual desire in women is extremely sensitive to environment and context." Dr. Laumann says boys will be boys *regardless* of age, "As men and women age, each fantasize less, but men still fantasize about twice as often."

Okay. Sounds right. But *why* is the female sex drive seemingly weaker? And why is it more dependent on relational connections than raw physical attraction? Sine says, "Some theorize it's related to the greater power of men in society, or differing sexual expectations of men when compared to women."

Not so, says Professor Laumann. He attributes it to *sociobiology*.

"Men have every incentive to have sex to pass along their genetic material," Dr. Laumann says. "By contrast, women may be hardwired to choose their partners carefully, because they are the ones who can get pregnant ... They are more attuned to relationship quality because they want a partner who will stay around to help take care of the child."

Sine also taps Dr. Roy Baumeister, a social psychologist at Florida State for insight. After analyzing numerous studies, he concluded, "Men reported more spontaneous sexual arousal and had more frequent and varied fantasies."

Again, not surprising. Baumeister nails it: "Men want sex more often than women at the start of a relationship, in the middle of it, and after many years of it."

Maybe they could have skipped all the research and just asked comedian Billy Crystal. He says, "Women need a reason to have sex. Men just need a place."

Forsaking all others.

Listen up, guys. I'm mostly writing to the women here, but I have some pointers for you as well, so stick around.

When Chris first asked me to write on this subject, I put it off as long as I could. But I had to speak up. Marriages can rise and fall on the success of your sex life, so it can't be ignored. Do you remember your wedding vows? Ours went something like: "Chris, do you take Melina to be your lawfully wedded wife, to love, honor, and cherish, forsaking all others ..."

Ladies, do I need to repeat that? "Forsaking *all* others." Think about what that means in practical terms. For Chris to keep his vow — his public commitment to me before God and a church full of witnesses — it meant no flirting, no affection, and certainly no sex with any other woman *for the rest of his life.*

That means I am his only sexual outlet. Forever. I am the only one who can meet his number one need. Forever. I have a responsibility to my husband and my marriage to meet that need because he has forsaken all others. Forever.

Ladies, please don't withhold sex from your spouse as a punishment or a bargaining tool. That's manipulation, and it's wrong. Imagine if *he* intentionally withheld affection or communication because he was upset. How would you feel? Would it build up your marriage or chip away at its foundation? Likewise, it's important we never use sexual access as a penalty or a weapon in an argument.

English comedian Les Dawson understood this punitive behavior. He said, "My wife is a sex object. Every time I ask for sex, she objects."

Men have a need for speed. Fast cars, fast food, fast results.

So it's hard for them to understand that women are not turned on by flipping a switch. For us, making love is like building a fire. The flame starts with a tiny spark and slowly grows when stoked properly. Too much too soon can put it out, but with care and attention a small fire can get roaring hot!

> Don't withhold sex from your spouse as a punishment or a bargaining tool.

Men, we wives really *do* love, enjoy, and desire to be with our husbands sexually. It just takes us time to ramp up (in the right atmosphere with the right conversation) and feel emotionally connected and ready for intimacy.

Gents, here's a tip that never, ever fails: If you want great sex, take your wife to a hotel or on a vacation.

Why is a change of scene so helpful? As Melina pointed out to me, a woman's home is her *workplace* (even if she has a job outside the home). The minute a woman walks in the door, she sees clothes on the floor, dust on the furniture, and dishes in the sink. She sees bathrooms to clean and mouths to feed. In the blink of an eye, she's hit with a huge to-do list. With all these tasks screaming for attention, it's difficult to shift into "romance mode" with her husband.

Men, put yourself in her shoes. Can you imagine if your wife walked into your office and expected sex in the middle of a meeting? What if she wanted some sugar while you're being hit from all sides with emails, deadlines, and customer complaints? What if your phone was ringing off the hook and she asked you to drop everything for some "afternoon delight?" You'd think she was crazy.

(If it were after hours and nobody else was at work, it would be quite a different scenario! But that's not the point I'm making here.)

By the time a wife makes dinner, cleans up the kitchen, packs the lunches, bathes the kids, and reads them a bedtime story, she's exhausted. And just as she walks into the bedroom, yawning and feeling drained, she sees one more "chore" to do before her head hits the pillow — sex with her husband.

Now does a change of scene make sense?

Obviously, it's not practical to book a getaway every time you want to make love. But creating some atmosphere at home can turn what's deadly familiar into something alluring. Do something surprising to help her detach from her daily work and responsibilities. Perhaps a candle or some incense? Maybe potpourri or a bubble bath? Or a foot massage? How about asking how her day was?

INSIGHT: Men, connect with your wife *emotionally* through unhurried conversation and active listening before attempting to connect *physically*. Make her feel special through acts of service (babysitting, errands, etc.) and acts of kindness (shopping spree, day at the spa, etc.). Give surprise gifts like flowers and coffee cards. Nonsexual touching (holding hands, hugging) at the grocery store or the kids' soccer game can set up a hot time in the bedroom later on.

Is there such a thing as too much sex?

Once a day. Once a week. Once a month. When it comes to sexual frequency, we've heard every number you can imagine.

Each couple must work this out on their own. But I do know this — too *much* intimacy is hardly ever the problem! In Chapter 5, we saw how ironic it is that Satan tempts us TO have sex before we get married, and then tempts us NOT to have sex after we're married.

Ladies, don't let him win. He's a liar. The Bible unmasks his motive, *"The thief's purpose is to steal, kill, and destroy."* Whether you're religious or not, trust me when I say there is an enemy, and he wants to steal your joy, kill your romance, and destroy your marriage. And judging by statistics, he's pretty effective.

> Sex is God's idea. He's not embarrassed by it.

Fortunately, God has an alternative, *"My purpose is to give them a rich and satisfying life"* (John 10:10 NLT). He wants to increase your joy, rekindle your romance, and preserve your marriage. How? According to *The Message* version of that same verse, with *"more and better life than they ever dreamed of."*

God wants your marriage to succeed in every possible way. But it does involve following his guidelines. More on that later.

Meanwhile, it's essential to get one truth down into your bones: Sex is God's idea. It's his invention. His gift to humanity. So God's not embarrassed by it. He designed marriage and he created intimacy between a man and a woman.

How "intimate" is intimate? Genesis says *"the two become one person."* You can't get more intimate or connected than that (Gen. 2:24 TLB).

––––––

When Adam saw the newly created Eve, he was thrilled.
Excited. Turned on.
He blurted out, *"Finally! Bone of my bone, flesh of my flesh."* That hints at

the incredible closeness God intends for husband and wife. I can honestly say that Chris and I experience a special connection after we are sexually intimate. It's like we're on the same team, joined at the hip. We laugh more. We see eye to eye on things. We don't argue as much. Life is good.

But let a little too much time go by without making love, and suddenly we're facing off against each other, toe to toe. Skip sex for longer than normal, and we're ready to rumble over just about anything.

As I said, there's no magic formula for sexual frequency.

It's up to you to discover the rhythm that works best. What's important is that you both talk about it candidly and come to a mutual agreement. Ladies, I suggest leaning a bit toward his side on this one. In our relationship, my husband would be happy (okay, *thrilled*) to connect physically every day. On the other hand, I would prefer less often. After discussing it, we found a happy middle ground.

Except for your honeymoon, it's rare for any couple to have an equal, simultaneous desire for sex. No couple's timing lines up perfectly every time. So success is based on compromise. Psychiatrist and author Dr. Gail Saltz says, "If your sex drives are out of balance, your aim is to meet in the middle, having sex a bit more than one partner likes, but probably a bit less than the other likes."

In 2011, Tim and Kathy Keller wrote a magnum opus on relationships called *The Meaning of Marriage*. When it comes to the frequency issue, Tim says it's typical that "one person wants sex more often than the other." His solution is counterintuitive but brilliant, "If your main purpose in sex is giving pleasure, not getting pleasure, then a person who doesn't have as much of a sex drive physically can give to the other person as a gift. This is a legitimate act of love."

That might ruffle a few feathers. But it's scriptural. I seem to recall a verse that says, "*It's better to give than to receive.*" That applies double in marriage.

The Kellers explain, "Each partner in marriage is to be most concerned not with getting sexual pleasure but with giving it. In short, the greatest sexual pleasure should be the pleasure of seeing your spouse getting pleasure."

At the Hann house, our frequency target leans a little more to the Chris side. Do we always hit it? Of course not, but we are very aware of each other's needs and how critical an active, "giving" sex life is to keeping our marriage healthy.

––––––––

Whether you make love a little or a lot, you cannot overestimate the importance of sex in your marriage. In an article that asks "How Often Do Normal Couples Have Sex?" Heather Montgomery quotes therapist Dr. Ian Kerner: "In my experience, when couples stop having sex their relationships become vulnerable to anger, detachment, infidelity and, ultimately, divorce. I believe that sex matters: It's the glue that keeps us together and, without it, couples become 'good friends' at best, or 'bickering roommates' at worst."

INSIGHT: Remember the old Krazy Glue TV ads? A man literally glued his helmet to a steel beam and dangled above the ground to prove how strong the bond was. Sex is like that when it's done right. In his book *Sheet Music: Uncovering the Secrets of Sexual Intimacy in Marriage*, Dr. Kevin Leman says, "A fulfilling sex life is one of the most powerful marital glues a couple can have."

Drenched in sex.

Every February, 170 million or so Americans tune into the Super Bowl.

For the most part it's good, clean fun. But over the years, the extravagant halftime shows have become problematic for parents. I won't name names, but the entertainment has too often devolved into a combination strip tease and erotic dance, with performers bumping and grinding in seductive choreography that would have made our grandparents faint.

It's not just pop stars that go over the top with R-rated content.

We live in a country drenched in sex. From daytime talk shows to music videos, we're inundated with lurid imagery and references. Mailers for risqué lingerie arrive uninvited. Ads for escort services and sex toys appear in mainstream publications. From the annual "swimsuit issue" to steamy soap operas, we're surrounded by sex.

And the internet? Experts report 21 billion visits to porn sites per year. Even checking a legitimate news network means exposure to clickbait teaser links to buxom starlets, wardrobe malfunctions, and virility enhancers.

And yet for all of this sexuality on display, U.S. couples are still unwilling — or unable — to talk openly about sex with each other.

Debbie Roffman, a sexuality and family life educator says, "It's like we are a nation that is culturally disabled about this subject." In a documentary film called *Let's Talk About Sex*, Roffman says, "We don't know how to think about it. We don't know how to talk about it. We don't know where to begin."

> We're up to our eyeballs in sex. But we can't have a normal conversation about it.

On one hand, we're up to our eyeballs in sex. But on the other hand, we can't have a normal conversation about it. Victor Hanson of the *Washington Times* says we've become "a nation of promiscuous prudes."

Hanson explains, "Graphic language, nudity and sex are now commonplace in movies and on cable television ... Yet at the same time, committed couples are often too embarrassed to discuss sex with their own partners."

Our culture has a conflicted (even schizophrenic) view on sex. From magazine racks to TV commercials, sex is everywhere. Yet we're inexplicably uptight when it comes to talking about it with our spouses or children.

Why the disconnect? Why the contradiction?

Talking about sex.

Great question, Chris. With so much emphasis on the *fun* of sex and so little on the *consequences* of sex, why the heck don't we talk about it with our loved ones?

In places like Europe and Scandinavia, sex is openly discussed at home and seen as a natural part of a healthy relationship. I am not condoning their "anything goes" policy on human sexuality. But I *do* admire their ability to speak candidly about the subject.

And that's our goal for your marriage.

"Sex talk is omnipresent in our culture," says Elizabeth Bernstein of the *Wall Street Journal.* "But it's rare to see examples of someone discussing sex with the person he or she actually has sex with."

In her article "What Couples Want to Know But Are Too Shy to Ask," she quotes psychologist Barry McCarthy. "Talking about sex as a personal, intimate experience with your partner is a totally different kind of talk. You have to be open to talking about what you value and your vulnerability."

No one teaches us how to do that.

A major study released by the Center for Sexual Health Promotion at Indiana University showed that married couples have *more* sex than dating couples or unmarried couples living together. (Hurrah for our team!) Dr. McCarthy says sex energizes the relationship, makes each person feel desired and desirable, and serves as a buffer against difficulties. But when a couple can't *talk* about sex, things can go wrong and actually end up hurting the relationship.

To repair the sexual bond, you have to talk.

Bernstein says, "Love's initial romantic phase lasts anywhere from 18 months to three years. During this time, our hormones are out of control. We are intoxicated with our partner and find it easier to talk about sex."

But as years roll on, talking about intimacy gets more difficult. So don't feel isolated or strange if you get tongue-tied on this tricky subject.

Bernstein offers tips for couples. Here are a few:

• **Be gentle.** Need an opening line? "I love you, and I'd like to feel even more connected to you."

• **Don't discuss sex right after having sex.** (Unless it's to praise your partner!) Talk about it outside of the bedroom — on a walk or a drive.

• **Never blame your partner.** Don't psychoanalyze. Just describe what you feel is the problem.

Remember, it may take several conversations. Rome wasn't built in a day.

Can discussing sex with our spouse *really* make a difference?

"Only 9 percent of couples who can't comfortably talk about sex with one another say they're satisfied sexually." That's relationship coach Kyle Benson. He feels the most important part of cultivating a healthy sex life is talking about it.

In his article, "5 Simple Ways to Make Sex More Romantic," Benson says we not only need to talk, we need to be *specific*. "When partners talk to each other about their sexual needs, their conversations are often indirect, vague, and left unresolved. Typically, both partners are in a rush to finish the discussion, hoping their partner will understand their desires without saying much."

Don't be vague or shy. He cautions, "The less direct you are about what you want, the less likely you are to get it." Makes sense.

Deepen your intimacy by saying things like, "When you do such-and-such, I feel very aroused." Or "I like it best when we make love in the morning before work." Or "It feels amazing when we start off by doing whatchamacallit."

> Both partners need to be clear about what feels good and exciting and safe.

Avoid ambiguity and you'll avoid frustration. Benson suggests:

• **Be kind and positive.** Many of us feel embarrassed about our bodies or about our performance. Criticism will only worsen these insecurities.

• **Be patient.** Talking about sex can be uncomfortable due to our upbringing.

• **Don't take it personally.** If your partner isn't in the mood, it doesn't mean they find you unattractive. Or that your lovemaking skills are poor.

Remember, both partners need to be clear about what feels good and exciting and safe — and what doesn't.

Sex permeates our culture, dominates our thinking, and drives our behavior. That's not a moral judgment. It's simply an observation.

We were created as sexual beings, so it's only natural it would garner a huge chunk of our attention and be an elemental part of the marriage relationship.

The reason you're alive and reading this book is because your biological parents had sex. God made it that way. Other species reproduce without much fun or any real bonding. But God designed humans to be *uniquely united, passionately involved,* and *emotionally in sync* during the act of creating new life.

God is a big fan of sex within the context of marriage, and it's referred to often throughout the Bible.

My girlfriends ask me all the time, "You mean sex is in the Bible?"

Big time. People hook up throughout God's Word, and you can read about the good, the bad, and the ugly sides of sex. Nothing is hidden.

> God is a big fan of sex in marriage. It's referred to often in the Bible.

But from start to finish there is only one context for sex that God ordains, condones, and blesses — and that's the kind of sex that happens in an exclusive, monogamous, sacred union between one man and one woman.

God's plan is for a couple to enter into a binding, lifetime covenant that exalts (and protects) sexuality. *"That is why a man will leave his father and mother and be united with his wife, and they will become one flesh"* (Gen. 2:24 NIV).

This bonding means our primary loyalty shifts away from our parents (and from any other potential mate) to our spouse alone. This kind of commitment builds trust and sets the stage for phenomenal, un-inhibited sex.

This "one flesh" union is the merger of two different but equal parts (male and female) uniting physically, mentally, and spiritually for life. And it was God's idea! Jesus said, *"The Creator originally made man and woman for each other."*

Jesus also said that through marriage, a man *"is firmly bonded to his wife, becoming one flesh — no longer two bodies but one"* (Matt. 19:6 MSG).

If that sounds too mysterious, think of it like chocolate and peanut butter morphing into the perfect Reese's Peanut Butter Cup. Pastor Tim Keller puts it this way, "Marriage is a union between two people so profound that they virtually become a new, single person."

The sexiest book in the Bible.

"Make me drunk with your kisses! Your sweet loving is better than wine."

That's not a line from a rock ballad or a Harlequin romance. It's the first verse from a book in the Old Testament called the Song of Songs.

It might make grandma blush, but God stuck a red-hot erotic poem smack dab in the middle of his book. It champions the beauty and grandeur of human sexuality and romantic love as he planned it from the beginning.

There is no doubt that God's idea was for a man and woman to have a passionate and satisfying sex life. Proverbs tells us married guys, *"Enjoy the wife you married as a young man! Lovely as an angel, beautiful as a rose — don't ever quit taking delight in her body"* (Prov. 5:19 MSG).

Now, that's advice I can follow!

As we discussed, men have a remarkably strong sex drive. It's our number one need, so "taking delight" in each other is essential to a healthy marriage. Another translation (NIV) of that same verse reads, *"May her breasts satisfy you always, may you be intoxicated with her love."*

We are to be intoxicated, head over heels in love with our spouses. So why do so many couples struggle in the bedroom?

Statistically, we know married couples have *more* sex (and *better* sex) than any other population group. But sometimes things go sideways. Sometimes we don't reach that high plateau of intimacy.

Why not? Why do we sometimes fall short of the most rewarding connection ever devised? Because, like everything else in marriage, nothing good happens automatically or without work.

Commitment, intentionality, and mutual *effort* are the keys to an extraordinary sexual connection for any married couple.

"I know how important it (sex) is in keeping a marriage going." That's from vivacious actress and devoted wife, Lisa Rinna. "Without it, you're roommates, you don't value each other, and boom — someone's going to have an affair and get divorced … So you really need to make the effort."

Remember the "3 Rs" from school?

Three keys to better sex are summed up by relationship expert Gladys Diaz as "Remember, Re-create, and Reignite."

She gives this advice to women, but it's equally valuable for us men. "I recommend women practice the '3 Rs' to create and maintain intimacy: *Remember* why you fell in love with him in the first place; *Re-create* the special ways you used to let him know you loved, admired, and wanted to be with him; and *Reignite* the passion by doing something new to take you and him out of your comfort zone!"

Pop culture is lying to you.

You may be the best lover in town.

You may have skill, stamina, and all the right moves, but real-life sex can never measure up to what you see in the movies. Or read about in romance novels.

Sorry, but your bedroom exploits will fall short by comparison.

After a good dose of hyper-sex on HBO or Netflix, a couple can't help but make comparisons to their own performance (or lack thereof). Mental blocks to having satisfying sex often stem from the misconceptions we pick up from pop culture. The fantasies portrayed in media create the image of an erotic playground that just doesn't exist. The exploits of lovers on the big and little screen cannot be lived up to and lead to feelings of frustration, guilt, and inadequacy.

Each spouse brings a different approach to sex. And different ways of talking about it.

On top of all this misinformation, each spouse brings a different approach to sex and different ways of talking about it. Many of our preconceived notions about sex are built on fiction, fueled by rumors, and complicated by our lack of ability to discuss the subject with our spouses.

INSIGHT: An additional obstacle can be the residual effects of sexual abuse. Melina and I have no specific expertise to offer in this area. But what we *can* say with confidence is that God loves you, and if you've been betrayed, he can bring healing to help move you beyond it. If you've been molested or abused, our strong recommendation is to find a therapist specializing in this area. Please don't go it alone; seek professional help.

As we've shown, our day-to-day world is sexually supercharged; the imagery is everywhere.

Sadly, the stereotypical images are usually dishonest.

These erroneous depictions are damaging to couples because they set false expectations. As a result, all newlyweds get two wakeup calls: First, SHE won't be begging him for sex at every possible moment. Second, HE won't be able to automatically make her swoon with pleasure.

In both cases, the disappointed spouse may begin to wonder, "What's wrong with him? He doesn't sweep me away with an irresistible force." Or, "What's wrong with her? She doesn't chase after me asking for sex."

Along with these false expectations (absorbed from our Hollywood role models), men and women simply approach sex from two very different starting points.

Men generally have a stronger drive than women. So the distorted portrayal of women aggressively craving sex fits their dream. When it doesn't happen, men are confused. We know of a couple who struggled and eventually got a divorce because they couldn't align their expectations with reality. There were other issues, but their weak sex life was the death blow. The problem was exacerbated by the husband's failure to try and understand his wife's needs — or to communicate his own in a respectful tone.

An irresistible force wanted sex with an immovable object.

In physics and in marriage that's an impossibility. This frazzled husband pushed and pressured his wife for sex. Without any warm-up conversation. Without any nonsexual touching. Without any romance earlier in the day. Nothing that would meet her need for affection and free her up to willingly engage later on.

No wonder she began to see sex as just one more item on her "to do" list to check off.

Barriers to amazing sex.

So how *does* a couple move past the misconceptions drawn from pop culture and the clear differences in the way genders approach sex?

To survive and thrive, every couple needs to:

1) **Understand the sexual differences between each other**

2) **Be able to communicate openly about their sex life**

That's it. Two things. Nail them and you're good to go.

Ready? Let's unpack this pair of undeniable, irrefutable, super-important areas you MUST get right to enjoy a fulfilling sex life ...

First, understand your sexual differences.

The average man pegs the sex-drive meter.

Most women barely budge the needle.

That's not to say wives don't enjoy sex, but they don't have the same intense physical need. For women, it's more about connection and relationship. That's why a man must meet his wife's need for affection and communication. If he does, she'll feel connected to him and free to let herself go sexually.

That's also why conflict resolution is so critical for a great sex life. If there are unresolved issues, a woman cannot feel connected or close to her husband. She may even build up resentment over time. As issues fester, there will be little or no desire for physical connection with her man.

In some mysterious way, a woman is connected to everything around her, with a million details flowing together simultaneously and seamlessly in her mind. At any given moment, she's focused on being a mom, balancing the budget, running the house, and processing a zillion contingencies: *Do we need milk? How are the kids doing in school? What did Sharon mean when she said my outfit was "interesting?"*

Men peg the sex-drive meter. Most women barely budge the needle.

And all that mental activity is not easily (or quickly) dismissed! From experience, I know that men need downtime to disengage from their workday in order to engage playfully with their kids. Likewise, women need time to unplug from all that's flowing through their mind in order to engage sexually with their spouse.

Right on, Chris! Another big difference is that we women are highly self-critical.

Men do *not* understand how hard women are on themselves, especially regarding their appearance. Women are bombarded with images of what they "should" look like. Of course, these computer-enhanced images are impossible to copy. Comparing ourselves to these picture-perfect examples can leave even the prettiest women feeling unsexy.

Here's something else men need to know. A woman's body naturally goes through changes after having kids. It's just part of life, but it's tough for most women to feel quite as beautiful after delivering children into this world.

If your wife isn't happy about her body (for whatever reason) it's harder for her to be enthusiastic about an activity that exposes her even more. A man can really help his wife here by building into her all that he finds sexy and attractive about her (remember how "eight-cow thinking" works).

Guys, watch for any and all chances to compliment her appearance — an outfit you think looks great, those jeans that make her look hot, a particular way she wears her hair, anything! Comment on how her glasses make her look classy … and how her heels make her look sexy. Be constantly mentioning things that *you* find attractive about her. Remember, she is continually bombarded with slicked-up images that can make her feel self-conscious and inadequate.

Regardless of your wife's age or beauty, it's likely she has a hard time seeing herself positively. The incessant media stream is dragging her self-image down.

You need to provide consistent, positive messaging to counter the negative influences. Husbands are in a unique position to counteract this self-critical tendency with an ongoing stream of affirmation, accolades, and compliments.

> **INSIGHT**: Chris *does* compliment me when I wear something new or get my hair or nails done. And believe me, it's a boost! But I'd like the ladies to do the same to their husbands now and then, too. Remind him he's a handsome, sexy hunk. Often. Even if his idea of high fashion is sweatpants and a flannel shirt.

You'll recall we said women are like Crock-Pots; we need time to "warm up" to the idea of sex and get cooking. That's because we often come to bed dragging our bag of things to do (kids, lunches, dishes, laundry, etc.). It seems like every room we pass by on our way to the bedroom reminds us of more work to be done.

Women see home as a jobsite. Men see home as a comforting shelter.

For guys, home is where you can take off your shoes and relax. For gals, home is where you pick up a bucket and get busy — a place of endless work that no one else seems to notice or care about.

And honestly men, you really *are* like a microwave, always ready to go. You take almost no time to heat up. Plus, you're so good at compartmentalizing. You can close the "responsibility door" and move right to the "sex compartment" without a hitch. But don't give up on us slow cookers. Like I tell Chris, "Honey, Crock-Pots still cook — it just takes a little longer for us to heat up!"

An actual Crock-Pot is simple to operate — you put your ingredients in (a roast, some vegetables, etc.) and let it cook all day until mealtime. A human Crock-Pot is also pretty basic. Just plug us in and give us time. Don't rush us, don't stand around worrying. Remember our needs (communication and affection) and address them with gusto. Ingredients could include rubbing our back or vacuuming the living room. The recipe might include giving us a foot massage or brewing some tea.

Before you know it, we're in the mood for love.

Chris will usually call on his way home from work and ask if he can stop and pick anything up for me. You men may not realize it, but he just expressed love by offering to help! *(My Crock-Pot just got plugged in.)* Then maybe a kiss on the neck while I'm in the kitchen. *(My Crock-Pot just got hotter.)* Later on, maybe some playful hugging with no strings attached. *(My Crock-Pot is ready to go.)*

> Women see home as a jobsite. Men see home as a comforting shelter.

Taking out the trash or giving a helping hand around the castle will also work wonders. Relationship expert Dr. John Gottman says, "Women find a man's willingness to do housework extremely erotic."

Amen to that.

Pompeii is an ancient Roman city frozen in time.

The bodies of men, women, and children are preserved by layers of volcanic ash that belched from Mount Vesuvius in A.D. 79. Archaeologists found the city virtually intact — shops full of merchandise, loaves of bread still in the ovens.

What nobody expected were the scores of erotic wall paintings and sculptures depicting graphic sexual themes. In one building — a brothel — a series of paintings depict an array of positions for sexual intercourse. The images were there to stimulate male customers into plunking down their money.

This preoccupation with eroticism shocked Europe, and the city's artwork was censored from view for two centuries. Even today, it's off limits to minors. From archaic frescoes to online videos, the power of seeing sexual images is proof that men are (and always have been) highly visual creatures.

None of that surprised me!

Just a glimpse of my lover's body is all it takes to arouse me. It's a total turn-on for a husband to see his wife naked. And if they put on some fancy lingerie, our pulse races even higher. Can you see the potential problem here? A man has a huge desire to see his wife's body, and a woman has an equally huge desire to avoid showing it.

As Melina discussed, women suffer from self-criticism based on conscious or subconscious comparisons to unattainable body ideals. As a result of this insecurity, many women want to "operate under cover" (literally hiding under the sheets) or keep the lights off in total darkness. Some wives will avoid any sexual encounters in daylight and even prefer to undress in private.

Melina was no different in that regard.

Fortunately, we found a compromise. We wanted to balance a man's need for visual stimulation and the woman's desire to conceal her body. The answer was as old as Pompeii — candles! Try using a candle or two as a romantic light source. It's bright enough for him, but discrete enough for her. *Scented* candles can further stimulate the senses for an even more amorous atmosphere.

> Men have always been highly visual creatures.

A note here to the ladies: We guys view you as incredibly sexy — just the way you are! Women don't understand this, but most husbands are not as fussy and perfection-driven as you are. We don't understand the feelings of insecurity and inadequacy you get from trying to match the enhanced images of idealized women. To us, you're *already* desirable and beautiful and alluring.

Being sexy in a man's eyes is more about how a woman carries herself than having the "perfect" body. For instance, a guy can find a woman of any shape or size very sexy if she presents herself with confidence, if she's happy and smiling and "in the game" with him. On the other hand, a woman with a so-called perfect body can be very undesirable if she's uptight, critical, and not in sync with her spouse. If a woman is frowning all the time or acting insecure, most guys will not find her attractive or sexy — even if she's a cover girl.

Second, communicate openly about your sex life.

Did you marry a psychic? Is your spouse a mind reader?

If not, this section is for you.

Communication is the cornerstone of a thrilling and fulfilling sex life. You must talk openly with each other about what you like and don't like, what turns you on and what turns you off. Without communicating, there will be a lot of guessing, missing the target, and sorry to be blunt — plain old *faking* it.

Ladies and gentlemen, your spouse will not be able to please you unless you tell them what's working and what's not. Without feedback, they won't even know *when* they should (or should not) initiate sex, let alone *how* to make you happy!

One important lesson I learned (Melina says this was absolutely huge for her) is to take no for an answer and not pout. I've learned not to pressure her and to be okay if she's not in the mood to make love at any particular time. She says my willingness to back off makes her feel honored and significant.

Trust me, *ladies* — it's not easy for a guy to stand down and take a cold shower, so to speak. But trust me, *men* — you're much better off if you do! Pressuring or guilting your wife about how unfair it is to leave poor little you all "hot and bothered" is childish, and a deterrent to ongoing trust and mutual respect.

As a man, I know that being turned down (for any reason) is rough. It's hard on our ego and our physical body. There are plenty of times when I think about making love all day at work. By the time I get home, I can't wait to hop in the sack. By bedtime, I'm *more* than ready to go. But maybe Melina's had a long, stressful day. Despite my eagerness, she indicates she's too tired or not in the mood on that particular night. What I've learned to do is to ease off and just hold her.

> Being sexy is more about how a woman carries herself than having the "perfect" body.

To avoid awkwardness, you may want a code word to signal each other. We've come up with a phrase that works for us. When Melina's not in the mood or she's tied up with something else, she asks, "Can I have a rain check?"

This communicates to me that she absolutely *wants* to make love, but the timing's not quite right. Hearing "rain check" lets me know that we *will* be together soon and keeps me from feeling rejected. This gentle, humorous approach is important for men, given our fragile egos.

We have fun with this code. After a few days of "rain checks," one of us may playfully say, "You know, it's been dry for a while, but the weatherman's predicting there might be a BIG storm coming tonight!"

Melina understands that *how* a woman defers her husband's advances is really important. Guys are sensitive about sex. It's hard for us to be rejected by the woman we love when we are turned on and vulnerable.

> Your spouse can't please you unless you tell them what's working. And what's not.

A wife needs to reassure her man that his needs are important to her. For example: "I love you and love having sex with you, but I'm so tired right now from the long meetings I had today. Can we have a rain check?"

Also, a smart wife doesn't criticize her husband for wanting sex. Reactions like, "You're such a horndog" or "Can't you think of anything else?" are not helpful! Ladies, sex is a man's number one need, and he's put it completely in your hands by forsaking all others. You need to treat his inclinations with tender loving care if you want an extraordinary marriage.

There's another myth that needs to be shattered: Sex in movies or novels always results in spectacular, simultaneous orgasms that "Rock the Casbah." So if you experience anything less, you feel inferior. Baloney. If the earth doesn't wobble every time you have sex, relax — you're normal!

Listen to me carefully. You are NOT going to both have "mind-blowing orgasms" every time. In fact, if that's your only goal, you need to check your priorities. A healthy sex life is *not* about performance but about having an intimate connection.

So what *about* "The Big O?"

Early in their marriage, Tim Keller's wife, Kathy, wrote, "We came to realize that orgasm is great, especially climaxing together. But the awe, the wonder, the safety, and the joy of just being 'one' is stirring and stunning even without that."

That concept removed the pressure, "When we stopped trying to perform and started trying to simply love one another with sex, things started to move ahead."

A word to my fellow men: We are goal setters by nature and very task-oriented — even when it comes to sex. Don't be too hard on yourself if you don't set the bed on fire every time. A loving wife understands and does not think less of you.

Don't turn sex into an Olympic sport. Best-selling marriage author Dr. Kevin Leman tells newlyweds (and veterans alike!) to chill out if things fall flat now and then: "Nobody's sex life is such that every experience is a ten. You may have to be satisfied with regular eights or sixes and even an occasional three."

> Don't be too hard on yourself if you don't set the bed on fire every time.

Relax and enjoy each other; remove the pressure to perform. It's not a competitive event. You have your entire lives to develop a wonderful love life together.

As I said earlier, it's helpful if couples openly communicate on how often they'll have sex. You don't have to carve anything in stone, but you need some alignment of expectations regarding frequency.

If the man wants sex every day and the wife prefers to wait for national holidays, there's trouble ahead. A large gap could have relationship-damaging consequences and erode closeness.

(On a humorous note, if you ask a couple how often they have sex in a month, the woman will usually guess high and the man will usually guess low. It's been proven!)

We know a woman whose grandmother had a "Rule of Three" that she passed down when her grandkids got engaged: *A married couple should not go more than three days without making love.* Can you imagine your granny telling you that? Not me. But I applaud her open dialogue on this important topic. Her sage advice improved her granddaughter's odds of having a successful, long-term marriage.

Kids: The antidote for sex.

Forget saving the world or fighting evil. The real *Mission Impossible* is finding time for sex after you have children.

Those bundles of joy that bring so much happiness can be passion killers for a couple who's sleep-deprived, overworked, and stressed out.

Life is already hectic and busy, and when children come along the work goes up exponentially. Both of you are worn out from the daily grind — bosses, meetings, checkups, spit-ups, cleanups — and carving out free time for regular sex can seem difficult if not impossible.

When the kids were young, our sex life took a nosedive, and we looked for every chance to find time alone. Even after finally getting the little ones to sleep, we'd worry about making too much noise. It's hard to focus on passionate, crazy sex when you're wondering, "What was that? Did one of the kids get up?"

> Those bundles of joy that bring so much happiness can be passion killers.

Nothing cramps your style more than envisioning the dreaded "walk-in" — a visit that could embarrass you *and* traumatize the munchkins.

As our family got older, things became easier. With only two children, we enjoyed conjugal bliss whenever they were both invited to sleepovers on the same night (can you say party time?). Bottom line is that even though life is busy and kids are demanding, your intimate together-time is foundational for marriage.

Warning: We know parents who pretty much hit the pause button on sex until the kids are grown up. Don't do that. If you delay gratification for too long, you'll look at each other one day and ask, "Who the heck are you?" Too many spouses who drift apart during the helter-skelter of child-rearing walk away from marriage when the kids leave the nest. This can happen to well-meaning couples who focus all their energies on the kids and neglect their own romantic relationship.

Don't settle for roommate status. Marriage isn't about being adult friends who inhabit the same house. It's about being *lovers*. So learn to pick your moments. Learn to drop the kids off with relatives. Learn to snuggle while the kids watch cartoons.

> Marriage isn't about being friends who inhabit the same house. It's about being *lovers*.

INSIGHT: Make it a habit to schedule romance. Book an appointment for a sexy rendezvous just like you do for an oil change or a dental cleaning. If you don't have time for long, luxurious sex, don't despair. A quickie can be thrilling! Sex on the fly can be satisfying and restore closeness. Not every event is a marathon.

Set the mood to be nude.

Let me talk to the guys about how to impress your wife.

First, remember that a woman can't "disconnect" as easily as guys can. If you want your wife to be open to sexual advances, do whatever you can to help her separate from the busyness that's tugging at her.

Instead of asking, "Honey, can we have sex tonight?" try asking, "Honey, is there anything I can do for you?"

While she recovers from the shock, get busy fixing whatever's broken, scrubbing whatever's nasty, and generally just making yourself useful.

No woman on earth can ignore that kind of unselfish helping hand. I've always said a wise man starts making love by helping with dinner, setting the table, and loading the dishwasher (would that be *chore-play*?).

"Good sex is an all-day affair. You can't treat your wife like a servant and expect her to be eager to sleep with you at night." That's Dr. Kevin Leman again. He adds, "Your wife's sexual responsiveness will be determined by how willingly you help out with the dishes, the kids' homework, or that leaky faucet that drips throughout the night."

I have girlfriends who come home beat from a long day. They help the kids get settled, cook dinner, and clean up while their husbands loaf around watching sports. As the burly men lounge in front of the TV, the women get the kids ready for bed, do a load of wash, and fall into bed exhausted.

Do you think they want to canoodle with Mister Couch Potato? Absolutely not, and you can understand why!

> A wise man starts making love by helping with dinner.

Smart husbands don't pop the question at bedtime. They start their seduction way back in the kitchen (or family room, laundry room, or wherever the need is greatest) by helping, laughing, talking, and flirting.

Want better sex? Put down the remote and grab a dust mop.

Some thoughts on pornography.

Question: "How can you tell if a man has looked at porn?"

Answer: "If he's breathing."

Although funny, it's painfully true.

I grew up in an era when boys passed around tattered copies of *Playboy* magazine. But the internet changed everything. Today, the sheer volume of online smut is mind boggling. Porn sites get more visits than Netflix, Amazon, and Twitter combined. To put that in perspective, porn rakes in more money than Major League Baseball, the National Football League, and the National Basketball Association combined.

Attitudes about porn are changing. Almost 80 percent of young adults (men and women) view pornography in some form. Kids in grade school "sext" each other with obscene material. One study found that teens and young adults consider "not recycling" more immoral than viewing pornography.

Today, many ordinary, decent people consider porn a good thing. In fact, some marriage books actually recommend couples watch pornography together to improve their relationship. Is that good advice? Let's ask the experts.

According to noted sociologist Jill Manning, research indicates pornography consumption is associated with:

> Almost 80 percent of young adults (men and women) view pornography.

• Increased marital distress, infidelity, and separation

• Decreased marital intimacy and sexual satisfaction

• Increased sexual activity that's abusive, illegal, or unsafe

Does any of that sound like the recipe for a healthy marriage?

Not according to The American Academy of Matrimonial Lawyers. They report that 56 percent of divorce cases involve one party having "an obsessive interest in pornographic websites."

That's staggering — *over half* of divorce cases have some porn causality.

According to the *Journal of Adolescent Health*, prolonged exposure to pornography leads to a series of marriage-killing behaviors:

• Diminished trust between intimate couples

• Belief that promiscuity is the natural state

• Belief that marriage is sexually confining

Does porn have *any* positive role in the bedroom?

Some therapists claim a dose of porn before sex can act as an aphrodisiac. But for us highly visual males, it leads to a desensitizing of what we find arousing. The result is we're less and less turned on by our wives. Here's why: Our brains release chemicals when we're sexually engaged. In the marriage bed, these help cement the intimate connection with our wives. However, when a man is viewing porn, that same chemical connection is bonding him with an *illusion*.

Over time, his brain's chemical connection with porn becomes stronger, making it harder to relate intimately with his wife. This chemical process can lead to porn addiction — moving from casual to obsessive viewing. Like a drug addict, a porn user needs to "up the dosage" to try and relive his original high. In some cases, this search for a bigger "fix" means having an affair or paying for sex.

Using porn erodes the intimate emotional connection between husband and wife. But did you know it also damages your physical *ability* to perform sexually?

An alarming study cited by the Covenant Eye organization confirms the danger. In it, Dr. Mary Anne Layden states, "Pornography viewers tend to have problems with premature ejaculation and erectile dysfunction. Having spent so much time in unnatural sexual experiences with paper, video, and cyberspace, they find it difficult to have sex with a real human being."

Over half of divorce cases have some porn causality.

Some guys use porn as a "training" regimen, hoping the "workout" will help their performance with their wife. Again, the opposite is true.

French author Virginie Despentes says, "Consuming pornography does not lead to more sex, it leads to more porn. Much like eating McDonald's every day will accustom you to food that (although enjoyable) is essentially not food ..."

Your battle is my battle.

Let's step away from the stats and get personal.

First, let me say I'm not making accusations or pointing fingers. In fact, I've struggled with porn for much of my life. From my own battle, I am intimately familiar with how seductive porn is and how hard it is to break free.

Guys, I know the drill. I know about hiding porn use from family and peers. I know about the guilt and fear that come from not being able to control yourself.

I totally get it because I've dealt with the same behaviors.

My first exposure to porn came at a buddy's house when I was about ten or eleven. Wanting to act "cool," he took me and a friend down to his basement where his dad had a huge box filled with *Playboy* magazines.

From that initial thrill, my problem lay dormant until I found a collection of *Penthouse* magazines someone discarded. Now I had my own little stash hidden between my mattress and box springs. I lusted after those photos during my teenage years, carving neurological pathways into my psyche.

Porn wasn't nearly as accessible as it is today, with unlimited material online. Back then, you had to physically walk into a local store to get it. I'm sure the sheer embarrassment of this ordeal kept many men (like me) in check. The easy, anonymous flow of porn today helps explain its explosion among youth.

During college, I lived in a house owned by a very successful man I had worked for. When he passed away, his estate asked me to stay on while they worked on selling it. One day, I came across the man's library of adult videos. This was my first exposure to hard-core porn. Like the mythical Sirens in Homer's *Odyssey*, the video vixens beckoned me again and again, saturating my mind with explicit, raunchy sex.

In Greek mythology, the Sirens were beautiful creatures who lured sailors to shipwreck. Like those doomed sailors, I was unable to resist the enticing pull of the girls in the porn videos. But something was wrong. Even though I wasn't a Christian yet, I always felt a little dirty and empty after watching them. At the time, I had no moral issue with the subject matter, yet it left me unsatisfied.

Soon, I noticed I was becoming desensitized to erotica. It was taking more and more exposure to turn me on.

Eventually, it hit me — by ingesting porn I was systematically lowering my ethical standards on acceptable interaction between the sexes.

> Today's easy, anonymous flow of porn helps explain its explosion.

Then I became a Christian. Boom. I threw all the videos away. This successfully removed the temptation from me. At least temporarily. Years passed without incident. I certainly wasn't about to walk into a store and buy porn myself! Without any materials to look at, the burning urge subsided. Mostly.

Fast-forward. Melina and I met, dated, got married. Our children were born. And then the Internet Age exploded and online porn was calling my name. All of a sudden, I was face-to-face with my old thorn in the flesh. But this time it was only a mouse click away. I gave in and explored the sites. Peeking at porn always brought anxiety about being discovered: *I was a Christian, right? Wasn't I supposed to be stronger than this? What was wrong with me?*

I learned that while I was a brand-new person *spiritually*, I was still living in a *physical* body that struggled with temptations. Although salvation is instantaneous, developing godly character is a process — and requires time, study, prayer, and plenty of patience.

Meanwhile, my lustful desires were still deeply ingrained, always lurking just beneath the surface, waiting for a trigger.

Early in our marriage, I was so busy with family and trying to launch a new business that I didn't have much time to view porn. But as the kids got older and financial success began to come, I had more idle hours — especially in the evenings. And that's when I usually gave in. Another weak spot was business travel. Having adult movies available in my hotel rooms was a strong temptation.

Sometimes I could resist, other times not. Whenever I gave in, I vowed to never slip again, but it was a seesaw battle. Soon I began noticing a slight change in my sex life with Melina. I wasn't getting quite as turned on as I used to. Worse yet, I occasionally needed to get "warmed up" beforehand by looking at porn.

This decline in my sexual attraction toward Melina scared me. It wasn't like I was a full-on addict wasting hours in front of porn. I was a light user, indulging my curiosity a few times a month. But even as a dabbler, I still felt the unhealthy effect it was having on our sex life and by default, our marriage.

I wanted to stop. I needed to stop. I tried to stop. But the urge was embedded too deep to quit cold turkey.

Then the breakthrough: Melina and I began talking openly about my struggles with porn, and she became my accountability partner. She was awesome. She encouraged me and empowered me to overcome this thing that had such a grip on my life. She never belittled me or made me feel like a loser.

Even with her help, the pull was strong.

I tried fighting it with sheer willpower. I could be successful for months on end, maybe even a year. But sooner or later, I'd be in a weakened state and slip up. Maybe I'd been on the road too long. Or maybe a couple of drinks would lower my inhibitions enough to sneak a peek or two. The trigger was usually some combination of physical exhaustion, a splash of alcohol, and too much time elapsed since our last lovemaking session.

After continuing to fail, I realized willpower alone was not cutting it. So with prayer and help from Melina, we came up with "built-in accountability" solutions.

First, we put a filter on our home internet that blocked all porn sites (and anything *resembling* porn). We wanted this for our teenagers anyway, but in reality, it was more for me. Today, the filter's zero tolerance for porn still forces me to seek out my beautiful, sexy wife when I'm feeling frisky instead of some hollow illusion full of empty promise.

Second, I cut off all porn sites in my hotel rooms. The minute I check in, I disable the adult movie channels. If needed, I call the front desk to have all content blocked and all access removed — *before* I have a chance to be tempted. Melina knows she is free (and encouraged) to check how I'm doing anytime day or night.

In my case, Melina is my accountability partner. But if your wife doesn't feel comfortable with that, choose a close friend to monitor you. Marriage is far too important to let any weakness rise up and corrode your intimate connection.

I encourage every man to take action and not let pornography steal the beauty from your love life. If you think you may be addicted, get help from a counselor or support group at your church. Don't be shy. Be intentional. Protect the most important relationship you have on this earth.

————

If you're inclined to wink at pornography, consider the unique viewpoint of Stephen Arterburn and Fred Stoeker. In their must-read book, *Every Man's Battle: Winning the War on Sexual Temptation One Victory at a Time*, they write: "For males, impurity of the eyes is sexual foreplay … Foreplay ignites passions … God views foreplay outside marriage as wrong … It's critical to recognize visual sexual impurity as foreplay."

Whoa! Is a life of visual purity even possible? Can a red-blooded man keep his eyes from wandering?

Arterburn and Stoeker believe we can: "We can't eliminate our maleness, and we're sure we don't want to. For instance, we want to look at our wives and desire them. They're beautiful to us, and we're sexually gratified when we gaze at them … In its proper place, maleness is wonderful. Yet our maleness is a major root of sexual sin. So what do we

Don't let pornography steal the beauty from your love life.

do? We must choose to be *more* than male. We must choose manhood."

The coauthors say that God is asking (and empowering us) to "rise above our natural tendencies to impure eyes, fanciful minds, and wandering hearts."

INSIGHT: Both men and women can be addicted to porn. You can help break the porn habit with internet accountability and online filters. By sending reports of your online activity to a friend or mentor, you can have open conversations about your struggle. Check out *covenanteyes.com* for free tools and resources.

Sex is better than you think.

Isn't the human body amazing?

God created our exquisite anatomy and our incredibly sensitive nervous system to give and receive pleasure for our entire married lives. Instead of treating sex like a taboo subject, shouldn't we honor God's creative skills and make our marriages the absolute best "between the sheets?"

The Bible not only condones erotic love, it virtually commands it.

The Apostle Paul spelled out the importance of marital relations: "*The husband should fulfill his wife's sexual needs, and the wife should fulfill her husband's needs*" (1 Cor. 7:3-5 NLT). This passage goes on to say the husband's and wife's bodies belong not only to themselves, but to *each other* for mutual sexual pleasure and satisfaction. The inference is that sex was to be frequent and reciprocal. (Remarkably, Paul's enlightened viewpoint was written in a time when women were treated like second-class citizens without rights.)

On the role of sex in marriage, Tim Keller says, "Kathy and I often liken sex to oil in an engine — without it, the friction between all the moving parts will burn out the motor. Without joyful, loving sex, the friction in a marriage will bring about anger, resentment, hardness, and disappointment. Rather than being the commitment glue that holds you together, it can become a force to divide you. Never give up working on your sex life."

So let's work. Let's take risks. Let's be creative. Let's communicate. Let's start conversations with our partners that we've been afraid to bring up.

And most of all, let's celebrate!

INSIGHT: Intimacy was intended for marriage. Any other sexual interaction is inferior, counterfeit, and ultimately harmful. For those of us who've fallen short, God offers forgiveness and a clean start. He created sex for procreation, pleasure, and to express love between a husband and wife. Enjoy.

TALK IT OVER.

These are touchy subjects, so be gentle with each other. No criticizing allowed!

1) Ask each other three questions: "How would you rate our sex life?" Then, "Do you have unmet expectations? What are they?" And finally, "What can we do together to improve?" (Caution — be extra affirming, sensitive and thoughtful in this discussion.)

2) Ask your spouse: "Are we having too much or too little sex?" Discuss your current frequency and timing with each other. Compare your answers and move toward a new rhythm that's better for both parties.

3) Has your sex become a dull routine? Discuss ways to recapture the spark (this chapter is full of suggestions). If you're not bored, discuss how to deepen your intimate connection and take your sex life to new heights of fulfillment.

TAKE ACTION.

This is the best homework assignment ever! Seriously, get naked and get busy:

1) Schedule a sexy getaway, the sooner the better. One night is okay, but if you can swing a weekend, go for it. Make it a romantic and exciting time for re-energizing your love life.

2) Set the mood. Purchase some candles, incense, and romantic music for your bedroom and commit to using them next time you make love.

3) Spice it up. Each of you will write down three new things you'd like to experience during sex. Then swap lists. Without telling your spouse which one you pick, surprise them by doing it.

CHAPTER 7

Finances:
Dollars and sense

Ever dream of winning the lottery?

The biggest Powerball jackpot in U.S. history was $1.6 billion, drawn in 2016. This record-shattering jackpot was split between just three tickets. That's over $500 million per winner.

No wonder a recent Gallup Poll found over half of all Americans play the lottery!

In fact, we spend more money playing the lottery than on books, video games, and tickets for movies and sporting events combined. According to an article in *The Atlantic*, Americans spend $70 billion a year on lotto games. That's $300 in tickets for each adult in the USA.

Obviously, people believe that winning a big pile of money would solve most — if not all — of life's problems. But is that true?

Turns out money is *not* a panacea. Far from it. In fact, 7 out of 10 people who receive a sudden windfall of cash lose it within a few years.

"Many winners befall the so-called curse of the lottery," warns *Time* magazine's Melissa Chan. "With some squandering their fortunes or meeting tragic ends."

In "How Winning the Lottery Makes You Miserable," Chan cites expert Don McNay, "So many wind up unhappy or broke. Terrible things happen. People commit suicide. People run though their money. They go through divorce or die."

But you don't have to be rich to run up big debts. The average credit card debt for U.S. households that carry a balance is now over $16,000.

So, we're all susceptible to overspending and stress. Especially in a marriage. If a couple lacks an agreed-upon budget, even mile-high stacks of cash won't keep them from arguing about money. And that's a poison pill for marriage.

> ## Arguing about money is the number one predictor of divorce.

In fact, arguing about money is the hands-down, *number one* predictor of divorce, according to Sonya Britt, a Kansas State University researcher.

Britt found that couples who argue about money early in their relationships are at the greatest risk for divorce, regardless of variables like income, debt load, or net worth. "It's not children, sex, in-laws or anything else. It's money — for both men and women."

Whether we're rich, poor, or somewhere in between, disagreements about budgeting and finances are marriage killers that need to be met head-on.

Wedding bells vs. wedding bills.

Every little girl dreams of having the perfect fairy-tale wedding when they grow up. And I was no different! I had met my Prince Charming, so why shouldn't our big day be just as perfect as a Disney fantasy?

We were engaged in May 1995, with our wedding date just four months later in September. We were very much in love and both looking forward to a "storybook wedding" that matched the magic and beauty of our unique relationship.

The challenge — as we'd find out later — was finding a way to pay for it.

We had limitless love, but a limited budget. Each of our fathers had graciously given us $5,000 for the wedding. From this $10,000 pot we had to pay for the entire wedding (invitations, rehearsal dinner, flowers, cake, wedding dress, tuxedo rental, reception, etc.) *and* our honeymoon. To make it even tougher, we were getting married in Southern California!

My home state has lots of benefits, but it is *not* the cheapest place to get hitched.

The gap between our expectations and our financial reality could have caused a huge fight. It could have driven us apart. Instead, it brought us closer together. In fact, Chris and I look back on our wedding as the experience that first taught us how to communicate with each other about finances.

As a newly engaged couple, we determined to only spend up to the combined $10,000 gift from our fathers. That would be our total budget, period. (This first big financial decision set the tone for thousands more since then.)

Once our spending limit was set in stone, we decided each of us would take responsibility for roughly half the work and half the budget. We also agreed to review our budgets regularly to make sure we were both staying on track.

How did we break it down? I would handle all aspects of the wedding (except for the groom's tuxedo). Chris would handle all aspects of the rehearsal dinner and honeymoon. Looking back, it was amazing to see what we were able to do with limited funds, active imaginations … and lots of *prayer*.

For example, I made a fantastic "flower arrangement" — no pun intended. The couple getting married immediately after us approached me about setting up their flowers before our ceremony. This was so convenient for them that they wouldn't take a dime toward the floral cost! Free flowers for us; less hassle for them. A total "win-win" for both couples.

My next challenge was the reception. After searching for bargains, I was able to find a place right on the water in Newport Beach. At the time, it was called Windows on the Bay. Having recently emerged from bankruptcy, they weren't booked for the day of our wedding. That in itself was a miracle! (If you've ever planned a wedding, you know decent places get reserved a year or more in advance.) Then I negotiated a discount price. By having a morning wedding, our reception could be a *lunch* — far less expensive than a dinner event.

Alcohol was another potential budget buster. In fact, it's a major expense at most weddings. We went back and forth — open bar, cash bar, no alcohol — weighing all options. Holding the reception as a luncheon was in our favor; people would naturally drink less at noon on Saturday than at an evening bash. After talking and praying together, we decided we couldn't afford an open bar. Instead, we opted for a cash bar that kept us within our budget. Another win-win.

I saved on everything from the cake to my wedding gown — even making our own invitations! It took prayer and planning, but I stayed within my half of the budget.

Heaven-sent honeymoon.

When it comes to post-nuptial fun, some guys would be satisfied with a Red Roof Inn. Not Chris. He envisioned a sensational, unforgettable honeymoon experience, one that would start our married life with a bang … and set the stage for excellence in every area of our relationship.

Unfortunately, his first-class aspirations hit the brick wall of financial reality. He only had $5,000 to cover our rehearsal dinner, transportation to our honeymoon destination, hotel, food, activities, and more.

Of course, Chris could have picked some drab, unexciting options. There are always boring ways to pinch pennies. But Chris had his heart set on surprising me (he knows I love surprises) and honoring our guests.

One result was an enchanting, exotic honeymoon (in Hawaii) that matched his dream (including totally surprising me) and more importantly, matched our budget. When the costs were tallied up (including limos, flights, meals, and activities), we met our budget!

Money lessons of a young bride.

Our wedding was beautiful. Our honeymoon was spectacular. And when all was said and done, we came in under budget.

Was it worth it? Absolutely! Was it easy? No way.

It took lots of work and consistent communication throughout the process, including regular checkups to discuss if corrections were needed. Most importantly, it set the stage for Chris and me to have open dialogue about finances going forward. By continually working on this area over the years, we've avoided many of the money-related issues that derail countless marriages.

Managing our *wedding* finances taught us much about *marriage* finances. We've continued to apply these five principles over the years:

1) **Communicate openly about finances** (no money secrets)
2) **Get on the same page regarding financial priorities** (be one team)
3) **Agree to discuss all purchases above a set amount** (for us, it's $100)
4) **Agree that all income is "our" money** (not "my" money)
5) **Designate a certain amount for each partner to spend as they choose**

Now let's unpack each of these five ground rules and apply them in practical ways ...

1. Be transparent about finances.

Do you keep money secrets from your spouse?

Lots of us do. A survey (conducted by *TODAY.com* and *SELF.com*) found that 37 percent of men and 56 percent of women have lied to their partner about money.

Is financial fibbing a big deal?

Apparently so. About two-thirds of those surveyed said that in a relationship, honesty about *money* is just as important as sexual fidelity.

In her article "Sometimes We Cheat on Our Partners About Money," writer Allison Linn says, "Sex and money do have something in common: They are two areas where one partner has the capacity to devastate the other."

And like sexual fidelity, financial fidelity is all about *trust*.

> Communicate openly and honestly. With no money secrets.

According to the survey, most of us have told "little white lies" about our spending — like fudging on the price of a purchase. It also found that women are nearly twice as likely as men to hide purchases or receipts from their partner.

This kind of petty fibbing is hard on a marriage. But the article's author says outright lying is even worse: "A pattern of hiding money or having secret credit cards could signal deeper rifts ... (it) could be as damaging as a one-night stand."

Nearly 1-in-3 Americans lies about money to their spouse.

That's according to a *Forbes* article called "Is Your Partner Cheating on You Financially?" Writer Jenna Gaudreau reports that dishonesty between spouses commonly includes hiding cash, making secret purchases, and not paying bills.

The results can destroy a marriage.

"Betrayal regarding money can be just as painful and damaging as other kinds of cheating," says Tina Tessina, psychotherapist and author of *Money, Sex and Kids: Stop Fighting about the Three Things That Can Ruin Your Marriage.*

Nearly 1-in-3 Americans lie about money to their spouse.

Tessina warns that when a partner is caught hiding debt or fudging income, it creates "total loss of trust, feelings of betrayal and destruction of the relationship."

If that's you, admit it, apologize and decide to be honest and open about money. Have weekly discussions about your finances. Review your accounts together and talk about your income, upcoming bills, and monetary goals. If necessary, consider financial counseling.

While preparing this chapter, Chris ventured a guess that the overall rate of divorce — about 50 percent — roughly correlates to the overall rate of spouses who lie to each other about money.

Turns out he was right. The percentage of spouses who "cheat" on each other financially (by keeping secrets or hiding purchases) actually is about the same as those who end up in divorce court. And the survey backed up his hunch.

We don't think this correlation is a coincidence.

Of course, financial issues aren't the only reason people break up. As we saw earlier, plenty of wealthy and financially secure couples split up (Hollywood, anyone?). The bigger issue is the lack of trust. The symptom of financial infidelity only reveals cracks in the foundation that were already there.

I have a married friend who handles the bills in her household. Every so often, she complains to me that her husband (the primary income provider) spends money they don't have without consulting her. Once he bought $2,500 of sporting equipment without discussing it. This impulse purchase totally stressed her out because money was tight at that moment. The husband didn't know where they stood financially (they didn't communicate about their budget). As the main breadwinner, I'm sure he felt "entitled" to purchase the gear on a whim. Unfortunately, he was clueless that other expenses had drained their finances that month. His surprise purchase put undue pressure on her as she tried to juggle the other bills. No wonder she felt devalued and marginalized.

> Financial infidelity only reveals cracks in the foundation that were already there.

Unhealthy attitudes and hurt feelings about money can harm a marriage. If they're not discussed and dealt with, they can threaten any relationship. Incidentally, the husband wasn't the only guilty party. Since his wife had freely agreed to manage the family bills, she should've reported that things were tight — telling him to delay any extra expenses. Instead of dealing with the budget crunch head-on, both sides put off a potentially tough conversation.

When couples clam up, a pattern of avoiding conflict and enabling bad behavior is established and the problems only get worse.

———

Chris and I have noticed a troubling cause and effect. Sometimes a couple avoids conflict over financial issues by hiding what they're doing. To rationalize their own behavior, each spouse will make up a generalization about the other ("He is such a tightwad; he needs to loosen up" or "She is so reckless, just spend, spend, spend"). Once they stereotype their spouse, they feel more justified in operating independently and secretly with regards to money.

A woman I know frequently made purchases behind her husband's back. Then she'd warn her daughter, "Don't tell your father about this."

A few years later, she came to me all upset about catching her daughter in several significant lies. She exclaimed in exasperation that she couldn't believe her daughter would engage in such blatant lying. She fumed, "Where is she learning this from?"

I responded to her outburst, "Where did she learn to lie? She learned it from you over all those years of lying about your purchases. You not only lied to your husband, you recruited her to help hide the truth."

An older gentleman we know is an excellent example in this area. Now that he and his wife are retired, stretching their budget is a key focus. Financial security (important for all women) was especially significant to his wife. Knowing that, he used to conceal his generosity toward his kids and grandkids from her. He loved to "treat" his offspring, paying for things like lunches and boat rides. However, he knew his wife wouldn't approve. So he'd avoid potential conflict by secretly splurging on the kids with the warning, "Don't tell my wife, she'll get upset."

One day it all changed. He told his daughter that although he wished he could still be extravagant, his first priority now was being fully honest with his wife. From then on, unless she approved an expense in advance, he would no longer indulge his family like before. He made a conscious decision to prioritize his marriage and not follow a path of well-intentioned deceptions.

2. Align your financial priorities.

Students used to take driving lessons in special cars equipped with *two* steering wheels. At any time, the instructor could take over and avoid disaster.

Now imagine you own such a car and you're going on vacation with your spouse. Neither of you have discussed where you'd like to go, so as soon as you leave the driveway you start steering in opposite directions! If the wife wants to go east and the husband wants to go west, they'll end up going nowhere.

That describes how some couples "steer" their finances.

While planning our wedding, we discovered just how vital it is to be on the same page regarding finances. The challenge for couples is to be in alignment regarding *where* and *how* and *when* they spend their resources.

What about the husband who spent $2,500 on sporting equipment? I can't answer that. We weren't in the couple's home. But let's run a hypothetical. Let's say the wife's priority had been saving for their kids' college fund. And let's say the husband's priority was getting in better physical shape. For him, the sports gear was a necessity to reach his goal. But for the wife, it was an extravagance that thwarted her plans. Both sets of priorities had value; neither spouse was inherently wrong, but they were headed in different directions.

They had two steering wheels.

Imagine the conflict and fights this kind of confusion can cause. The word alignment means "a state of agreement or cooperation among people with a *common cause*." (That's a pretty good definition of a successful marriage!)

Being in alignment — living in cooperation and agreement — could be a central theme running through every chapter in this book. But perhaps nowhere is alignment more important and problematic than in our finances.

In the case of our wedding, Melina and I were aligned on sticking to our $10,000 budget. That was the non-negotiable, bottom-line priority we agreed on. The details of "how" were yet to be worked out, but we had one common goal.

To function in financial alignment, couples need to discuss areas like creating and sticking to a budget, paying off debt, and saving for the future.

Decisions on investing, using credit, and making major purchases need to be mutually agreed on. Big goals like leasing a car or taking out a mortgage should never be unilateral. Sometimes, women like to abdicate and not take any responsibility in this area. They figure ignorance is bliss. Same for men. Sometimes, the guys just let their wives handle it all. Bad idea. You are a team, and you need to work this money thing out together so there are no surprises.

Don't do anything in the dark; be transparent and open about all your expenses — from a family vacation to a home improvement to a piece of furniture.

INSIGHT: Opposites attract. So typically, one of you will be a saver and the other will be a spender! That makes it even more critical that you discuss your *individual* priorities in relation to your *family* priorities. Without this alignment there will always be friction around finances because you will be pulling in different directions, fighting each other instead of working in unison.

3. Discuss purchases above a set amount.

While planning our wedding, Chris and I developed a simple rule that we still follow today — neither of us will make a purchase over $100 without first talking about it with the other.

The specific amount we chose as a limit isn't important. That's something each couple will come up with ($50, $150, $1,000, whatever). The important thing is it forces us to keep dialoguing about money and remain in alignment. This rule may seem restrictive to some, but for us, it's liberating. And it's a safety net against needless consumptive spending ("Wow, that's a really lovely antique carousel unicorn you have there. How much did *that* cost?").

I hate buyer's remorse. Checking in with each other before spending our hard-earned cash gives us a great second opinion! It ensures we are jointly moving our finances in the direction we agreed upon together. Early on, this simple rule got us into the habit of frequent conversations about finances — more than most couples ever dream of. Over time, our "full disclosure" policy has built tremendous trust and reinforced the solid foundation of our marriage.

INSIGHT: Remember, if you're doing something that seems "crazy" or strange to most ordinary married people, you're more than likely on the right track! As financial consultant Dave Ramsey says, "Being broke is normal. 75 percent of Americans are living paycheck to paycheck. That's why you want to be weird. You've got to look at what everyone is doing and then run the other way."

4. It's *our* money. Not *my* money.

"His" and "Hers." It's a great idea for bath towels, but a bad idea for finances.

Many couples struggle whether to pool their income or divide it up. If both spouses are working, they may tend to look at their respective incomes as "my money" and "their money" instead of "our money."

In the Hann family, I'm the primary income producer. That's a result of our mutual decision (every couple should determine what works best for them). Because I'm the breadwinner, Melina used to make remarks like, "Well, it's your money anyway." I always responded by reminding her it is not "*my* money" but "*our* money." Being the main income generator doesn't change anything. All the money that comes in is both of ours. Equally. In no sense is it mine.

This is a key point that many couples miss. Remember our teaching on "*the two shall become one*?" If you can't be "as one" with your finances, how can you expect to be "as one" in other areas?

Money is a complicated issue, and it can entail family history, emotional baggage, and disinformation. But how we *use* it, *save* it, and *divide* it reveal what matters most to us. Billy Graham said, "Give me five minutes with a person's checkbook and I'll show you where their heart is."

3-out-of-4 Americans live paycheck to paycheck.

In a marriage, every problem matters, big or small.

To understand how even small misalignments can have a big effect, let's hop in the cockpit of an airplane. If our compass is off by just *one* degree, we'll stray off course by one mile for every 60 miles we fly. If we flew from New York to Los Angeles like that, we'd miss the LAX airport by 50 miles!

Many couples struggle whether to pool their income or divide it up.

Disagreements over finances may seem trivial, but "one degree" problems can escalate. For an airplane to stay on course, the crew must constantly *evaluate* their situation and make the necessary *corrections*. Likewise, keeping your financial priorities and goals on target requires ongoing communication and plenty of "in flight" adjustments as you go.

No spouse is perfect — we all make mistakes. Especially in financial matters. But with lots of face-to-face communication, we can keep small, fixable errors from growing into marriage-killers.

If you're not dealing with the "little" things as they arise, statistics show you're headed for a crash landing — with emotionally painful, financially devastating consequences. Stop being possessive or controlling about whose money it is, and get on the same team. The Hann family believes in the "one bucket theory" — viewing any and all money that comes in as being "ours."

5. Money of our own to manage and spend.

The final lesson we learned while planning and paying for our wedding actually had to be *relearned* during our first year of marriage.

Leading up to our wedding, we each had clear-cut responsibilities. We split the money and the workload 50/50. We had equal ownership.

But as we moved into married life, we shifted into a lopsided situation where Chris handled virtually all of the finances and monetary decisions.

This imbalance was probably an outgrowth of him being the primary income provider. Whatever the cause, I quickly became very frustrated with the situation. In my mind, I had recently demonstrated that I had much to offer to our marital finances. But Chris was inadvertently ignoring my talents.

I remember complaining to my friend Susan that Chris ran the checkbook, paid the bills, and controlled the finances. She stopped me abruptly, "Melina, do you know how many women *wish* their husbands would take control and lead in their finances?"

Maybe some women, but not me! I admired and respected Chris for taking on the burden, but I still wanted to be partners in the process. I felt we needed to share the load in handling our money, and it led to some negative feelings on my part.

Later on, Chris told me this initial imbalance of responsibilities was a blind spot for him. He really didn't see it as an issue until some heated arguments made it abundantly clear the way things had developed wasn't working.

Fortunately, we had the opportunity to sit down with an older couple who served as mentors to newlyweds. One of the first things they asked us was how we handled our finances and whether it was causing any friction. That was all I needed to jump in and get going! Kidding aside, this was a significant breakthrough in our marriage. With wisdom and grace, this older couple helped get us on a better track concerning the way we approached our finances together.

> Communication keeps small, fixable errors from growing into marriage-killers.

The mentors made two key points that changed our lives:

First, they said each of us needed to have an active role in handling our finances. We had done this while planning our wedding, but then drifted away from that model. This shift in responsibility left me feeling excluded and opened the door for misunderstandings and arguments about money.

Second, they said we each needed to have a certain amount of money (whatever worked in our budget) that we could use for anything we wanted. We would each have complete discretion over this allocation and could do whatever we wished with it. Older generations called it "pin money" or "mad money" and it was any sum set aside for nonessential expenditures. We called it "running money."

Without realizing it, we had fallen into a "parent-child" or "boss-employee" type of scenario. Because I had no part in our finances and no discretionary money of my own, I felt like I had to ask permission to use our money — obviously not a healthy situation over the long term!

> **Don't fall into a "parent-child" or "boss-employee" financial scenario.**

Coming out of that session, we agreed that I would now handle a meaningful portion of our monthly expenses. I would take care of areas like the groceries, the kids' clothing, the pets, the cars, and the property taxes. To cover these and other areas, I would get a "paycheck" of sorts each month that I was responsible to manage. Including me in our marital finances significantly reduced the fights over money we'd been experiencing.

Interestingly, even in this case, we still continued to discuss all purchases over $100, even with our personal running money.

Opposites tend to attract.

So it's likely that one of you is better with handling money than the other. And one of you is more of a saver while the other is more of a spender.

This isn't a question of right and wrong. One personality type isn't superior to another. What's important is that couples recognize the inherent differences and varying strengths each spouse brings to the table regarding finances.

In our case, Melina was very good at handling smaller, short-term money issues (such as saving for a car, a vacation, or the kids' braces). On the other hand, I was proficient at handling larger, long-term money issues (like retirement and investing). She was thrilled that the "big picture" stuff fit my abilities.

Likewise, because I am more detail-oriented, we decided that drafting the family budget was a logical, natural fit for me to do.

Please understand — there is NOT a "man's role" and a "woman's role" in terms of finances. Give the jobs to whoever has the strengths in that particular area, regardless of gender.

You have to figure out what works for *your* team (there's that communication thing again). Your division of labor may not look anything like ours. The critical things are that both spouses are included, and that neither is using money to control the other.

In finances, one-sided arrangements always breed distrust and will chip away at the foundation of your relationship.

Be quick to praise.

A marriage is like a garden. To make your relationship grow, it should be watered daily with praise, compliments, and words of support.

Notice what your spouse does right and praise them for it. Often. For instance, when Melina asks me if we have enough money to get her hair done, I let her know I appreciate the question — that I'm grateful she is conscientious about cash flow.

When I recognize her ability and support her for using a particular skill — like saving money — it inspires her to do even more. Here's an example: When we recently purchased a "new-to-us" car, she took on the task of saving extra to pay it off as quickly as possible. Through her efforts entirely, we added a substantial amount to each month's payment and paid it off early.

> Give the jobs
> to whoever has
> the strengths
> — regardless
> of gender.

Once we owned the car free and clear, she took that same amount and applied it to a self-managed "escrow" for our property taxes. This was a huge relief to me. I used to avoid even thinking about property taxes until they were due — and then scrambled madly to come up with the funds. When Melina took it over, she began setting aside 1/12 of the yearly total each month in a separate account. When the property tax bill arrived (and I started stressing), she gently reminded me that she had it covered.

I can't tell you how much I appreciate Melina for using her unique abilities as a saver. Likewise, make sure to praise your spouse for whatever they do — big or small — to help the marital finances. If things aren't perfect, communicate it, then communicate it some more until you're aligned.

Above all, please don't be critical or nitpicky. Dale Carnegie got it right when he said, "Any fool can criticize, condemn or complain — and most fools do!"

INSIGHT: Melina and I learned many financial lessons through trial and error. But we've also benefited from some easy-to-understand experts who teach finances in a way that makes sense to us. We'll leave the in-depth planning to them! Their advice will benefit you for a lifetime. Here are three high-impact resources:
- Dave Ramsey's Financial Peace University *(daveramsey.com/fpu)*
- Crown Ministries Small Group Financial Study *(crown.org)*
- David Bach's book *Smart Couples Finish Rich*

Lifestyles of the (not so) rich and famous.

Do you fantasize about exotic vacations, luxury cars, and elegant mansions? It's fun to have "champagne wishes and caviar dreams."

But money has a practical side, too. We absolutely need it for basics like food, clothing, shelter, education, health care and more. Maybe "the best things in life are free," but without a good supply of cash, we're pretty much toast.

Motivational speaker Zig Ziglar used to say, "Money isn't the most important thing in life, but it's reasonably close to oxygen on the 'gotta have it' scale."

I don't know about you, but I can only hold my breath for about one minute. After that *I need oxygen*! Same for money.

In our world, your success (and survival) is largely determined by attaining sufficient income and using it wisely. Nowhere is that truer than in our marriages. Learning and employing financial wisdom, fiscal restraint, and budgeting skills are huge factors in whether or not your marriage will last long term.

There are two basic rules of finance that couples need to address and work through. These two are dealbreakers — if you don't come into alignment in these twin areas, money problems can become the wedge that drives you apart.

> Financial wisdom and budgeting skills protect the health of your marriage.

First, stay out of debt.

"To spend or not to spend, that is the question." With apologies to Hamlet, couples must understand the practical aspects of handling money. To have a viable marriage you need to at least cover the basics. Here are six tips you could call the "nuts and bolts" of staying out of debt:

- Spend less than you make
- Devise and live by a budget
- Save methodically for the future
- Create an emergency "rainy day" fund
- Do not run up or carry credit card balances
- Do not compulsively buy non-necessities

Having guidelines is critical to the longevity of a marriage. Why? Because mismanaging money creates *stress*. The anxiety and uncertainty caused by ignoring the principles of good money management become an increasingly heavy weight that slowly crushes the life out of your marriage.

Financial expert Dave Ramsey says, "Bankruptcy and divorce are brothers." He's right. In fact, there's a grim joke among lawyers that most referral business for divorce attorneys comes from bankruptcy attorneys.

Humor aside, here's the bottom line: If you don't keep your financial house in order, the resulting stress will create a toxic environment for your marriage. Arguments over money will steal your joy, wreck your peace of mind, and make you bitter. When debts pile up, it'll feel like you're dragging around a ball and chain. The Bible says, *"The borrower is slave to the lender"* (Prov. 22:7 NIV).

Don't be a slave.

> **INSIGHT**: Dr. James Dobson asked financial expert Larry Burkett to summarize all of his financial advice to couples in a single statement. Burkett replied: *Stay out of debt.* He says the misuse of credit has enormous potential to destroy a family. "I tell couples to label their credit cards: 'Danger! Handle with Care!'"

Second, get on the same page.

We know couples who *technically* had their finances in rock-solid shape, but still ended up in divorce over money issues.

Why? The breakups came because they didn't effectively communicate to each other about finances. For whatever reason, the subject was off limits. They could not (or would not) have honest, open dialogue on the subject of money.

"Money is either the best area of communication in a marriage or the worst." That's from author Larry Burkett again. He says couples must deal with tough questions (*Who's going to balance the checkbook? How often will we eat out? Will we rent or buy?*). Burkett says, "If a husband and wife can't have meaningful discussions and reach agreement over these questions, they probably can't talk about the other areas vital for a healthy relationship."

After decades of observing couples, we agree.

Ongoing disagreements and deception over money are the leading causes of separations and divorce (up to 80 percent of couples seeking divorce cite money issues). Dave Ramsey quips, "If we can agree on the checkbook, there would be nothing left to fight about except who gets the remote!"

On a more serious note, Ramsey explains that difference between genders often cause friction. "When it comes to money, men tend to take more risks and don't save for emergencies. Men use money as a scorecard and can struggle with self-esteem when there are financial problems."

The typical male propensity for risk is true

> If you don't keep your financial house in order, the resulting stress *will* create a toxic environment.

for me. And in our home, Melina is definitely more fiscally conservative. Ramsey concurs. "Women tend to see money more as a security issue, so they will gravitate toward the rainy-day fund. Because of their need for security, ladies can have a level of fear."

In some couples, the "traditional" roles may be reversed. In others, both spouses may have identical tendencies. However you're wired up, the key to success is acknowledging and embracing your differences.

Fortunately, big spenders and tightwads *can* both get on the same page — *if* they talk openly and honestly.

Money talks. So should you.

At your wedding you probably vowed to stick together "for richer or poorer." But did you understand the ramifications of that pledge?

Being transparent about money issues is almost as hard for couples as discussing sexual needs. As a result, many are in the dark about their joint financial picture. A survey from Fidelity Investments says 43 percent of people do not know how much their spouse earns — and a large percent are off by $25,000 or more!

Landon Dowdy wrote "How to Talk with Your Partner About Money" for CNBC. She says, "Having regular money talks that are transparent is key to financial success as a couple. Take a look at your credit score, your credit history, your debts and assets so that you know exactly what you are working with."

It's ideal to do this assessment during your engagement period or as newlyweds. But wherever you're at, it's never too late for full disclosure. "Being a couple, it's going to be an adjustment thinking in terms of 'my' finances' to 'our' finances."

Dowdy emphasizes togetherness: "A good way to plan together as a couple is to make a budget. Figure out what you each bring in, then try making a list of your monthly income and expenses. That includes your expenses that are a must, like your rent or mortgage, utilities and insurance."

Great place to start talking. But it's often the money spent on *nonessentials* that drive couples into conflict. Dowdy continues, "Figure out what extra spending is most important to each of you, such as your gym membership or her manicures."

That, my friends, is where the rubber meets the road. Or the checkbook.

> Being transparent about money issues is almost as hard as discussing sexual needs.

Sometimes because of guilt, fear, or just to avoid awkwardness, one spouse hides the truth. For instance, a spouse drags a truckload of personal debt into the marriage without mentioning it. Or a spouse incurs significant debt without sharing the news. Or a spouse makes a secret investment that flops spectacularly.

Folks, this comes under the "for better or for worse" part of your wedding vows. Hiding a problem, an addiction, or a mistake never helps.

Historically, couples used to merge their bank accounts when they got married. But today, some view that as a loss of financial independence.

Our advice? Of course, this depends solely on the couple, and their level of trust. But as Chris said earlier, *we* believe being married means one bucket of money to budget and spend from. It symbolizes unity.

But here's the rub — you may have drastically different spending habits. When one partner is a loose goose (like Chris) and the other is conservative (like me), some opt for a *hybrid* situation — a joint account for shared expenses and separate accounts for personal expenses.

After you have an honest talk about your financial history (What were your wins and losses?) and your budget (How is it working out?), shift gears and discuss your long-term, big-picture goals, like saving for college and retirement. Again, the sooner the better, but it's never too late to come up with an allocation plan.

For instance, some couples live on 70 percent of their income. That allows them to save 10 percent, invest 10 percent for retirement, and donate 10 percent to charity. (In our case, we give to our local church and other ministry projects.) But each couple is unique and needs to run their own numbers. The overarching goal for any budget is that both spouses harmoniously end up on the same page.

INSIGHT: Larry Burkett says family budgets fail for three reasons: First, some men think it's a weapon to attack their wife's spending habits. So it leads to conflict. Second, some establish an unrealistic budget that inevitably ends up in the trash. Third, some try to fix three years of bad spending habits in three months. They become disillusioned and quit. The right balance? A proper spending plan doesn't *limit* expenditures; it *defines* them.

Take a chill pill.

Here's our last tip and it's designed to lower your blood pressure.

A study commissioned by *SmartMoney* and *Redbook* found that "Most of us don't know *how* to talk about money."

That's from Mary Claire Allvine, a certified financial planner. "People tend to be emotional and reactive about money, not strategic," she says.

No kidding. And when emotions run high, we tend to make financial mistakes — and say unkind things we regret later. Kansas State researcher Sonya Britt says, "It takes longer to recover from money arguments than any other kind of argument."

And such arguments are more intense. Britt says, "Couples often use harsher language with each other, and the argument lasts longer."

The way to reduce (or avoid) these heated altercations is to communicate rationally before things reach a flash point. Once you're stressed out and the verbal barbs are flying back and forth, it's hard to see things clearly. When you're agitated, you lose perspective. Britt says, "People who are stressed are very short-term focused. They don't plan for the future."

How to stay cool, calm, and collected?

Perhaps you should think of your home as a *corporation*. Writing for Key Bank, Aleksandra Todorova suggests couples approach the family finances as if they were running a business. "If you put a business metaphor into the picture, you'd be surprised how much more methodical people are."

Just be sure to conduct your "board meetings" on a regular basis and always with both "board members" present!

TALK IT OVER.

Money talks. So start talking! If it's awkward, don't worry — it will get easier with time:

1) How well (and how often) do you communicate as a couple about finances? How could you improve it together?

2) In terms of financial priorities, how well aligned are you? How can you get more on the same page?

3) Ask each other, "Am I more of a *saver* or a *spender*?" What are your other respective strengths and weaknesses?

4) How similar or different were your family backgrounds in terms of how finances were handled and discussed growing up? How does that influence your current approach?

TAKE ACTION.

Take control of your money together. Reaching your financial goals starts with a series of small steps. Ready?

1) Each of you write down your top five financial priorities. Then trade lists and discuss what's similar and what's different.

2) Find a Financial Peace University class near you and enroll to attend together *(daveramsey.com/fpu)*. This is so beneficial that many couples do it every few years.

3) If you don't have a budget (or wish to improve yours), download a free budget form at *daveramsey.com/budgeting*. Or get Ramsey's free budget app at *everydollar.com*.

4) Agree to consult each other before spending over a certain amount. Set that threshold number, then promise to discuss any purchase above that figure.

CHAPTER 8

The Perfect Storm:
Hurricane-proofing your marriage

In October 1991, an electronic buoy off the coast of Nova Scotia reported a wave height of just over 100 feet, the highest wave ever recorded offshore.

The combination of meteorological events that produced such towering seas was dubbed the "perfect storm." It began when Hurricane Grace formed near Bermuda and swept north toward the southeastern coast. Grace continued north, where it bumped into a massive low-pressure system moving south from Canada. This once-in-a-century clash of systems wreaked havoc over the Atlantic, with enormous waves driven by winds gusting up to 78 mph.

For one historic week, the freak storm flooded coastlines as far south as Florida and as far north as Newfoundland. Ships of all sizes took emergency shelter. One did not. Despite worsening conditions, the crew of the 70-foot fishing boat *Andrea Gail* continued chasing swordfish about 60 miles south of Martha's Vineyard. It was a fatal decision. Battered by gigantic swells, the *Andrea Gail* sank without a trace, killing her crew of six and inspiring the best-selling book and movie, *The Perfect Storm*. Neither the boat nor the men were ever recovered.

Weather forecasters use the term "perfect storm" to describe an unusual combination of unrelated factors that add up to create catastrophe. Melina and I use the term to describe an emotional crisis triggered by a combination of unhealthy behaviors or negative events. These contributing factors can be obvious or hidden, current or buried in our past.

In both cases, a perfect storm is a critical situation created when multiple circumstances combine to create a disastrous outcome — the kind that can capsize and sink even the strongest marriage.

Drowning in sight of land.

Brian and Tiffany were the "All American" couple.

Brian was tall, athletic, and handsome. His winning personality and sales skills led to owning a successful business. Tiffany was blonde, blue-eyed, and cheerleader-pretty. Her charm and sense of humor seemed the perfect complement to the duo's wholesome image.

Sadly, just as blue skies can hide approaching rain clouds, outward appearances can disguise an upcoming marital storm. Few would have suspected this picture-perfect couple was running headfirst into an emotional hurricane …

———

Mr. and Mrs. Right started out as high school sweethearts. They continued dating off and on during college. One day, Brian caught Tiffany flirting with another guy; she was obviously seeking and enjoying the attention. Brian was hurt by what he considered disloyalty and broke up with her. Before long, he found that he really missed her, and a couple weeks later they got back together. They actively dated through the rest of their time in school.

Soon after college, Brian realized he loved Tiffany deeply and wanted to marry her. After seeking the counsel of close friends and asking her dad for approval, he popped the question. To his delight, she happily agreed to marry him.

Everything seemed ideal. Everyone celebrated. But at that joyous time, Brian didn't know that Tiffany carried a deep emotional wound. A wound with profound implications that would be the root of many future struggles.

When Tiffany was 14 years old, tragedy struck her close-knit family. On a

> A perfect storm is created when multiple circumstances combine to create a disastrous outcome.

cold winter night, Tiffany and her brother each went off to enjoy slumber parties with their respective friends from school. While the two siblings were away, a fire broke out in their family's home due to a faulty heater. Everyone was able to get out safely except Tiffany's sister, Jane, who perished in the fire.

Tiffany and Jane normally shared a bedroom on the second floor, but on this particular evening, Jane had fallen asleep in the basement. Because the fire started close to where she was sleeping, thick smoke prevented her from escaping.

In one terrible night, the lives of Tiffany's entire family were shattered forever.

Tiffany's parents were traumatized by the tragic fire. As a result, they were unable to adequately focus on the needs of their surviving children. To deal with the pain, her father became increasingly detached from normal life. He turned completely inward and withdrew from all social contact. Her mother was so hurt by the loss that she stayed in bed for several months, emotionally paralyzed and numb from the anguish.

Tiffany felt crushing remorse: *It should have been me instead of her … If I hadn't selfishly spent the night with my friend I might've saved her … It's my fault my sister is dead.* During counseling, Tiffany learned she was dealing with "survivor guilt" and other issues from the trauma. She would also learn that part of her coping mechanism was a powerful need to feel attractive, to be noticed, and to get attention — especially from men.

After months of grieving, her parents decided they could all benefit from moving. To distance themselves from the scene of the tragedy, the family relocated from northern Michigan to the Detroit suburbs. Tiffany was a junior in high school when they moved downstate, and being ripped away from her schoolmates only added to her pain. To cope with her ongoing grief and strange new surroundings, she hid her true emotions and pretended to be fine. To the other students, she seemed to have it all together.

It was at this large suburban high school that the beautiful Tiffany met her handsome Brian, and their life journey together began.

Brian and Tiffany had a picture-perfect wedding.

They soon settled into married life and experienced the normal growing pains that any relationship goes through. They were ecstatic to learn of Tiffany's pregnancy with their first child — a happy, healthy baby boy. Four more boys would follow over the coming years, each one special in their own way.

From the outside, things looked great. But all was not well with their marriage.

Along with the normal pressures of modern life — careers, school activities, social obligations — there were issues from the past lurking under the surface of their relationship. They started fighting. And arguing.

A *lot*.

Recognizing their need for outside help, they wisely sought out a Christian counselor. They also attended gender-specific small groups through their church. Nothing seemed to help. After 17 years of marriage, they were spinning their wheels and getting nowhere. Their oldest son was 12, their youngest was 3.

Brian's sales career was financially rewarding but very demanding. On top of that, he was the busy director of Men's Ministry at their large church. Ironically, he was counseling scores of men on how to have successful, rewarding relationships.

All the while, his own life was unraveling.

Grudgingly, Brian began coming to grips with an ugly truth.

He had suspected for some time that Tiffany was not being faithful. At first, the idea was so appalling that he was unwilling to admit it to himself. After taking steps to validate his suspicions, Brian confronted Tiffany with her infidelity.

What came out rocked him to the core — Tiffany had been having a six-month affair with someone she had known in college. Brian was shaken and understandably furious. But he didn't throw in the towel. Contemplating the future, Brian decided not to give up on his family and marriage by reacting in anger and filing for divorce. He pushed the pain aside and made the conscious decision to fight for his marriage and for his five young boys.

He went back to their marriage counselor and explained why their sessions had been so unfruitful. He shared the devastating revelation from Tiffany and asked what could be done to salvage their shipwrecked marriage. The counselor agreed to help, but only under the condition that Tiffany submit to a full battery of psychiatric testing. To Tiffany's credit she was willing to do so; she also wanted to make their marriage work and decided to fight for its survival.

Through the testing, the couple learned that Tiffany had an exceptionally high IQ. In addition, they learned she had severe survivor guilt and detachment disorder as a result of her sister's death. Utilizing a Christian counselor also helped them understand the *spiritual* component of her issues. They had an "enemy" who very much wanted their marriage to fail. To do that, this enemy was barraging Tiffany with lies about how worthless she was, how unattractive she was, and how she was to blame for her sister's death.

Voices in her head taunted: *How could anyone love someone as awful as you?*

While writing this book, Melina and I interviewed Brian and Tiffany. I asked Brian about the impact of spiritual warfare. He said, "Satan loves to camp out at traumatic situations with the full intent of taking us out, like a sniper on a battlefield. He engaged in an invisible spiritual attack on a vulnerable teenage girl when her sister died. He began by whispering lies that it was Tiffany's fault, then continued the insidious poisoning of her spirit over the next 20-plus years."

Though it was painful and hard, Tiffany and Brian were both determined to make their marriage work. It was a careful, rational decision, not based solely on emotions. Soon after the revelation of her "secret life," Brian asked his wife to move out of the house for a month. This separation was recommended by their counselor to help them begin the healing and restoration.

Brian emphasized, "To Tiffany's credit, she really sought God to help her and to help heal our marriage. She was as committed to it as I was."

Brian sat his five boys down and explained that Mommy had to leave for a short time while she and Daddy worked through some things. The tone was optimistic, the goal was reconciliation. After she left the house, Brian invited a group of close friends and trustworthy people from their church to come over and pray over their marriage, their physical dwelling, and their individual lives.

In addition, Brian and Tiffany both invited people into their lives to encourage them and to hold them each accountable to the restoration process. These accountability partners would not let either of them get away with any of the behaviors that had hamstrung their marriage in the past.

During our interview, Tiffany shared another important lesson: "Past trauma — trauma that isn't dealt with — is a huge barrier in a person's life. In my case it was the deep, festering wound that led to my unhealthy need for attention and to seeking validation apart from God and from Brian."

Turns out the trauma in Tiffany's past was so impacting that she could actually *disassociate* her secret affair from her day-to-day marriage. In her mind, having illicit sex was completely separated from daily life. In fact, this psychological disconnect was a big reason it went undetected.

Tiffany explained, "You can't move on in your marriage unless, and until, you address your own wounds and issues, and I hadn't done that."

There's a larger application here. Tiffany had feelings of inadequacy that most (if not all) spouses struggle with to some extent and never resolve. Like many of us, she had the false, underlying feeling that, "If anyone knew the real me they wouldn't like me, certainly couldn't love me, and would reject me."

Sound familiar?

By getting help, she found the freeing principle that *authenticity leads to true connection.* "When you come clean and let your walls down — that's the only time you can truly feel loved. But you have to be real."

> Most (if not all) spouses struggle with feelings of inadequacy.

Brian told us that counseling also confirmed that their personalities were polar opposites. "I've always heard that opposites attract, but in reality, it made things very difficult." In fact, he and Tiffany viewed the world so differently it was hard to agree on much of anything.

This incongruity may have been a blessing in disguise.

Because of their past issues and personality differences, they knew they *had* to rely on God — together and individually. There was a chasm between them they could never fill themselves; they needed a "Higher Power" to bridge that gap. In no uncertain terms, Brian told us how they intentionally put Jesus Christ at the center of their marriage and looked to him to guide them and heal them.

Brian said, "Eight years ago, it got really simple for me. I would wake up in the morning, ask for God's daily direction, then shut up, listen, and obey."

What did that look like? Brian recalled, "One day while I was still completely revolted by Tiffany — soon after her affair came to light — she walked into the garage. I felt God telling me to give her a hug. Believe me, that was the last thing on earth I wanted to do. Little did I know it was exactly what she needed at that particular moment. It was a little thing, but it was huge in moving us forward to healing and restoration."

Throughout the long process, Tiffany was working hard and getting better.

Brian was *also* getting healthier. He began to realize what a lingering impact his mother had made on his adult life. A schoolteacher by trade, she was very controlling and wore the pants in their family. Inversely, his father was overly passive. This pair of unhealthy role models led Brian to become very controlling, and he struggled with what it meant to be a "man" throughout his 20s and 30s.

Shortly after college, he had a spiritual awakening.

He described his life change as, "Broken before Christ at 24 years old." Despite his genuine conversion, he had plenty of personality flaws that plagued his marriage. Looking back, he readily admits his controlling nature had exacerbated the couple's issues. He didn't listen very well to Tiffany and tended to take a my-way-or-the-highway approach to conflict resolution. He was highly controlling and tried to apply logic instead of compassion when addressing situations.

While working on their marriage, Brian recognized his own negative tendencies and traits. Most significantly, he realized that their problems as a couple were attributable to *both* of their past issues and behaviors.

The combination of Brian's personality flaws, Tiffany's traumatic past, and a series of poor choices by each of them created the conditions for a *perfect storm.*

The question is, did they sink or swim?

Mostly sunny, no chance of divorce.

I'm sitting on a soft, cushy couch in Brian and Tiffany's living room. Looking up, I see one of their teenage sons walk by. He's wearing a college sweatshirt — emblazoned with the same school emblem his parents wore when they were dating. The residence is beautifully decorated. It's large and spacious. But it's more than just a great house; it's a warm and loving *home.* This peaceful environment is a sharp contrast to the chaos and turmoil their marriage was embroiled in before they decided to fight to restore their relationship.

"We're the classic redemption story," says Brian. "And it's even more special for us because of the pain and difficulties we've been through together."

Melina and I sat down with this remarkable couple to hear for ourselves just what it takes to save a marriage from the brink of disaster. Among other qualities, it takes a sense of humor. That sense of fun is evident when Brian quips, "We've been married now for 25 years — 'happily,' for the last eight."

To keep their romance kindled, they make it a point to regularly go out on dates together. They also decided to not let their lives and marriage revolve strictly around their kids. "Our five boys know they are a welcome addition to our home but that they are not the center of our family."

I'm thrilled to report that Brian and Tiffany enjoy their new life together. It's obvious they genuinely love being in each other's company. They share fun and laughter, fully appreciating the blessings of their renewed commitment.

And thanks to God, "Divorce is no longer an option."

Seven ways to survive the big one.

Chris and I asked Brian and Tiffany what lessons they'd like to pass on to other couples going through difficult times. They were eager to share, hoping their struggles and recovery could help others facing crisis.

They boiled their advice down to seven principles to apply whenever black clouds threaten your most important relationship:

1) **Give it time.** Don't panic. Don't follow the crowd. Don't run to divorce. Pursue temporary separation if needed, and look for slivers of hope to give encouragement during the difficult times. Don't rush into a bad decision.

2) **Submit to Christ.** Wake up in the morning with the attitude of "Private Smith reporting for duty — what are my orders for the day?" Then be quiet, be listening, be willing to obey. If the directions you receive seem strange, compare them to the Bible to make sure they don't contradict Scripture. This helps validate that whatever you sensed was indeed God's prompting. Like any relationship, you will eventually get more familiar with God's voice, but it takes time.

3) **Get wise counsel.** We are in daily battles. Don't fight alone! The Bible indicates that we're attacked by the *world* (the pull of money, fame, and popularity), the *flesh* (lust, greed, and selfishness), and the *devil* (an enemy who is actively trying to take us out of the game). To survive, we need reliable allies and reinforcements — seek out trusted friends and discrete advisors to help you stay accountable.

4) **Be fighters for your marriage.** You both must decide to fight tooth and nail for your marriage — it won't just get better on its own. It will not be easy, but it will be worth it. When one of you is down, the other can help pull the marriage back up. When you're both down, invite trusted people into your lives. Give them "refrigerator rights" — permission to walk into your house and help themselves to the food in the fridge. Give them full access to your lives.

5) **Be vulnerable and be real.** Take off the mask. Any feedback you get from people invited into your process will not be effective (or ultimately helpful) if you're not being authentic with them or your spouse. If you're pretending, withdrawing, or concealing, even the finest marriage counseling won't work. As Tiffany said earlier, "When you come clean and let your walls down — that's the only time you can truly feel loved." Or make progress!

6) **Look internally.** Past trauma needs to be dealt with or it will lurk under the surface and continue sabotaging any efforts to heal your marriage. Sometimes there's a partial memory loss or mental block about

traumatic events. Find a reputable Christian counselor with the expertise to help you work through issues and wounds from your past that may be hampering you.

7) **Physical intimacy is critical.** During the early stages of their restoration, Brian did not want to have sex with Tiffany. Nonetheless, it was important for her (and for him) in the overall healing. It validated *her* in terms of being *wanted*, and it helped *him* feel *tender* again. As an integral part of God's plan for marriage, sexual intimacy brought them closer physically, spiritually, and emotionally. At first it just felt like going through the motions. But it soon led to deeper connection, and eventually rekindled desire and feelings for each other. All of which smoothed out the bumps and setbacks during the restoration.

———

Life is full of surprises, some good, some awful.

Things can go bad "in a New York minute." Before they do, make up your mind that bailing out on your spouse is not an option! In his song "New York Minute," Don Henley warns us to hang on tight: *"(When) you find somebody to love in this world, you better hang on tooth and nail, the wolf is always at the door."*

Until death do us part?

I'm all for personalized marriage vows. But today's trend to inventiveness is producing some pretty unusual verbal exchanges at the altar.

One skeptical couple concluded their vows with a promise to "love and be faithful for *as long as we can stand each other.*" Good luck with that.

One of the strangest vows I've seen packs an odd condition: "I take you as my lawfully wedded husband, until death do us part or you turn into a zombie. Because then we're going to have to start seeing other people."

If the zombie apocalypse happens, this bride has an escape clause!

In one way or another, marriage vows express an unending

commitment — and that's *wayyy* easier said than done. By this point in the book, you've realized that marriage is hard.

And not just for some unlucky folks, but for *every* couple. No matter how good your intentions are, there will be turbulent waters that can tempt you to break your vows and sink the "marriage ship" you set sail on.

In search of the one percent divorce rate.

External stresses put pressure on your marriage — illness, relocation, financial difficulties, job loss, pesky in-laws. Even happy events like having a baby or getting promoted at work can significantly strain your relationship. It's been said, "In life you're either in a crisis, just coming out of a crisis, or headed toward a crisis."

That's kind of grim, but that's life, and life can be tough.

Mix in some "internal" stressors like marital unfaithfulness, relational boredom, or emotional detachment, and it's just about impossible to stay married.

Or *is* it?

Of course, difficult situations are very real, and they can be incredibly painful. But are they *really* so insurmountable?

To put that question in perspective, we looked at arranged marriages, a common practice in many parts of the world. I was shocked to learn that according to UNICEF statistics, only 4 percent of arranged marriages end in divorce globally. In India — where about 90 percent of marriages are arranged — the divorce rate is just 1 percent. That's not a typo! Compare that to America's 50 percent rate.

> Marriage vows express an unending commitment ... easier said than done.

What's the secret?

In a *New York Times* article on arranged marriages, Brian Willoughby of Brigham Young University said arranged marriages have one huge advantage: "They remove so much of the anxiety about 'Is this the right person?'" The professor notes, "Arranged marriages start cold and heat up and boil over time as the couple grows. Non-arranged marriages are expected to start out boiling hot, but many eventually find this heat dissipates and we're left with a cold relationship."

He also credited supportive parents (after all, they arranged the darn thing!). "Whether it be financial support for weddings, schooling and housing, or emotional support for either partner, parents provide valuable resources for couples as they navigate the marital transition."

An article by Paul Bentley in the *Daily Mail* agrees. "They are seen by many as business deals that have little to do with love. But arranged marriages are far more likely to lead to lasting affection than marriages of passion."

He points out that couples who don't marry in a burst of passion are more likely to commit for life and to stick together through rocky patches. On the other hand, those who marry for love tend to bail out when the storms hit — as if adversity is fate telling them their romantic dream was not meant to be.

Bentley cites Harvard academic Dr. Robert Epstein. For eight years, Epstein researched arranged marriages within Indian, Pakistani, and Orthodox Jewish cultures.

His work suggests that feelings of love in non-arranged matches begin to fade by as much as a *half* in eighteen months! In contrast, the love in the arranged marriages tends to grow gradually, surpassing the love in the non-arranged marriages at the five-year mark. Ten years later, the affection felt by those in arranged marriages is typically twice as strong.

> You're either *in* a crisis ... or headed *toward* a crisis.

Dr. Epstein believes this is because Westerners leave their love lives to chance or fate (think about every romantic comedy or chick flick you've ever seen). While we're waiting for a "love-at-first-sight" fainting spell, other cultures consider character and compatibly more valuable than Hollywood-style serendipity.

What can we learn from this disparity?

Epstein says, "We must not leave our love lives to chance. We plan our education, careers, and finances, but we're still uncomfortable with the idea that we should plan our love lives ... In the West, physical attraction is important. But people must be able to distinguish lust from love."

And ironically, good looks can actually get in the way. "Strong physical attraction is very dangerous," warns Epstein. "It can be blinding."

There's one last lesson. In America, divorce is seen as an acceptable option with little or no stigma. If things get rough, we call the lawyer. "In the West marriages are easy to get out of. But in arranged marriages, the commitment is very strong. They get married knowing they won't leave, so when times are harder — if they face injury or trauma —they don't run away. It brings them closer."

> In America, divorce is seen as an acceptable option with little or no stigma.

Kiss Cupid goodbye?

Chris and I are not saying that arranged marriages are the way to go. After all, we met each other on spring break during college!

We're simply pointing out the obvious — although arranged marriages face the same challenges as other couples, they have a drastically lower failure rate. Francine Kaye, author of *The Divorce Doctor*, thinks she knows why. "There's an awful lot to be said for arranged marriages," says Kaye. "They are determined to make it work."

If they can do it, why not us? If two people in an arranged marriage (who were not necessarily in love at the beginning of their marriage) are able to make it work 96 percent of the time, why shouldn't a couple that starts out head-over-heels crazy in love be able to do even better?

We discussed this with Eva Kraus-Turowski, the marriage counselor we quoted in Chapter 3. We asked her to estimate the success rate of couples who were *both* 100 percent committed to making their marriage work. Her answer? A whopping 95 percent! That shouldn't really be a surprise — it aligns very closely with the global success rate of 96 percent for arranged marriages.

INSIGHT: When storms hit, it's easy to think your mate isn't doing their share. "Keeping score is one of the worst things you can do, because partners rarely keep score fairly." That's from Scott Stanley, author of *Fighting for Your Marriage*. "You see everything you do that's positive in the relationship, but only a fraction of what your partner does." And stress makes it worse. "Couples facing a difficult situation start thinking the other is not pulling their weight … that creates a sense of divisiveness … me versus you." Don't let storms divide you. Present a united front, working together.

Batten down the hatches.

As we've noted, our family has attended Saddleback Church in Lake Forest since moving to Orange County. On one memorable Sunday, pastor Rick Warren and his wife, Kay, spoke on "Fighting for an Awesome Marriage." It was a fantastic message, full of practical wisdom for couples looking to beat the odds.

Kay delivered some particularly compelling points on making it through tough times in your marriage:

• *"A great marriage is the union of two great forgivers."* What a terrific concept! Being willing to forgive one another (and to seek each other's forgiveness) is so important. Yet how many of us are unwilling to do such a basic and simple thing?

• *"Close the escape hatch."* Although Kay and Rick faced some rocky and turbulent times (especially early on), they had both agreed "Divorce was never even an option for us." Interestingly, this approach is one of the main factors that researchers credit for the enormous success rate of arranged marriages.

• *"A happy marriage is two people who are 'happily incompatible.'"* Kay explained that we're all different, with our own baggage, our own faults, and our own idiosyncrasies. The idea that there's somebody out there who is your "perfect match" is a complete myth.

Truth is, we all need to work at being — as Kay so eloquently put it — happily incompatible.

In that same message, Rick made a comment that stuck with me, "The grass isn't greener on the other side, it's greener where you water it."

Got that? Stop looking over the fence and wishing you were single again or that you married someone else or that your spouse would change. Get over it.

Stop whining, start watering.

Riding the storm out.

Back in Chapter 1, we said most couples get married with good intentions. They want to succeed, they want things to work out. But in reality, many are not willing to put in the effort to get through the storms of life. They "let nature take its course" until there's no feeling left for each other. Then they go their separate ways.

Our friends Brian and Tiffany proved it is possible (even in a perfect storm of problems) to replant and nurture the seeds of love in a marriage — if each spouse is determined to make it work. Ideally, this kind of rock-solid commitment is in place at the start of a marriage. That's the case in cultures where arranged marriages are the norm — but it can be true for *all* of us if we're willing.

> Finding your "perfect match" is a complete myth.

Trouble is, people have all kinds of excuses for mediocrity, for not giving the 100 percent commitment that's required. I once heard a speaker say, "The price of success in anything is non-negotiable. You either pay it, or you don't."

That's doubly true in marriage.

Excuses like, "We're staying together for the kids" may sound noble, but they're hollow words describing two people who are passively accepting a declining relationship — instead of trying to rekindle the flame. If they really cared about the kids, they'd work 24/7 at resuscitating their dying marriage.

Another excuse spouses use to justify quitting is, "It would be better for the kids to not see us fighting so much." I get pretty emotional about this cop-out. Listen up, parents! It's better for the kids to see genuine conflicts (*and* resolutions) as Mom and Dad fight for their marriage. Get solid counseling if needed, but stick together.

I've had many friends tell me, "But you don't understand how bad he is," or "You don't understand how poorly she treats me," or "You don't understand how much he's changed."

My response is, "I *do* understand! I understand that at one time you were madly in love, but at some point, you both stopped dealing with issues and started sweeping them under the rug. You stopped communicating and quit putting maximum effort into your marriage."

> Stop wishing you were single again or that you married someone else.

That doesn't always go over so well, but it's true. Like Chris says, all success comes with a cost attached. Nothing worth having comes easy.

Advice from the best.

Gone to a class reunion lately?

One woman went to her 20th high school reunion and was shocked at how many classmates were on their second or third marriages. To help avoid a similar fate, she wrote into Billy Graham's website with a burning question, "Why aren't marriages lasting today?"

Mr. Graham responded with wisdom based on experience. In August 1943, he married his Wheaton College classmate Ruth Bell. They remained married for almost 64 years until her passing in 2007. That's going the distance!

He shared some secrets to their long-lasting relationship:

1) **Cherish.** Let your spouse know how special they are. You are God's gift to each other. Take time to express your love, not just by your words, but by random acts of kindness — a surprise gift, a favorite café, or an outing together.

2) **Communicate**. Keep the lines open! Don't clam up. Let each other know what's going on in your life at home or work. Be sure not to nag, complain, or only express yourself when you're upset about something. Keep it upbeat.

3) **Compromise**. Remember that none of us is always right! We are born selfish, and problems naturally occur when we can't always have our own way. Marriage is a partnership where we must master the art of give-and-take.

> It is possible to *replant* and *nurture* the seeds of love in a marriage.

I'm not a pastor, priest, or rabbi. But I know from experience that the more you invite God into your marriage, the closer you grow as a couple. And the more often you turn to God for wisdom, the better your relationship will be. In fact, studies show that less than one percent of marriages where spouses pray together daily end in divorce!

Okay, sermon over.

———

Many marriages fail today because spouses don't even understand what it means to really love another person. Media and entertainment tell us that love is an emotion. But the trouble is, feelings can fade — and then so does your relationship.

Chris and I believe love is not so much an *emotion*, but an act of your *will*. A decision. A commitment. We made a commitment to make our marriage the highest priority and to fight for it whenever necessary.

INSIGHT: Love is not a warm fuzzy feeling. It's not even an intense emotional attachment. And it's certainly not having sex with someone you think is hot. Biblical love is doing for others what you'd want them to do for you (even if they can't pay you back). Biblical love is unselfish and unconditional. It's treating others according to God's moral character. In Corinthians 13, Paul lists the characteristics of real love — things like patience, kindness, humility, forgiveness, and truthfulness. That's the kind of love that keeps a marriage intact forever.

What's your first thought of the day?

I'm hoping it's not about what to have for breakfast.

Cornell professor of family sociology Karl Pillemer writes, "When you wake up in the morning, think: *What can I do to make his or her day just a little happier?*"

Pillemer suggests this morning ritual: "You need to turn toward each other, and if you focus on the other person even just for that five minutes when you first wake up, it's going to make a big difference in your relationship. Start each day thinking about what you can give that special person in your life."

That advice is from an article in *BuzzFeed* that collected opinions on what it takes to stay married from 19 widely different sources. Consider these crowd-sourced tips:

• **Keep dating.** Sexual integrity mentor Jay Pyatt says, "Dating is an important part of keeping the relationship healthy. If you are not dating, start. Make it simple. Go to the park and eat sandwiches. Talk about good memories and future plans. Don't talk about work, breakdowns, or difficult issues."

• **Know when to give in.** Coffee shop owner and part-time philosopher Kapil Aggarwal suggests the key to surviving conflicts is being willing to let it go: "In any argument, know when to back down. Let go of your ego. Relationships don't die. They're murdered by ego."

• **Be a unit.** Marriage blogger Oliver Marcelle says, "No matter what comes at you in your relationship, it is never you against your spouse. It is *always* you and your spouse against the issue. Often, we get caught up in placing blame and designating responsibility to only one person … Tackle all issues as a unit."

Embrace the change.

To those tips, I would add this blockbuster — *learn to deal with change.*

I wish I had a dollar for every time we've heard a couple try to explain their breakup by saying, "We just grew apart." Or some other equally weak variation of blaming gradual *change* as their grounds for divorce.

I get it. Change can be scary. And it can be upsetting. But it should never come as a surprise! All of us are changing — every month, every year, every decade. That's the nature of life, and it's true in every single marriage.

"At some point in any long-term relationship, each partner is likely to evolve from the person we fell in love with into someone new — and not always into someone cuter or smarter or more fun."

In her *New York Times* article "To Stay Married, Embrace Change," author Ada Calhoun, tells it like it is: "Each (spouse) goes from rock climber to couch potato, from rebel to middle manager, and from sex crazed to sleep obsessed."

Can you relate? I understand the confusion that change can bring. It may feel like you fell in love with one person and ended up with another! Given enough time, your spouse may *look* and *behave* differently than the one who stole your heart and ignited your dreams. When that happens, you may feel cheated, or like your spouse somehow violated the marriage contract.

I hate to break it to you, but change is a two-way street.

Both spouses are susceptible to "remodeling by nature." Waistlines expand. Hairlines recede. Wrinkles emerge. As we age, we may pick up annoying habits — we slurp our coffee, we take naps in movies, we lose our car keys. Over time, we have less energy. Less sex drive. And that's just the *physical* stuff!

Our spouse's personality, ambitions, and interests may also shift over time. They may become more emotional ... or more detached. More affectionate ... or more aloof. More outgoing ... or more withdrawn. Don't take it personally.

It's perfectly natural for our dreams and desires to evolve. What consumed us as newlyweds may be replaced by things that are equally valid — but different.

Calhoun puts it this way, "Several long-married people I know have said, 'I've had at least three marriages. They've just all been with the same person.' I'd say Neal and I have had at least three marriages: Our partying 20s, child-centric 30s and home-owning 40s."

Melina and I have already experienced a few different seasons of life, and adjusting to each has required some flexibility (and fighting back some nostalgia for the "way things used to be").

To make it even tougher, husbands and wives don't change at the same rate.

Couples can be disoriented by this disparity. For instance, one spouse develops social skills and their partner doesn't. One pursues higher education, and the other binges on Netflix. One advances at work while one gets demoted. That kind of inequity causes issues. When one spouse stops learning or growing or reaching for goals, it can aggravate the one who's motivated. If that's you, I suggest some honest, loving conversations about this situation.

Bottom line? Like I said, change can be puzzling. Frightening. Even painful. But it's not a valid reason for divorce. None of us are static. We're all changing, for better or worse. A committed stormproof relationship must take both in stride.

"Human beings are works in progress that mistakenly think they're finished." That wisdom is from Harvard psychologist Dan Gilbert, in a TED Talk he called "The Psychology of Your Future Self."

It may feel like you fell in love with one person and ended up with another.

Gilbert described research that he led in 2013. His study subjects (ranging from 18-to-68 years old) reported changing *much more* over a decade than they expected to.

If science says change is inevitable and ongoing and profound, we need to embrace it.

Granted, that's not always easy. Change rocks our world. Upsets our apple cart. Resenting (and resisting) change is human nature. But it can be overcome.

Ada Calhoun agrees, "Being forever content with a spouse … requires finding ways to be happy with different versions of that person."

From page one, we've said a good marriage takes work. But the results are worth it. Even when it means accommodating change. Leadership expert Robin Sharma says, "Change is hard at first, messy in the middle, and gorgeous at the end."

Let's all be gorgeous!

Fireproof your marriage.

Can a dead marriage come back to life?

A movie that explores that possibility became the highest grossing independent film of 2008. The surprise hit was called *Fireproof* and starred Kirk Cameron and Erin Bethea. In it, a highly decorated firefighter is a hero to his community but a failure as a husband. On the job, Caleb Holt (Cameron) teaches the importance of marriage, but at home he and wife, Catherine (Bethea), argue constantly. Their ongoing fireworks cause Catherine to demand a divorce; an angry Caleb reluctantly agrees.

After seven years, they've given up.

The movie's realistic fights and frustrations are what most marriages deal with, and the struggles they face make for a gripping plot. Using God as a last resort, the reluctant Caleb embarks on a 40-day mission to rescue his marriage — after divorce proceedings have already been filed.

Plan a date night with your spouse built around viewing this movie together. Please, watch it no matter where you are in the cycle of your marriage. Whether your love is hot, cold, limp, or on life support, see it and talk about it. Whether you are passionate, affectionate, or obstinate, please rent it and discuss it. Whether the results are preventive or corrective, you'll benefit either way.

Who knows? It may be the spark of something amazing in your marriage.

> Change can be puzzling. But it's not a valid reason for divorce.

TALK IT OVER.

Every family needs a plan in case of severe weather. Likewise, every marriage should openly discuss their strategy for the storms of life in advance:

1) How have you handled tough times as a couple in the past? If a storm hasn't hit your marriage yet, discuss how to survive one when it does come.

2) Discuss how to best apply Rick and Kay Warren's advice ...
   • *"A great marriage is the union of two great forgivers."*
   • *"Close the escape hatch ... Divorce was never an option."*
   • *"A great marriage is two people who are 'happily incompatible.'"*

3) Arranged marriages have a 96 percent success rate. As a couple that started out with much more in common (and actually being in love!), what lessons can you learn from them?

TAKE ACTION.

Storms hit everyone. Sometimes you need an umbrella, sometimes a life jacket. Either way, success depends on being prepared. Here's a start:

1) Plan an undistracted date night to watch *Fireproof* as a couple. What are your key learnings and main takeaway?

2) Find the married couples you respect most (including parents). Ask them what the biggest storm was to hit their marriage — and how they lived to tell about it.

3) If either of you have issues from the past that are buried or bubbling up and negatively affecting your marriage (like Brian and Tiffany), find a reputable counselor and start the healing process.

CHAPTER 9

Head Over Heels Forever:
Staying madly in love no matter what

After 69 years of marriage, an Illinois couple died within minutes of each other while holding hands.

"They were always in love, literally to the end. To the last second," said Rabbi Barry Schechter, who led their joint funeral service.

Isaac Vatkin was devoted to his bride, Teresa, since the day they met. He was well into his eighties when she was diagnosed with Alzheimer's. When she had to be removed from their home for specialized care, he visited her every day. Even as his own health deteriorated, he clung to life so he could comfort his ailing wife.

Isaac was 91 and Teresa was 89 when their respective conditions worsened, and they were both admitted to Highland Park Hospital in Skokie. Soon, they both became unresponsive. When their breathing grew shallow, the medical staff wheeled the longtime lovers into the same room and put their beds side by side.

Family members positioned their hands so they touched.

Teresa died first. Moments after they separated the couple's hands, Isaac passed.

At the memorial service their daughter said, "Their love for each other was so strong, they simply could not live without each other."

That's the kind of love that goes the distance.

How does one couple stay married to their last dying breath, while others fizzle out in the first years of marriage?

Part of the answer is found in "Escape (The Piña Colada Song)," by Rupert Holmes.

Disclaimer: I get it. This tune is ancient. But hey, I'm stuck in the '80s.

Back in the era of wide ties and leisure suits, Holmes sang about a married couple bored with their stale relationship. Looking for romance and adventure, they each secretly check out other "options" by running personal ads in the paper. Ironically, they answer each other's ad. Husband and wife end up seeing their spouse in a fresh new light and fall passionately back in love (probably wearing flared pants).

This fictional couple discovered they could refresh and revitalize their love life by getting a new perspective. Together. They didn't need an *affair* to spice up their marriage; they needed a *strategy*. Tropical drinks aside, there's a lesson: To keep the fires of love burning, both spouses need to constantly fan the flames.

Without attention, romance flickers and dies like an untended campfire.

Again, Hollywood has messed with our brains.

Thanks to fictionalized tales of romance, most westernized couples think they just "fall" in (or out) of love — with little or no influence over its duration or outcome. In the movies, love is blind, arbitrary, and totally beyond an actor's control.

Consequently, real-life couples don't realize they actually can have significant control — especially if they continue doing the *actions* that preceded their *feelings* in the first place.

> To keep the fires burning, both spouses need to constantly fan the flames.

Does it work? Yes! After 20-plus years of marriage, strangers still come up and ask Chris and me if we're *newlyweds*. The secret sauce to staying head over heels in love (feelings) is to keep going back to what you did (actions) when you were dating, courting, and enjoying your "honeymoon period."

The trick is to recollect and recreate the romantic activities from early in your marriage as you go through later seasons of life. If your feelings have cooled off, take action. To paraphrase the mysterious voice in the movie *Field of Dreams*, "Build it (actions) and they (feelings) will come."

INSIGHT: "Love is a decision." That deceivingly simple key to avoiding marital burnout is from *Love Is A Decision*, by Gary Smalley and John Trent. They assert that the *feelings* of love follow the *actions* of love — and actions are a conscious decision of the human will. Smalley says, "Love is not an emotion, love is not a feeling, love is not happenstance. Love is a decision. Love is waking up every day committed to honoring your mate. If you want to have a great relationship, guess what, it's up to you."

I'm not a big gardener, but I admit I have "lawn envy."

No matter what I do, my neighbor's landscaping seems to look better than mine. Greener. Lusher. Healthier. In the previous chapter, we discussed Rick Warren's quote about keeping your marriage going strong, "The grass isn't greener on the other side, it's greener *where you water it*."

That's it in a nutshell — we need to put energy into "watering" our marriages if we want them to flourish. Beautiful marriages (and lawns) don't happen by accident! If we water them, nourish them, and carefully nurture them, they grow and thrive. Conversely, if we neglect their care, they wither.

Guys in particular seem slow to grasp this concept. That's because men tend to be task oriented. Once we "finish the task" of winning our spouse with courtship and romance, we can slip into thinking we've "checked that box" and move on to other big goals. Like building a career, growing a beard, whatever. This is a tragic (and sometimes fatal) mistake in terms of marital health and vitality.

Bottom line? You don't plant a rose bush and forget about it. You don't water your lawn once and then quit. Nurturing your marriage is a daily choice. Like a flower, your marriage is either growing or dying; there is no "pause" button.

Stick these seven tips on the bathroom mirror.

Call me crazy, but why settle for a dull, passionless marriage when you can choose excitement and romance — today? Over the years, Melina and I have come up with seven areas to focus on daily for an intimate, fun-filled marriage.

Grab some Post-it notes. And put these seven tips where you'll see them every day:

1) **Never stop dating.** Someone said dating is pretending you're someone you're not to impress someone you don't know. But for all its pitfalls, most married couples can look back on the time they were dating with fond memories.

> Your marriage is either growing or dying. There is no "pause" button.

A proven way to nurture your marriage is by turning back the clock and doing what you enjoyed so much during courtship — *dating* each other. I know, it sounds too simple. But it's frequently overlooked in marriage. The pull and pressures of daily life (careers, kids, finances, health issues) can crowd out the time we spend with each other. Without intending to, we end up giving our spouse the "table scraps" and "leftovers" of our day. Our crazy, busy lives are so overbooked that we can barely wave to each other as we fall exhausted into bed.

No wonder relationships suffer in this stressed-out environment.

What's more important — a business meeting or saving your marriage?

The key to sustaining a fun and functional relationship is to *intentionally* carve out time for each other, just like you do for any other important appointment. Meeting your fitness trainer or taking the car in for service are important appointments. So is spending a pre-planned, cut-in-stone connection with your spouse.

Remember the quote about the price of success? It's non-negotiable. You either pay it or you don't. Same for marriage. The key is *intentionality.*

Ladies, dating is important. Our *children* need to see us model a healthy marriage, and our *husband* needs to know we're 100 percent committed to him — that we love spending quality time together.

Don't have time to date? That's a big red flag. We must give our spouses top priority. If we don't, nothing else works. I have a friend who realized that her husband needed more of her time, energy, and focus. But they had a young son who took up much of her time. *Too* much, as it turns out.

"I figured I could wait and focus on my husband when our son was older," she told me. "I thought I could catch up on our marital relationship later on." What happened next was sad but predictable. It's impossible to put a relationship on the "back burner," thinking you can just pick up where you left off at some future date. Her husband felt neglected and ended up having his need for attention filled elsewhere. He ultimately left her.

Today, their son (the one who demanded so much of her time) is a grown man and out of the house. My friend is alone, wistfully thinking of what might have been if she had not put off nurturing her marriage.

"Never, ever stop dating."

That's advice from two self-described "65-year-old romantics." In an article for *All Pro Dad*, the husband explained, "We go out once a week. Money or no money, we find something special to do together. Sometimes it's just a long walk on the beach and ice cream. Sometimes it's a fancy restaurant. We never take it for granted ... ever."

Want the best marriage possible? Commit to dating and courting each other for a lifetime. It won't be easy. You'll have to adjust your priorities. Scheduling a time-out — an oasis of togetherness — needs to become part of your rhythm. We recommend doing it weekly, but I must admit we don't always hit our goal (remember, we're just like you!). If we do have to miss, we are painfully conscious of it and get together as soon as possible.

> **INSIGHT**: Relationship expert Jim Burns recently posted, "Your spouse deserves your best. A good question for evaluation is: At the end of the day, do I only give my spouse emotional leftovers? You can never overdo showing your spouse that you love them and that they are still the one you cherish above all others."

2) **Get away together.** Hit the road, Jack. And take Jill with you.

Early in our marriage, we recognized the value of getting away — just the two of us — at least once a year. The escapes range from a few days to a week. Of course, this was much easier before the birth of our kids, but it's a non-negotiable, life-giving habit we insist on, often as an anniversary celebration.

To create anticipation, we make a game out of it. I pick the location and drop only a single clue — I tell Melina it's within a certain distance (a three-hour drive, a five-hour flight, etc.) of our home. This way, she gets the fun of trying to guess. (If she happens to guess correctly, I keep a poker face.) These surprises don't have to cost a ton of money. But if you do have the means, a more exotic trip can be just what the doctor ordered to shake up and reinvigorate a relationship. If money is tight, consider getting away for a weekend camping trip. If you don't like roughing it, use a discount travel site to find great deals on local hotels.

> Get away, just the two of you. It's non-negotiable.

"Vacations can help to refresh and revive relationships. It is like breathing fresh air into them, reenergizing them with greater intimacy and deeper love."

That's from psychologist Krystal Kuehn. In her article "Save Your Marriage With a Getaway," Kuehn writes, "Without devoted time for rest and relaxation, we get burned out on our jobs, and lose our effectiveness and interest. How about our marriages? They suffer also. Couples grow apart, experience less satisfaction, and are more irritable with each other."

Can't clear your calendar? Even the briefest mini-vacation can reap great rewards. The key is setting time aside in a location that separates you from anything and everything that normally competes for your attention, keeps you on edge, or distracts you from connecting with your spouse.

Kuehn says, "Studies show that couples who schedule periodic dates and spend more time together are more satisfied with their marriages than those who don't." Isn't that what we all want?

> Shut off the demands of everyday life. And rev up your romance.

Periodic getaways — a night, a weekend, or a weeklong adventure — give us an invaluable chance to be alone with our spouses. When we shut off the demands and clutter of everyday life, we have time to focus on each other, create memories together, and simply rev up our romance. Pulling away from the problems and stress of the rat race is do-it-yourself therapy.

The daily grind is rough on couples.

It can even make you wonder if you married the right person. Israeli psychotherapist Mike Gropper says couples need vacations. "Otherwise, it's too easy to forget why you got married in the first place."

It's tough to break away from your routines. We get that. People have told us that they can't afford a vacation or they can't miss work or worst of all — they feel guilty for leaving the kids with someone else.

Sorry. Excuses don't cut it. Neglecting your marriage hurts everyone sooner or later. Couples need quality time away from the kids and the pets and the job. Time off rejuvenates your relationship and makes you a better spouse, parent, and caregiver.

Gropper asserts a "couples vacation" has many benefits:

• *It's a chance to rediscover one another.* Spending quality time alone can help you remember what made you a great couple in the first place.

• *It increases the fun and friendship in a relationship.* Focus on enjoying each other's company; maybe try a new sport or explore a new place.

• *It can rejuvenate your sex life.* Daily hassles and routines leave many married couples too tired to enjoy romance by the end of the day.

In addition, it sends your children a message that your marriage matters — and that you treat it with importance in terms of time, money, and commitment.

Best of all, the benefits follow the couple long *after* the vacation. Don't worry about the details; follow Nike's classic advice and JUST DO IT!

INSIGHT: Start packing. Get off the grid. Leave your laptop home and turn your cell phones off. Forget about work, bills, and obligations. Forsake your Facebook. Ignore your Instagram. Only answer emergency calls from family. Don't let your co-workers follow you. Stay off the internet unless you're using it to find a great dinner spot! Take a news blackout. Leave your cares behind and just treasure the gift of love and the beauty of nature.

3) **Do little acts of kindness.** Comedian Jim Gaffigan says, "Why should we make our beds? We don't tie our shoes after we take them off."

I agree with that logic, but Melina is a stickler for neatly made beds. I mean, you can bounce a quarter off our bedspread. As a bachelor, I didn't bother smoothing out my sheets and blankets because I knew I'd be messing them up by nightfall. But as a husband, I've learned that doing this small act of kindness makes a *big* difference for Melina.

Another priority for my wife is doing the dishes and putting them away. Like making the beds, it's a symptom of her THS (Tidy House Syndrome) — a noncontagious condition Melina's afflicted with. For her, having a spotless kitchen is a magnificent obsession. For me, stacks of dirty dishes are no big deal — isn't that what sinks are for? But I gladly pitch in because it means a lot to her and doesn't take much effort on my part.

If it's a big deal to her, why wouldn't I help out the woman I love? Why wouldn't I go out of my way to make her day a bit easier? It's worth just about any effort to put a smile on her face. Incidentally, she does the same for me by complying with *my* pet peeves. For instance, it's important to me that the toilet paper roll has the loose end coming over the top and not hanging down the backside. While it means absolutely nothing to her (or any other sane person), it's important to *me*. I love that she takes the time to do this little quirky act of kindness!

> Small acts of kindness make a big difference.

Now imagine if *I* refused to do the dishes and *she* refused to install the roll correctly. Imagine that instead of complying, we fought about all the minutia of life — always arguing about our different preferences. Over time, the negative chatter and lack of cooperation would slowly choke the joy out of our marriage.

Here's another little Hann tradition: Since I'm the one who usually wakes up first, I make a Starbucks run and get our morning coffee. We could just make it at home, but we both like the Starbucks brew better. Best of all, I enjoy bringing her the little "cup of gold," as she calls it. This small act of kindness brightens her day and tells her she is important to me and that I love her. It may not look like a big deal, but carrying out this morning mission means a lot to our relationship.

I'll have a Venti Americano with a splash of coconut milk, no sugar. Just talking about coffee makes me want to hug Chris! When he used to travel a lot for work, I'd make it a point to find out when he'd be coming home. Then I would draw a hot bath for him as a welcome-home treat. I knew this was his favorite way of detaching from work so he could freshly engage with me and the kids. Helping him soak in a tub of hot, soothing water was a small act of kindness. I could have easily skipped that little gesture and expected him to jump in right away with the family (especially if I'd been flying solo with the kids for a while).

From a hot cup to a hot soak, look for things your spouse likes and surprise them.

I loved that treat (still do!). Taking the time to get my bath ready lets me know I'm important to Melina and that she loves me.

A simple way to get started is by asking "What can I do for you?" and really mean it. Listen actively to your spouse's reply and take action on it. For example, I've made it a habit to call Melina on my way home from the office. As we chat, I always ask if she needs me to swing by the store to pick up anything. Most of the time she doesn't, but just my asking makes her feel valued. Even though I might be wiped out (death by meetings) and eager to get home, I honor her by my willingness to see if she needs something.

My fellow men, I'm talking directly to you here. Do you take the time to open her car door when you're out? Yes, it may be "old fashioned," but it communicates to your wife (and to others around her) that she is important and valued by you.

Look for things your spouse likes and surprise them.

A few years ago, I was picking my daughter up from volleyball practice. She was 16 then, and as we were walking to the car I went to the passenger side and opened the door for her. A teammate of hers was leaving at the same time and sent her a text saying, "Holy #@*%, your dad just opened the #@*% door for you!" How do you think that made my daughter feel? Did she feel special that her friend noticed how highly I valued her? Absolutely!

More tips for guys: When you're walking with your wife, make it a point to reach over and hold her hand or put your arm on her shoulder. If you're out together and an attractive woman walks by, make the choice to look directly at your wife (and not stare at the competition, no matter how good she looks).

Let's say you're at the mall or out jogging. Or at the beach. When a pretty gal comes into view, give your wife a touch or a squeeze to let her know that you are hers and she is yours. She'll love you for it. Trust me on this.

Again, every spouse has little niceties and gestures they like. Tune in, you'll find some. And your return on investment will be stellar. Hint: It's actually easier in the long term to comply than to argue about their requests (or worse yet, ignore them).

> It's never too late to break bad communication habits.

Pour into your marriage during the *easy* times and you'll be strong enough to withstand the hard times that are sure to come.

4) **Pay attention to your words**. Someone said the tongue has no bones, but it's strong enough to break a heart. Words matter. What we say, and how we say it matters.

Author Yehuda Berg agrees, "Words have energy and power with the ability to help, to heal, to hinder, to hurt, to harm, to humiliate, and to humble."

How spouses speak to each other is critical: *Are we being harsh or loving? Are we being kind or crass? Do we sound complimentary or demeaning?*

When you're at a party sometime, tune in to some conversations. Complete strangers are usually polite and gracious. But married folks (who should know better) are often gruff and dismissive to each other. Listen to the tone of their voices and watch their body language for clues about their love life. It's better than a soap opera.

Thankfully, it's never too late to break bad communication habits. How we engage or respond to each other is a *choice*. I know. I'm weak in this area. I have a tendency to respond too quickly and too harshly. When I slip, I quickly ask Melina for forgiveness. Choosing kind and appropriate responses is a constant battle for me, and quite honestly, I don't always win.

Say "I love you" to each other. Say it often. Say it all the time.

Maybe you've heard the story about the man who said, "I told my wife I loved her when we got married. If anything changes, I'll let her know."

That's not enough! We need to constantly reinforce to our spouses (and to ourselves) that *we love them*. Tell them when you wake up. Tell them when you go to bed. Tell them when you leave the house. In the car. On the phone. At the store. When you're reading the paper or watching TV. Tell them as often as you can.

> Say "I love you" to each other. Say it often. Say it all the time.

Words are like containers for emotions. America's poet laureate, the late Maya Angelou, once said: "I've learned that people will forget what you said ... but people will never forget how you made them feel."

Listen to yourself speak. Be aware of your words with each other. Be sure they're used for positive affirmation instead of criticizing, condemning, and complaining. Negative speech patterns can erode your relationship. Someone has said, "Don't mix bad words with your bad mood. You'll have many opportunities to change a mood, but you'll never get the opportunity to replace the words you spoke."

INSIGHT: If you've stopped talking, maybe it's because you focus too much on "business" — work, budget, chores, problems. If talking isn't fun, why bother? Writing for Focus on the Family, Gary Smalley urges, "Ask open-ended questions. Your spouse desperately wants to be known." So let's open up. Let's share "non-business" words that convey our deepest emotions, opinions, dreams, beliefs, and hopes.

5) **Say goodbye to toxic friends**. Are your friends *helping* or *hurting* your marriage?

That's a tough question every couple should ask themselves, but many avoid. The power of association is one of the strongest influences on our character and behavior. Have you ever warned your kids not to hang around with a particular person because they were a bad influence? As the old saying goes, "If you lie down with dogs you're going to get fleas."

You may even find yourself living in the doghouse.

Whether we're aware of it or not, we tend to become like the people we spend the most time with. The same principle is in play for couples, and the people you choose to associate with will most certainly affect how you relate to each other — and ultimately affect the quality of your marriage.

> If your friends are critics of your spouse, it's time to find new friends.

Can I be candid? If your current crop of "friends" are self-appointed critics of your spouse, it's time to find new friends. If they egg you on and exacerbate divisions and arguments between you and your spouse, they don't deserve your friendship. Even if you were BFFs when you were single, they may be inappropriate now that you're married. This reality can be hard to handle. It's painful to jettison toxic friends, but you need to protect your spouse and your relationship at all costs.

How can you tell a *booster* from a *basher*?

Marriage experts Robert and Jeannette Lauer came up with some "tough questions" to ask yourself about your friendships:

- Do they make you feel better about your spouse?
- Do they enjoy activities and conversations that strengthen marriage?
- Do they respect and support your need for couple-time?

You can't judge a book by its cover, but you can *always* judge a tree by its fruit. Same for people. Before you take advice from anyone, look at the results their philosophy is having on their own lives! Make sure you're spending time with people who have outstanding marriages and who align with you in building yours up. If they don't celebrate marriage as a rich human experience well worth preserving, bid them adieu.

Bottom line? Don't pal around with anyone who is negative about their own marriage — let alone about *yours*.

One of my good friends, Meghan, was in a fight with her husband. After the spat, she got some advice from our mutual friend Kelly regarding the disagreement. Basically, Kelly suggested that Meghan "tell her husband off" and lob some nasty verbal bombs his way to "teach him a lesson."

I quickly told Meghan she should do the exact opposite! To back up my advice, I simply asked: "How did Kelly's marriage work out?" She thought about it and replied, "Good point." Not only was Kelly divorced, she was constantly having difficulty getting along with men in general.

> Don't pal around with anyone who is negative about their own marriage.

Hmm, probably not the best one to be giving relationship tips!

We usually can't pick who our co-workers are. But in our personal lives, we can pretty much control who we spend time with — and the choices we make *will* have an impact on our marriages. Whether it's a positive or a negative impact depends on how seriously we screen out the bad apples.

Motivational speaker Jim Rohn said we are the average of the five people we spend the most time with.

Choose wisely.

> **INSIGHT**: The right friends can inspire, support, and build up. But the wrong friends can tear us down. They can give bad advice. They can desert us when times are tough. They can have hidden agendas. They can hold grudges. They can gossip about us. They can provide false comfort. They can tempt us to do bad things. They can even lead us astray in our marriages. The Bible is right when it says, *"Bad company corrupts good character"* (1 Cor. 15:33 NLT).

6) **Don't let the kids wreck your marriage.** If you ever attend a football game or a volleyball match that my kids are playing in, you'll be able to spot me quite easily. I'll be the deranged man jumping up and down and cheering wildly from the sidelines.

Full disclosure: We absolutely love our kids. Samantha and Alex (now both young adults) are amazing siblings, and have been a total joy. So we completely understand how couples can be hyper-focused on their kids. Personally, I am a bona fide crazy dad — completely passionate about my kids and their world. But as our friends Brian and Tiffany shared in Chapter 8, children need to be a welcome *addition* to the home, not the all-consuming *center* of it.

Having children is a primary reason God brought humans together as husband and wife in the first place. And it's a fabulous privilege. But too many couples make their kids the core of their universe and neglect their marriage. Ironically, this neglect can ruin a marriage — and the resulting divorce shatters the lives of the very kids the couple was so focused on benefiting.

Some marriages blow up quickly from spousal neglect. Others disintegrate slowly, via "death by a thousand cuts." When the children grow up and leave the nest, the doting parents wake up one day and look at each other as strangers!

Only then do they realize they've drifted apart over the past eighteen-plus years of child-centered marriage. Without noticing it, their relationship had gradually faded away while their attention was fixated on child raising.

Couples need to remain *intact* and *devoted*. Before, during, and after the kids come.

God's plan for Adam and Eve was to "*become one flesh,*" to bond with each other before they had kids to divide their attention. Once they were solidly bonded, they were allowed to procreate, to "*be fruitful and multiply.*" But please note — the kids weren't supposed to come between Adam and Eve, nor were they supposed to live with them forever. On the contrary, the children were to "*leave and cleave.*" That means leave the parents and cleave to their new spouse.

Each man-and-wife team is a core unit, a couple that needs to remain intact and devoted to each other — before, during, and after kids come on the scene.

That's the natural order of things, but today's hypervigilant, overindulgent, helicopter parents often have it out of whack.

When our kids were young, Melina and I struggled to balance their needs with our needs as a couple. Then we discovered a valuable concept called "couch time" that really helped us in this area.

Here's the basic idea: When I got home from work, the first thing I would do was join Melina on the couch. We'd spend twenty minutes or so talking about how each of our days went. In the beginning, it was difficult because the kids kept climbing onto the couch, trying to be the focus of attention. Each time, we would gently put them back on the floor and let them know that "Mommy and Daddy are having couch time." We believed our children needed to see that Mom and Dad came first, as husband and wife. Soon, the kids got used to it and even looked forward to it! Over time, seeing Mom and Dad honor each other with "couch time" gave our kids security and comfort.

For example, Melina always made me feel super appreciated when I came home from work. As I walked in the door, the kids would be totally engaged with her, playing, laughing, and hanging on tight. When they felt her breaking away to greet me, they'd yell loudly for attention — "Mommy, mommy!" Some moms would have caved in. Instead, Melina made a big production out of my arrival. She'd excitedly declare, "Look kids, Daddy's home! Let's go say 'Hi,' and then Daddy and I will have our couch time."

Like all couples, Chris and I occasionally got into fights (still do, actually). Whenever it happened, our preschool kids would intervene in a very sweet way. They would tell us they wanted us to have "couch time" and would take our hands and lead us to the couch! They really understood the concept, even as toddlers.

That was encouraging. And *humbling*.

Practicing couch time was one way Chris and I prioritized our marriage as the cornerstone of the family unit. Another way

> Kids instinctively know how to play parents against each other.

was by honoring each other in front of the children. We weren't perfect parents. But our kids grew up knowing that their dad honored and respected me, and that he would protect me and care for me in any way possible. And they knew I felt the same about Chris.

That consistent image of mutual respect was, and is, setting them up for success in their own future marriages.

As kids grow up, they're constantly presenting new challenges to your marriage. That's one reason it's so important that you back each other up on any issue pertaining to them. When the kids get older, they also get "wiser" — they'll manipulate you in a hundred different ways (can you say "passive-aggressive?"). Somehow, they instinctively know how to play Mom against Dad, or have one parent become the "bad cop" versus the "good cop."

Sadly, some parents play along — even trying to win a child's favor by working against their spouse. Bad idea. The Bible says *"a house divided against itself will fall."* And sadly, many families have fallen. Make the decision to always support each other in front of the kids. Never undermine your spouse's authority. If you disagree on how something should be handled, discuss your differing opinions in private.

Always present a united front from the two of you.

Your spouse deserves to know (and be constantly reminded) that you are their rock-solid ally and will always, always, always have their back.

7) **Never stop cuddling.** "I am the planet's most affectionate life-form, something like the cross between a golden retriever and a barnacle." Does that describe you? If so, you can skip this section because you're probably hugging someone right now.

Meanwhile, the rest of us need to brush up on the importance of physical touch. The quote came from Elizabeth Gilbert's bestseller *Eat, Pray, Love.* And it reminds me of the joy I get when Melina and I cling to each other like "barnacles."

The need for physical touch is so universal and so powerful that an entire industry of "cuddlers for hire" has sprung up. Writing for *The Atlantic,* Olga Oksman reports that professional cuddlers "will hold clients close, in a platonic manner for $60 to $80 per hour."

Oksman says, "The idea of paying to cuddle may sound laughable or desperate." But business is booming. "Some clients seek companionship — two recent surveys found that 40 percent of adults say they're lonely." (That's a huge increase over the 20 percent of adults who said the same back in 1980.)

This loneliness epidemic seems to parallel our obsession with social media. "The advent of professional cuddling and friend rentals seems to be serving a distinctly modern need." The companionship industry exists because digital technology "doesn't provide physical touch and can't replace real-life friendships."

But benefits go beyond emotional, says Oksman. "Human beings have been shown to benefit from touch — in studies, it has been linked to feelings of relaxation, increases in the hormone oxytocin, and decreases in blood pressure."

All over the country, people are paying $1 per minute to have someone touch them. Would you be surprised to know that many of the clients are *married*?

One professional hugger told *Prevention* magazine that the only cuddling most adults get is associated with sex. And many get none at all. She describes a man who weeps during his sessions — lasting 60 minutes or more — because he is so deprived of touch. "He's happy in his marriage, but he loves to cuddle and doesn't know how to talk about it with his wife."

> The loneliness epidemic parallels our obsession with social media.

Why is our basic, genetic need for touch a taboo subject to discuss? And why hire a stranger when you could be in the trusted arms of your loving spouse?

Here's why: Many couples drift away from nonsexual touching as years go by. They get busy. Distracted. Tired. People can be living in the same house and sleeping in the same bed but be starving for physical touch. This unmet need prompted one paid cuddler to ask, "Why isn't there a Starbucks for hugs?"

So ramp it up, couples. Start hugging again. Start cuddling and spooning and canoodling. And maybe best of all — start holding hands!

If you're like me, you always smile when you see a couple holding hands — especially if that couple is up in years. Their public display of affection speaks volumes about the quality of their relationship. But those cool seniors didn't start holding hands yesterday! It probably began when they were dating and just got better over time.

Family expert Mark Merrill thinks all married couples should hold hands. Frequently. Merrill writes, "It's a simple sign of solidarity, and a symptom of a good relationship. But it can also strengthen the marriage."

In his excellent blog *(markmerrill.com)*, he lists these benefits:

- **Lower stress.** Research shows that holding a spouse's hand in a stressful situation is calming. Science suggests it reduces stress-related activities in the brain. The resulting lower cortisol level boosts your immune system.

- **Stronger emotional bonding.** It's in our DNA. Human touch releases special hormones that increase a sense of trust and security. A feeling of well-being is critical to emotional and physical intimacy in a healthy marriage.

- **Acceptance and love.** Squeezing your spouse's hand sends a message: "I love you and accept you." Interlocking *fingers* is symbolic that our *hearts* are also interlocked and woven together. This unspoken signal is louder than words.

There's another benefit. Whether you realize it or not, you're a role model to younger generations. When married couples hold hands it makes an impression. The act of holding hands is universally understood across cultures as a sign of togetherness. It declares you are in it together for the long run.

I totally remember the first time I held Melina's hand. I was wondering: *Will she be mad or upset if I reach for her? Will she accept my gesture?*

My palms were sweaty and my pulse was pounding. Happily, she responded positively to my first attempt, and today, holding hands is still a way we show the world and each other that our love relationship is dynamic and meaningful.

Cuddling is one of the great pleasures of life. But it's healthy, too. In his book *The Cuddle Sutra*, Rob Grader says, "Human beings simply cannot survive without the touch of another person … Infants who go without being touched show developmental delays from weight gain to cognitive and motor skills. Throughout life, the touch of another can have a dramatic effect on depression, arthritis, asthma, ADHD, autism, hypertension, and migraine headaches."

> **INSIGHT**: Cuddling and touching increase the so-called "feel good" chemicals serotonin and dopamine in the brain. Get a dose of God's own antidepressants — with no negative side effects!

Hit me with your best shot.

Rock star Pat Benatar is over 65 and madly in love.

With her husband, no less.

The hard-rocking couple met back in 1979 when Neil Giraldo auditioned to play guitar for Benatar's band. It was love at first sight. But that's the easy part. Against daunting odds, Pat and Neil have *stayed married* for close to 40 years. The lovers have collaborated on recording projects for almost four decades, resulting in Benatar winning four Grammy Awards and a string of platinum albums.

What's their secret to marital longevity? Benatar explains that her long, happy relationship with her husband is a result of mutual respect — and simply accepting that ending the marriage was never an option.

"It's kind of an incestuous relationship," she told *Parade* magazine of her marriage. "There isn't any part of our lives that isn't intertwined — so even when there's a conflict, you just have to resolve it."

Conflict resolution. Hmm. Benatar should know. Her hit song, "Love is a Battlefield" sold over a million copies.

The couple have two daughters and obviously prioritized creating a loving, secure home environment. "Touring for us is like breathing," Benatar said in 2015. "It's an amazing life. But when we're home, we're home, with big Italian dinners on Sundays. Family — that's the focal point."

Pat and Neil just might be rock and roll's greatest love story. "It was a partnership from the very beginning," Giraldo says. "We were just two missing pieces that found each other."

Whether you're a banker or a janitor or an MTV legend, your marriage can go the distance. You *can* beat the odds. And your love *can* last forever. The woman who sang "We Live for Love" has a lifetime crush on her hubby: "I feel about him now the way I felt about him the very first moment I saw him."

Benatar confessed to *Parade*, "We're nuts about each other."

If that's what it takes, let's all go nuts.

TALK IT OVER.

Keeping your marriage healthy takes teamwork. Go for a walk together and talk through these issues candidly. Holding hands will help!

1) What are some little things your spouse likes that you could easily do? What's been keeping you from doing them?

2) When's the last time you went on a date (the fun, romantic kind like before you got married)? If it's been a while, make it job one!

3) If you have kids, have you been prioritizing your relationship as husband and wife? Does your spouse come first before your children? If not, what steps can you take together to improve this?

4) Have your *feelings* for your spouse changed since you were newlyweds? Have your *actions* changed since your courtship?

TAKE ACTION.

Feelings follow *actions*. To rekindle the passion and fun of your early years, begin doing the same things you did as young lovers. Here's a start:

1) Guys, plan a date with your wife and don't disclose where you're going. Plan a "magical mystery" date that fits your budget. Just before you need to leave, go buy some flowers — then return and ring the doorbell to "pick up your date."

2) Ladies, plan a surprise for your husband that would be meaningful to him. Consider doing something he enjoys (but you're not so crazy about personally). Be creative, bring a camera, and make some cherished memories.

3) Put on some vintage polyester and Google the lyrics to "Still the One" by Orleans. Read the words out loud to each other and discuss how they apply to your marriage (Are you *still* having fun? Is your spouse *still* your better half?).

4) Find a marriage conference near you (sometime during the next three months). Make plans to attend as a couple.

CHAPTER 10

Marriage Tool Kit:
Must-have resources for making it work

Can Albert Einstein save your marriage?

The father of modern theoretical physics said, "Once you stop learning, you start dying."

That's true for individuals, more so for couples. Once we stop learning and growing, even dedicated spouses can drift apart. Our conversations and interactions can feel stale, boring, and repetitive. Without learning new relational skills (and polishing old ones), a marriage can become, well, a real drag.

If we're not committed to lifelong learning, we can lose perspective and forget why we even got married in the first place! Business trainers call this "vision leak," and companies fight it with ongoing training and motivational seminars.

In most aspects of life, we understand this.

For instance, we know that success in the workplace depends on learning new skills and constantly improving. Many professions — like medicine and education — require people to not only recertify existing skills, but to systematically attain new levels, with fresh certifications marking their progress.

As married couples, we can't let *our* skills get rusty, either.

Maybe you're thinking, "But my marriage is in great shape. No problems. No conflicts. No crises."

If so, consider this: When an athlete hits the zenith of their career (think Michael Jordan, Tiger Woods, or Alex Rodriguez in their prime), do they stop practicing? Do they fire their coaches and trainers?

Just the opposite.

"The best keep getting better." That's from performance coach Justin Foster. "It isn't that they demand perfection, but excellence." Those at the top share what Foster calls "a tremendous drive to master every aspect of their sport."

Can you say that about your *marriage*?

Substitute the word "couples" for "athletes" and listen to Foster: "Great athletes pursue excellence at every opportunity. They act like hard work pays off. They act like success is in the details. Great athletes act like they can always get better."

Great couples — like great athletes — always strive to get better. They're not content to rest on their laurels or past achievements.

And it makes all the difference.

Psychologist Carol Dweck, author of *Mindset: The New Psychology of Success*, says this desire to learn often makes the difference between success and failure. Dweck says we either have a "fixed mindset" or a "growth mindset." People with a growth mindset "believe their intelligence, talent, and abilities can be developed through persistence and hard work."

Catch that? Good intentions aren't enough. It takes persistence and hard work. That's the message of this book.

Learn it or lose it.

Do you exercise regularly?

Chris and I do. Working out helps us look and feel better. But if we start skipping it, the benefits start wearing off. Muscles lose tone. Brains get dull. Unwanted pounds come back. The time we spent sweating in the gym five months ago (or five years ago) does not carry over.

So we keep at it. We keep pushing ourselves.

Same is true for keeping our marriage in shape. It's easier to sit around and eat Chunky Monkey than it is to hit the treadmill. But "Ben & Jerry" won't help us attain our goals. Only "Chris & Melina" can do that.

———

One way to stay sharp is an idea we borrowed from the business world.

Back in the '80s, the Big Three automakers were plagued by poor quality and outdated engineering. Why? They had stopped learning and improving. As a result, Toyota, Nissan, and Honda grabbed huge market shares. Today, U.S. cars are back on par with the world's finest.

What happened? James Surowiecki talks about this seismic shift toward excellence in his *New Yorker* article, "Better All the Time." Surowiecki says, "The ethos that underlies all these performance revolutions is captured by the Japanese term *kaizen*, or continuous improvement."

Imagine with me what a "*kaizen* marriage" would be like!

Issues like communication, finances, and sexual satisfaction would not be static, fixed entities, but the targets of continuous improvement. Opinions and ideas would be mutually respected. Both spouses would be dedicated to openly discussing every aspect of life — from romance to retirement.

Of course, upgrading a marriage is not the same as upgrading an assembly line. But many *kaizen* principles can apply to a relationship:

- Start by questioning current practices and standards.
- Replace conventional fixed ideas with fresh ones.
- Think of how to do something, not reasons why it can't be done.
- Implement a solution right away, even if it's not perfect.

This notion of continuous improvement will impact your marriage, and you can integrate it anytime from newlywed to grandparent.

Your friends will think you're nutso.

It bears repeating: Doing the same thing over and over and expecting to get different results is insanity. Which explains why so many marriages crash and burn — couples make the same mistakes over and over yet expect a different outcome.

The bottom line is we *all* invest TIME, ENERGY, and RESOURCES in whatever we value most. For some it's a career. Or a favorite hobby. For us, it's our marriage, hands down. We have an almost insatiable desire to learn, improve, and grow as a couple. So learning how to do it better never gets boring.

Ironically, the same skeptics who tease us for being obsessed with improving our marriage gladly work on improving *other* facets of life:

• They invest TIME coaching their kids. ("Don't let anyone outwork you — look at J.J. Watt's work ethic and strive to get better.")

• They invest ENERGY upgrading their job skills. ("Just 15 more credit hours of night school and I'll get my MBA — and a promotion.")

• They invest RESOURCES improving their games. ("I'm having my swing analyzed with a computer. I'll spend whatever it takes to get my handicap down.")

These are all fine things to do by the way, but their proliferation proves my point — people instinctually know that constantly improving their skills can make them more competent and capable in virtually any endeavor.

> Couples make the same mistakes over and over yet expect a different outcome.

Why don't we apply that same logic to our marriages?

In life, nothing gets better without putting time and energy into it. Does your body slim down on its own? Do you get strength and vitality just by wishing? Or does it take dedicated effort at the gym and discipline at the dinner table?

I find it amazing that some husbands spend more time prepping for their fantasy football draft than they do on strengthening their marriage. I mean, it's only the most important relationship on earth!

(Note: One tweet said, "I work 40 hours a week. I do fantasy football 24/7." I wonder how many breakups stem from *this* obsession?)

Ladies, we can have misplaced priorities, too.

By nature, we can get so focused on mothering, housekeeping, or socializing with friends that we forget about learning new skills (and refreshing old ones) that can make our marriages better. If we don't intentionally expose ourselves to teaching resources — seminars, books, broadcasts, whatever — we can start slipping back into bad habits ... or get stuck settling for mediocrity.

In my experience, too many women just "hope for the best" in their marriages instead of being proactive learners with a growth mindset.

———

Are you the same couple you were on your honeymoon?

Yes and no.

Lifelong learning is essential because the dynamics of our marriage are constantly changing. For one thing, we're getting older (sorry, ladies). In addition, our incomes can vacillate, we might relocate, and of course, children can come along. The way we handle parenthood, money issues, division of labor, and so on must evolve to adapt to new circumstances. And handling change is a lot easier when you're constantly learning from the experts — reading books, listening to podcasts, whatever.

Couples that survive the ups and downs of life are the ones who discuss potential problems in advance and make expectations clear. But marriage therapist Eli Karam says most couples just fumble along on what he calls *autopilot*. "Couples operate on what they assume in their head because they grew up that way; they think that if it works for them, it works for their partners."

> In life, nothing gets better without putting time and energy into it.

Wrong.

Living a relationship on autopilot can lull us into drowsiness. We may not even notice that things aren't as good as they used to be. But reading a marriage book or joining a discussion group can be a well-timed wakeup call. Learning new skills forces us to reevaluate who we are individually and what our goals are as a couple.

Dr. Karam says married people often "operate on out-of-date knowledge."

Folks, we cannot get by on what we learned years ago. We must update our relational skills. "It's a myth that a good marriage sustains itself," Karam says. "It's learning yourself, learning your partner. What you are at age 24 is not what you are at age 34."

And I would add, not what you are at 44, 54, 64 or 94. Which is why we must keep learning and growing — to stay ahead of the inevitable changes.

> **INSIGHT**: Like an LPGA golfer who hires a swing coach, an opera diva who relies on a voice tutor, or a gymnastic star with a personal trainer, we all need experts to teach us new skills — and remind us of old ones. Same for solidifying a marriage.

People sometimes ask us for the "secret" to a happy marriage. Truth? We would not have the marriage we have today if it wasn't for the books, messages, and marriage conferences we've invested our time and money in. This commitment to learning goes back over twenty-plus years of marriage *and* during our courtship.

Seven ways to bring out the best in each other.

Paul Simon sang about 50 ways to leave your lover. As we near the end of our book, here are 7 ways to *keep* your lover. Over the years, we've road-tested a zillion ideas. May this batch of proven principles serve you well!

1) **Be supportive of your spouse's passions.** Melina's great joy has always been riding her horse and spending time at the stable. For me, it's been martial arts and physical fitness. Support and encourage each other

as you pursue your passions. Leave little notes for your partner expressing admiration for how good they are at what they love doing most. (They'll probably frame them.)

2) **Understand the ebb and flow.** Romantic feelings come and go. Relationships are fluid. Like the tides, our moods will rise and fall. Recognize that emotional swings are a *normal* part of marriage! Otherwise, when adversity (or boredom) hits, you'll think you married the wrong person ... that the good times are gone forever. Couples give up and quit when they don't realize that a "slump" or a "dry spell" is just a phase — not a permanent downward spiral. Don't jump overboard because the tide is changing. Hold tight and stay the course.

3) **Tune in to the small things.** Little things add up over the long term and bring success ... or failure. Everything matters. Nothing is insignificant in your relationship. Here are some positive little things: *Open the car door. Carry the groceries in. Say "thank you" several times a day. Swing by Starbucks without being asked.* Here are some negative little things: *Don't pick up your clothes. Never gas up the car. Dominate the TV remote. Stay glued to your smartphone.* Life coach Stephen Covey said, "I am not the product of my circumstances. I am the product of my decisions." Make a decision to work on the small things.

4) **Serve each other.** We're selfish by nature. Programmed to look out for "Number One." A good marriage requires you to reverse that policy. Relationship blogger Dave Willis says, "Marriage is not a 50/50 proposition, divorce is!" Marriage means hard work and putting your spouse's needs above your own. Willis says, "It isn't dividing everything in half, but giving everything you've got." Always be willing to serve your spouse. Even when it's not convenient. Always ask, "What can I do for you?" Even when you don't feel like it.

5) **Always show love and respect.** Ladies, let your man know you respect him and be specific about why. Appreciate and value his masculinity. Let him know he's your hero; let him be your knight. Build him up and watch him grow, lead, and live up to his God-given potential. Men, let your wife know you love her and treasure her. Wives have a deep (sometimes unspoken) need to be loved unconditionally and sacrificially. They feel most secure and empowered when a husband shows his true devotion by putting her needs above his.

6) **Have a vision of what you want your marriage to be.** Ours came from a lyric I sang to Melina when I proposed. The song is "True Companion" by Marc Cohn. Near the end Cohn pledges his love, "When the years have done irreparable harm, I can see us walking slowly arm in arm, just like that couple on the corner do." Growing old has brought pain and diminished abilities to the elderly couple, but they're still deeply committed. Our goal is to be "just like that couple on the corner." We visualize ourselves holding hands in our golden years, still passionately in love.

> Unveil some new lingerie. Or maybe get tickets to a tractor pull.

7) **Surprise them with romantic gifts.** Guys, never stop buying flowers. After 20-plus years, I'm still sending Melina a dozen red roses "just because." Include a message saying you appreciate, value, and love her — my wife has kept *all* the notes I've sent. (Tip: Know your wife. Some frugal gals prefer flowers from Trader Joe's; others prefer something pricier. Spend accordingly.) Ladies, men love romantic gifts, too! Plan a hot night out and a surprise unveiling of some new lingerie. Or maybe get tickets to a tractor pull. Men are not all that complicated.

Ladies, here's a question for you: *If your husband used to get you roses or candy, but stopped at some point, is there a reason?* Did you bash him with harsh words about being wasteful? Were you blasé or dismissive of his efforts? Remember, men are just "little boys with hairy legs" and respond well to appreciation and positive words from the women they love. On the flip side, they react poorly to nagging, complaining, and negativity from us.

With God's help, your marriage *can* be exceptional. It *can* be a role model for your children. It *can* be a positive, shining example to everyone around you.

Even if your relationship is currently in a rocky place, it can recover and be everything you've wanted and more. It just takes focused commitment and intentionality from each of you — for as long as it takes. The outcome is in your hands ... we're excited to see how beautiful and vibrant you choose to make it!

Priceless resources to grow on.

Smart investors want a big return on investment (ROI) for their money.

Based on experience, we can assure a huge ROI for your marriage if you invest in learning new relational skills. We owe much of our success to the effort we've both made in listening to, reading, and watching the best teachers out there. We've listed many of the resources that've helped us; our hope is you'll not stop with this book but become a lifelong learner. Going forward, our website will offer updates from us and links to brand-new resources *(chrisandmelina.com).*

Triple your chances for a great marriage.

Every marriage is a "work in progress." No relationship is static — your bond is either growing or dying. It's not enough to coast along on momentum and good intentions.

So use the tools, check our website, and above all, choose to *love* each other even when it's a challenge just to *like* each other! Remember, problems come and go, but keeping a relentless, positive focus is critical. Here are three insider tips to drastically improve your odds:
1) **Read and discuss at least one marriage book a year.**
2) **Join a small group focused on marriage skills** (check with your church).
3) **Attend one marriage seminar or conference annually.**

> **INSIGHT**: We've accessed a lot of great materials. But even more important is our mutual willingness to *put in the work*. In this section, we list books and resources that've made a huge difference for us — as a couple and as individuals. We pray these materials will fuel your desire to constantly grow and get better.

Recommended reading.

These books are all available at sites like *amazon.com* — including the out-of-print titles. As you shop, note that many of the older classics now come in revised and expanded editions.

Listed alphabetically by author, here's our hot picks:

Intimate Allies: Discovering God's Design for Marriage and Becoming Soul Mates for Life. Dan Allender and Tremper Longman. Tyndale House, 1995.

Every Man's Battle: Winning the War on Sexual Temptation One Victory at a Time. Stephen Arterburn and Fred Stoeker. Waterbrook Press, 2000.

Different Children, Different Needs: Understanding the Unique Personality of Your Child. Dr. Charles F. Boyd. Multnomah Books, 2004.

Love After Marriage: A Journey into Deeper Spiritual, Emotional, and Sexual Oneness. Barry and Lori Byrne. Chosen Books, 2012.

The Five Love Languages: The Secret to Love That Lasts. Gary Chapman. Moody Northfield Publishing, 1992.

Kiss Me Like You Mean It: Solomon's Crazy In Love How-To Manual. Dr. David Clarke. Revell, 2009.

Love for A Lifetime: Building a Marriage That Will Go the Distance. Dr. James Dobson. Multnomah Books from Questar Publishers, 1993.

Love Must Be Tough: Hope for Marriages in Crisis. Dr. James Dobson. Word Publishing, 1996.

What Wives Wish their Husbands Knew about Women. Dr. James Dobson. Tyndale, 1997.

Uncommon Marriage: Learning about Lasting Love and Overcoming Life's Obstacles Together. Tony and Lauren Dungy. Tyndale Publishing, 2014.

What They Never Taught Us About How to Get Along with Each Other. Judson Edwards. Harvest House, 1991.

Love & Respect: The Love She Most Desires; The Respect He Desperately Needs. Dr. Emerson Eggerichs. Thomas Nelson, 2004.

For Women Only: What You Need to Know About the Inner Lives of Men. Shaunti Feldhahn. Multnomah, 2004.

For Men Only: A Straightforward Guide to the Inner Lives of Women. Shaunti and Jeff Feldhahn. Multnomah, 2006.

Men Are from Mars, Women Are from Venus. John Gray, Ph.D. Harper Collins Publishing, 1992.

His Needs, Her Needs: Building an Affair-Proof Marriage. Willard F. Harley, Jr. Revell, 2001.

What the Bible Says About Love, Marriage, and Sex: The Song of Solomon. David Jeremiah. FaithWords Publishing, 2012.

The Meaning of Marriage: Facing the Complexities of Commitment with the Wisdom of God. Timothy Keller with Kathy Keller. Dutton Publishing, 2011.

Light His Fire: How to Keep Your Man Passionately and Hopelessly in Love with You. Ellen Kreidman. Penguin-Random House, 1991.

Light Her Fire: How to Ignite Passion, Joy, and Excitement in the Woman You Love. Ellen Kreidman. Penguin-Random House, 1992.

Sex Begins in the Kitchen: Creating Intimacy to Make Your Marriage Sizzle. Dr. Kevin Leman. Revell, 2006.

Have a New Sex Life by Friday: Because Your Marriage Can't Wait Until Monday. Dr. Kevin Leman. Revell, 2017.

The Christian Husband: God's Vision for Loving and Caring for Your Wife. Bob Lepine. Vine Books, 1999.

Silver Boxes: The Gift of Encouragement. Florence Littauer. Thomas Nelson, 1989.

Personality Plus for Couples: Understanding Yourself and the One You Love. Florence Littauer. Revell, 2001.

Hot, Holy, and Humorous: Sex in Marriage by God's Design. J. Parker. Broadstreet Publishing Group, 2016.

Trading Places: The Best Move You'll Ever Make in Your Marriage. Les and Leslie Parrott. Zondervan, 2008.

Preparing for Marriage: Discover God's Plan for a Lifetime of Love. Dennis Rainey. Bethany House, 1998.

Building Your Mate's Self-Esteem. Dennis and Barbara Rainey. Thomas Nelson, 1995.

Hidden Keys of a Loving, Lasting Marriage. Gary and Norma Smalley. Zondervan, 1993.

Love Is a Decision: Proven Techniques to Keep Your Marriage Alive and Lively. Gary Smalley and John Trent. Thomas Nelson, 2000.

Marriage from Surviving to Thriving: Practical Advice on Making Your Marriage Strong. Chuck Swindoll. Thomas Nelson, 2006.

Devotions for a Sacred Marriage. Gary Thomas. Zondervan, 2005.

The Purpose Driven Life: What in the World Am I Here For? Rick Warren. Zondervan, 2002.

Vertical Marriage: The One Secret That Will Change Your Marriage, Dave and Ann Wilson. Zondervan, 2019.

Recommended online resources.

Why not click on a few of our cyber favorites? Many offer free videos and downloadable materials to strengthen your marriage. Others highlight live events you can attend:

All Pro Dad. Be a hero to your kids. This group is on a mission to help men love and lead their family well. Check out *allprodad.com*.

Bible in One Year. Free Bible reading app with helpful commentary by Nicky Gumbel, founder of the Alpha Course. Get it daily via email, text, or audio podcast. Check out *bibleinoneyear.org*.

Covenant Eyes. Live a porn-free life. Break free with resources including Internet "accountably software." Check out *covenanteyes.com*.

FamilyLife. Champions of biblical marriage. Books, videos, and daily radio broadcasts. Exceptional "Weekend to Remember" (live events) and "The Art of Marriage" (video events). Check out *familylife.com*.

Focus on the Family. Founded by Dr. James Dobson in 1977. Renowned for daily broadcasts and marriage events. Online Focus on the Family Store offers an in-depth catalog of marriage materials. Check out *focusonthefamily.com*.

Mark Merrill. Terrific blog, podcasts, and articles on marriage, parenting, and relationships. All free. Check out *markmerrill.com*.

Joyce Meyer. God loves you and wants to improve your life — and your marriage. Joyce can help. Free message videos, email studies, and daily devotionals. Check out *joycemeyer.org*.

Beth Moore. Living Proof Ministries helps people come to know and love Jesus through the study of Scripture. Moore's audio and video messages are amazing. Check out *lproof.org*.

Dave Ramsey. Dump debt, build wealth. Give your marriage a total money makeover. Enroll in Financial Peace University. Check out *daveramsey.com*.

Andy Stanley. North Point Ministries in Atlanta is an epicenter of biblical truth that challenges today's pop culture. Messages by pastor Andy Stanley are available online for free — including marriage topics. Check out *northpointministries.org*.

Rick Warren. We attend Saddleback Church in Lake Forest, California. Our pastor, Rick Warren, is known worldwide for life-changing, purpose-driven messages. You can view any of them for free — there's a huge archive, including marriage topics. Check out *saddleback.com*.

Dave and Ann Wilson. Back in Michigan, we attended Kensington Church. Dave and Ann were teaching pastors, and greatly influenced our marriage. Keep an eye out — the Wilsons speak at FamilyLife marriage retreats around the country. (They host the daily radio program *FamilyLife Today*, heard nationwide.) Check out *kensingtonchurch.org* or *daveandannwilson.com*.

Our Story:
Everything that could possibly go wrong

Our paths first crossed during spring break in Mazatlan, Mexico.

It was a typically rowdy fun-in-the-sun beach party scene. We were both single, both in college, and lived approximately 2,246 miles apart.

Melina was there with her girlfriends. I was there with two of my classmates. At the time, I was living in Mexico for a semester abroad at the University of Guadalajara. Melina and I ran into each other several times over the course of the week, but we didn't actually connect and talk until her final day.

That afternoon we sat by the pool and chatted for five hours. Conversation came easily, and because she was on her way home I didn't feel the usual "dating scene" pressure. On top of that, she lived in Southern California and I lived in Michigan! We were just strangers in paradise being spontaneous and real with no strings attached. When it was time for Melina to catch her train, I handed her the business card of my friend who lived in Los Angeles. I figured since I'd never see her again, the least I could do was set my buddy up with this remarkable person. I knew he'd be a gentleman and that she'd have a good time.

Melina politely accepted the card, but had no intention whatsoever of going out with him. Several weeks later, I received an unexpected letter from her in Guadalajara — even though we hadn't exchanged contact information. What followed was a long-distance relationship with lots of letters and huge phone bills ("No, *you* hang up first"). That was followed up with visits to each other's homes. It was going along great — until it wasn't. After one year, Melina decided to break off the relationship because the distance seemed too hard to overcome.

From that day our lives took totally different paths.

If you had told me I'd end up marrying Melina Swanson, I would have chuckled. It was an appealing thought, but I was positive I'd never see her again.

———

On January 17, 1991, I became a Christian. I accepted God's forgiveness for all of my sins and became a follower of Jesus. For some unknown reason, I decided to send a letter to Melina telling her about my conversion.

We hadn't communicated in years.

When Melina broke off our relationship, she stopped responding to my calls and letters. Totally. No tapering off; it was like a door slamming shut. So deciding to write her about my newfound faith in Christ was a bit strange to say the least.

As usual, my letter received no reply or acknowledgment.

Two years later, in February 1993, I began praying that someone special would come into my life. I was trusting God to bring me *his* choice of companion so I could experience the kind of deeply satisfying relationship he intended.

Imagine my surprise when six months after that — in September 1993 — I received a voicemail message from Melina. The recording said: "Hi … this is Melina Swanson from California. I'm not sure if you remember me, but I wanted to let you know some great news. I recently became a Christian."

Of course, I called her back and soon we started dating long distance again. This time was different. Our relationship began getting serious very quickly.

Maybe too quickly.

The following summer, Melina became uncomfortable because she didn't share my deep feelings. She was worried about not having "that mushy, in-love feeling." She even began pushing me away so I would break up with her.

In August we had a canoeing and camping trip planned with my father. We would be staying in Canada, just north of Minnesota, in a lovely Provincial park called Quetico. Given her misgivings about our relationship, Melina didn't want to come. Her mom pushed her to go, and she reluctantly acquiesced.

By this time, I was ticked off about how Melina had been treating me. Her attempts to goad me into breaking off the relationship were painful.

As we prepared to head north we were both pretty upset. And nervous. From the minute we pulled out of my driveway it was tense and awkward. The 16-hour car ride from Detroit to Quetico was a disaster. We literally fought the entire way. There was no bloodshed, but we screamed at each other for most of the ride, trying to figure out what was going on and what we wanted.

It was horrible. Then it got worse. We got lost.

I remember it was about 2 a.m. Pitch black. We were somewhere around Thunder Bay, Canada. I can't say for sure — this was long before GPS and smartphones. All I knew was that we were exhausted, deep in the woods, and hundreds of miles away from any real civilization.

I'm not proud to admit this, but I came really close to just hitting the brakes and telling Melina to get out and walk. Even though we were in the middle of the wilderness. And surrounded by bears. Fortunately, God intervened.

At that exact moment, under the vast canopy of stars, I had an epiphany. I began silently talking to God. "Lord, I understand … I thought Melina was the answer to my prayers about bringing someone special into my life … But obviously I was mistaken. She must have just been a sign that you had *someone* for me, but not her. I get it now … I'm okay with that."

Up until that night I had never felt a direct impression from God. And I haven't since. But on that deserted road, deep in the wilderness, I felt clearly in my spirit two words, "Trust me."

To which I silently replied, "Lord, I don't want to trust you, this is too painful and too difficult."

Two more times, the Creator of the Universe came back with, "Trust me."

And I did. Tentatively at first. Then with reckless abandon.

That tempestuous night was the start of a miraculous transformation, the seeds of a lifelong journey full of big risks and even bigger rewards. Our week together in the wilderness completely changed our relationship.

Our prayer today is that our experiences will help transform *your* relationship as well. Great marriages don't just happen. Not for anyone. They take a lot of intentional effort by both partners — but the result is well worth it!

ABOUT THE AUTHORS

Chris and Melina Hann

Goodbye romance? No way! Chris and Melina were married in 1995, but still feel (and act) like newlyweds on a honeymoon. How they manage that is the subject of their first book. Ironically, the Hanns both had family backgrounds that offered little or no hope for a lasting marriage. After beating such tough odds, they are "passionate about helping couples achieve long-lasting, vibrant relationships." In addition to mentoring couples, they gratefully share what they've learned through blogging and speaking to groups around the country. When he's not writing (or practicing martial arts), Chris works as sales manager for a Silicon Valley tech firm. Melina is a California native who enjoys riding her horse, Brandy, and taking hikes in the canyons with her German shepherd, Nala. She is a licensed real estate agent and volunteers her time with foster children as a CASA (Court Appointed Special Advocate). The Hanns have two college-age kids who make sure they practice what they preach! Daughter Samantha recently graduated from UCLA with a degree in political science; son Alex is majoring in computer science. The family attends Saddleback Church in Lake Forest, California.

Karl Nilsson

A Detroit native, Nilsson enjoys collaborating with authors who "publish the positive." That includes pairing up with Jeff Petherick (*Grace Like Rain*), Mike Komara (*Life in the Balance*), and John Anderson (*Replace Retirement*). He's also written numerous novels, stage plays, and videos, including a short film on human trafficking in Nepal. In addition, Nilsson consults businesses and nonprofits on branding their message. Prior to that, he was Communication Director at the multi-site Kensington Church. He's been happily, devotedly married to his best friend Marie for over three decades. They have two adult children, Britt and Karl.

SOURCES

Introduction & Preface

Background info from: "Marriage and Divorce," *American Psychological Association*. Adopted from *Encyclopedia of Psychology*. (Accessed at *apa.org/topics/divorce*.)

"Do Half of All Marriages Really End in Divorce?" *LifeWay*. Published January 1, 2014. With quotes from *Good News About Marriage* by Shaunti Feldhahn and Tally Whitehead. (Accessed at *lifeway.com/en/articles*.)

Shaunti Feldhahn and Tally Whitehead, *Good News About Marriage: Debunking Discouraging Myths About Marriage and Divorce*. Multnomah Books, 2014.

"O.C. Divorce Rate One of Highest in Nation," David Whiting. *Orange County Register*. (Posted August 21, 2013, at *ocregister.com/articles/diamond*.)

"The Booming Business of Divorce Parties," Martha C. White. *Time*. October 15, 2012. (Also posted at *business.time.com*.)

"Shacking Up on the Rise? Ho-Hum," Rebecca Hagelin. *World Net Daily*. July 31, 2008. Article also references *USA Today/Gallup* poll. (Accessed at *new.wp.wnd. com/2008/07/710291*.)

Nicholas H. Wolfinger, *Understanding the Divorce Cycle: The Children of Divorce in Their Own Marriages*. Cambridge University Press, 2005.

Chapter 1. Together Forever

"World's Longest Lasting Couple Has the Secret of Lasting Love," Janelle Harris. *The Stir*. Published April 18, 2012. (Sourced from *thestir.cafemom.com*.)

"Rick and Kay Warren's Painful, Gradual Love Story," Jeffery Sheler. *Christianity Today*. (Posted November 10, 2009 at *christianitytoday.com*.) Excerpted from *Prophet of Purpose*, Jeffery Sheler, Doubleday Religion, 2009.

"The Purpose Driven Marriage," Sam House. *Lifeway*. (Posted at *lifeway.com*.)

Rick Warren, *The Purpose Driven Life: What in the World Am I Here For?* Zondervan, 2002-2012.

"Infidelity at Trade Shows?" Chris Matyszczyk. *C/NET Tech Culture*. (Posted August 18, 2012, at *cnet.com*.)

"E-Motional Affairs: How Facebook Leads to Infidelity," Ian Kerner. *CNN The Chart*. (Posted March 3, 2011, at *thechart.blogs.cnn.com*.)

"The Four Stages of Temptation," Dan Black. *Covenant Eyes*. (Posted February 26, 2016, at *covenanteyes.com*.)

Timothy Keller with Kathy Keller, *The Meaning of Marriage: Facing the Complexities of Commitment with the Wisdom of God*. Dutton Publishing, 2011.

"Kay Warren Shares About Early Years of Marital Hell as She and Rick Renew Their Vows," Lucinda Borkett-Jones. *Christian Today*. (Posted June 15, 2015, at *christiantoday.com*.)

Chapter 2. Sticks and Stones

"Johnny Lingo's Eight-Cow Wife," Patrica McGerr. First published in *Woman's Day*, 1965. Reprinted by permission of Curtis Brown, Ltd.

Dr. James & Shirley Dobson, *Night Light: A Devotional for Couples*. Multnomah Books, 2000.

Dr. Charles F. Boyd, *Different Children, Different Needs: Understanding the Unique Personality of Your Child*. Multnomah Books, 2004.

Dale Carnegie, *How to Win Friends and Influence People*. Gallery Books, 1998. (First published in 1936.)

"Positive and Negative Words," Peggy Bert. *Today's Christian Woman*. (Posted September 12, 2008, at *todayschristianwoman.com/articles/2008*.)

Florence Littauer, *Silver Boxes: The Gift of Encouragement*. Thomas Nelson, 1996.

"Love One Another with Brotherly Affection," John Piper. *Desiring God*. From a video message. (Blog posted December 12, 2004, at *desiringGod.com*.)

Chapter 3. Can You Hear Me Now?

Information from Eva Kraus-Turowski, MSW, LICSW. Associated Clinic of Psychology. 6950 West 146th Street, Suite 100, Apple Valley, MN 55124.

Willard F. Harley, *His Needs, Her Needs: Building an Affair-Proof Marriage*. Fleming H. Revell Company, 2001.

Dr. Kevin Leman, *Sex Begins in the Kitchen: Creating Intimacy to Make Your Marriage Sizzle*. Fleming H. Revell Company, 2006.

"When Couples Stop Talking: Reasons and Remedies," Suzanne Phillips. (Blog posted April 24, 2013, at *psychcentral.com*.)

"10 Reasons Couples Don't Talk," Dr. Barton Goldsmith. *Psychology Today*. (Posted August 5, 2009, at *psychologytoday.com*.)

Zig Ziglar, *Zig Ziglar's Secrets of Closing the Sale*. Berkley Books, 1985.

Gary Thomas, *Devotions for a Sacred Marriage*. Zondervan, 2005.

"Albert Mehrabian's 7-38-55 Rule of Personal Communication," Nagesh Belludi. (Posted October 4, 2008, at *rightattitudes.com/2008/0/04/7-38-55-rule*.)

"Is Nonverbal Communication a Numbers Game?" Dr. Jeff Thompson. *Psychology Today*. (Posted September 30, 2011, at *psychologytoday.com*.)

Gary Chapman, *The Five Love Languages: The Secret to Love That Lasts*. Moody Northfield Publishers, 1992.

Chapter 4. Conflict Resolution

Larry Crabb, *The Pressure's Off: There's a New Way to Live*. Waterbrook Press, 2002.

"Apollo Expeditions to the Moon," James A. Lovell. Excerpt from Chapter 13. (Accessed from *history.nasa.gov*.)

"Five Consequences of Going to Bed Angry," Mark Merrill. (Blog posted February 2, 2015, at *markmerill.com*.)

"How and Why to Ban the Silent Treatment from Your Relationship," Elizabeth Bernstein. *Wall Street Journal*. Updated June 16, 2014.

"The Lord's Prayer," Dr. Rowan Williams. BBC Broadcasting. (Posted August 6, 2009, at *bbc.co.uk/religion/Christianity*.)

"The Power of Forgiveness: Why Revenge Doesn't Work," Dr. Judith Orloff. *Psychology Today*. (Posted September 18, 2011, at *psycholgytoday.com/blog*, search words: *Emotional Freedom*.)

Nancy Leigh DeMoss, *Choosing Forgiveness: Your Journey to Freedom*. Moody Press, 2006.

Emerson Eggerichs, *Love and Respect: The Love She Most Desires; The Respect He Desperately Needs*. Thomas Nelson, 2004.

Emerson Eggerichs, *The Language of Love & Respect: Cracking the Communication Code with Your Mate*. Thomas Nelson, 2007.

"God Loves Imperfect People," Nicky Gumbel. *Bible in One Year* (daily readings), Holy Trinity Brompton Church, UK. Accessed September, 17, 2017, at *bibleinoneyear.org*.

Dave Willis. Marriage author and teacher. Check him out at *sixseeds.patheos.com*.

Chapter 5. Understanding Each Other's Needs

John Gray, *Men Are from Mars, Women Are from Venus*. Harper Publishing, 2012. (First published in 1992.)

Willard F. Harley, *His Needs, Her Needs: Building an Affair-Proof Marriage*. Revell Publishing, 2011.

"The Art of Non-Sexual Touch," Dr. Corey Allan, Ph.D. (Accessed on *simplemarriage.net*.)

"Fast Food Still Major Part of U.S. Diet," Andrew Dugan. Article published in *Gallup Poll* website on August 6, 2013. (Accessed at *gallup.com/poll*.)

Shaunti Feldhahn, *For Women Only: What You Need to Know About the Inner Lives of Men*. Multnomah, 2013. (Originally published in 2004.)

"Portrayal of Married Sex in the Movies," J.M. Dempsey and Tom Reichert. Article in *Sexuality & Culture*, September 2000, 4(3): 21-36.

"Gender Jabber: Do Women Talk More Than Men?" Nikhil Swaminathan. *Scientific American*. (Posted July 6, 2007, at *scientificamerican.com*.)

"Are Women Really More Talkative Than Men?" Matthias R. Mehl. *Science Magazine*. July 6, 2007, Vol. 317, Issue 5834, p 82. (*science.sciencemag.org*.)

"8 Questions with Krista Tippet — Interview," Elizabeth Dias. *Time*, December 12, 2016.

Robert and Pamela Crosby, *Creative Conversation Starters for Couples*. Honor Books, 2000.

Robert and Pamela Crosby, *Now We're Talking: Questions to Build Intimacy with Your Spouse*. Focus on the Family, 1996.

"What Makes Marriage Work?" John Gottman and Nan Silver. *Psychology Today*, Published March 1, 1994. Last reviewed on June 9, 2016. (Accessed at *psychologytoday.com*.)

"National Marriage and Divorce Rate Trends." *CDC/National Vital Statistics System. Centers for Disease Control and Prevention*. Page last updated November 23, 2015. (Accessed at *cdc.gov*.)

Dennis and Barbara Rainey, *Staying Close: Stopping the Natural Drift Toward Isolation in Marriage*. Thomas Nelson Publishers, 1989.

"The Number One Problem in Marriage," Dennis Rainey. (Accessed on FamilyLife website *familylife.com/articles*.)

Tony Dungy, *Quiet Strength: The Principles, Practices & Priorities of a Winning Life*. Tyndale Publishing, 2007.

Tony Dungy, *Uncommon Marriage: Learning about Lasting Love and Overcoming Life's Obstacles Together*. Tyndale Publishing, 2014.

Dr. Gary Smalley & Norma Smalley, *Hidden Keys of a Loving, Lasting Marriage*. Zondervan Publishing, 1993.

"Sex Differences in the Implications of Partner Physical Attractiveness for the Trajectory of Marital Satisfaction," Andrea Melzer. American Psychological Association (APA PsycNET Direct), *Journal of Personality and Social Psychology*, Vol. 106(3), March 2014, pp 418-428. (Accessed at *psycnet.apa.org*.)

Chapter 6. Sex

"So How Often Does He Have Sex on His Mind?" Tom Chivers. *The Telegraph*, February 2, 2012. Quoting Professor Nicholas Eply of the University of Chicago and evolutionary psychologist Dr. Diana Fleischman of the University of Portsmouth. (Accessed at *telegraph.co.uk.*)

"Men Think About Sex Every 7 Seconds? What Study Says," Ryan Jaslow, CBS Health Editor. *CBS News*, November 29, 2011. (Accessed at *cbsnews.com.*)

"Sex Drive: How Do Men and Women Compare?" Richard Sine. *WebMD*. Quoting Dr. Edward Laumann, Ph.D. from University of Chicago and Roy Baumeister, a social psychologist at Florida State. (Accessed from the *WebMD* archives at *webmd.com.*)

Timothy Keller with Kathy Keller, *The Meaning of Marriage: Facing the Complexities of Commitment with the Wisdom of God.* Dutton Publishing, 2011. (Quoted multiple times in Chapter 6.)

"How Often Do 'Normal' Couples Have Sex?" Heather Montgomery. *Everyday Family.* Quoting Dr. Ian Kerner and Dr. Gail Saltz. (Accessed at *everydayfamily.com.*)

Debbie Roffman, quoted from *Let's Talk About Sex.* 2009 documentary film, directed by James Houston, produced by Neal Weisman. Info at *letstalkaboutsexthefilm.com.*

"A Nation of Promiscuous Prudes," Victor David Hanson. *The Washington Times*, April 19, 2013. (Accessed at *washingtontimes.com.*)

"What Couples Want to Know but Are Too Shy to Ask," Elizabeth Bernstein. *Wall Street Journal*, June 7, 2012. Quoting psychologist Barry McCarthy. (Accessed at *wsj.com.*)

"5 Simple Ways to Make Sex More Romantic," Kyle Benson. *The Gottman Institute Relationship Blog*, February 14, 2017. (Accessed at *gottman.com.*)

"Lisa Rinna on Writing a Book About Sex," Nicki Gostin. *CNN Network*, May 16, 2012. Commenting on *The Big Fun Sexy Sex Book* by Lisa Rinna & Ian Kerner. (Accessed at *cnn.com.*)

"3 R's" quote from Gladys Diaz, relationship expert and co-founder of *Heart's Desire International.* (Accessed at *heartsdesireintl.com.*)

Dr. Kevin Leman, *Sheet Music: Uncovering the Secrets of Sexual Intimacy in Marriage.* Tyndale House Publishing, 2002. pp 9, 35, 39.

"Pornography Statistics" from *Covenant Eyes* website. The report quotes sociologist Jill Manning, the American Academy of Matrimonial Lawyers, *The Journal of Adolescent Health*, and Dr. Mary Anne Layden. (Access superb materials and free downloads at *covenanteyes.com.*)

"Family Group Releases Study on Effects of Pornography," Nathan Black. *Christian Post*, December 2, 2009. Refers to American Academy of Matrimonial Lawyers. (Accessed at *christianpost.com/story.*)

Stephen Arterburn and Fred Stoeker, *Every Man's Battle: Winning the War on Sexual Temptation One Victory at a Time*. Waterbrook Press, 2000. p 50.

Chapter 7. Finances

"Biggest Lottery Jackpots in U.S. History," Jackie Wattles. *CNN Network*. January 31, 2016. (Accessed at *money.cnn.com*.)

"About Half of Americans Play State Lotteries." *Gallup – Social Issues*. (Posted July 22, 2016, at *gallup.com/poll*.)

"Lotteries: America's $70 Billion Shame," Derek Thompson. *The Atlantic*. May 11, 2015. (Accessed at *atlantic.com/business*.)

"Here's How Winning the Lottery Makes you Miserable," Melissa Chan. *Time* magazine. January 12, 2016. (Accessed at *time.com*.)

"Researcher Finds Correlation Between Financial Arguments, Decreased Relationship Satisfaction," Sonya Britt. *Kansas State University News*. July 12, 2013. (Accessed at *k-state.edu/media*.)

"Sometimes We Cheat on Our Partners About Money," Allison Linn. *TODAY*. April 24, 2012. (Accessed at *today.com/money*.)

"Is Your Partner Cheating on You Financially?" Jenna Goudreau. *Forbes*, January 13, 2011. (Accessed at *forbes.com/sites/jennagoudreau*.)

"Financial Cheating: Being Secretive About Money Can Be a Big Betrayal," Sheri Stritof. *Very Well Mind*. Updated May 23, 2018. (Accessed at *verywellmind.com/financial-cheating*.)

"The Truth About Money and Relationships," Dave Ramsey. *The Dave Ramsey Blog*. (Accessed at *daveramsey.com/blog*. We highly recommend this site.)

Dr. James Dobson, *Love for A Lifetime: Building a Marriage That Will Go the Distance*. Multnomah Books from Questar Publishers, 1993. (With quotes from Larry Burkett.)

"Do You Know What Your Spouse Makes?" Ben Steverman. *Bloomberg*, June 24, 2015. Citing Fidelity Investments survey. (Accessed at *bloomberg.com/news*.)

"How to Talk with Your Partner About Money," Landon Dowdy. CNBC Network, July 1, 2015. (Accessed at *cnbc.com*.)

"The Six Financial Mistakes Couples Make," Aleksandra Todorova. *KeyBank National Association*. With references to *SmartMoney* and *Redbook*. Quotes by Mary Claire Allvine. (Accessed at *key.com*.)

Chapter 8. The Perfect Storm

Sebastian Junger, *The Perfect Storm: A True Story of Men Against the Sea*. W.W. Norton, 2009.

"Weirdest Wedding Vows Ever," Anne Roderique Jones. *The Knot*. (Accessed at *theknot. com/content/unique-wedding-vows*.)

"Funny and Hilarious Wedding Vows," *Inspired Bride*. (Accessed at *inspiredbride.net/ hilarious-wedding-vows*.)

"Arranged/Forced Marriage Statistics," *Statistic Brain*. Research date: August 16, 2016. (Accessed at *statisticbrain.com/arranged-marriage-statistic*s.)

NOTE: Other information on arranged marriage is available via UNICEF/United Nations International Children's Emergency Fund. (Access them at *unicef.org*.)

NOTE: We are strongly opposed to arranged marriage that results in any form of exploitation. This includes early marriage (prior to age 18), human trafficking, abduction, forced marriages, or any violation of human rights.

"Modern Lessons from Arranged Marriages," Brian J. Willoughby. *New York Times*, January 18, 2013. Willoughby is assistant professor in the School of Family Life at Brigham Young University. (Accessed at *nytimes.com*.)

"Why an Arranged Marriage Is More Likely to Develop into Lasting Love," Paul Bentley. *The Daily Mail*, March 4, 2011. Quotes Dr. Robert Epstein. (Accessed at *dailymail.co.uk/ news/article*.)

Francine Kaye, *The Divorce Doctor*. Hay House, Inc. 2009.

Information from Eva Kraus-Turowski, MSW, LICSW. Associated Clinic of Psychology. 6950 West 146th Street, Suite 100, Apple Valley, MN 55124.

Scott Stanley, Howard Markman, and Susan Blumberg, *Fighting for Your Marriage: Steps for Preventing Divorce and Preserving a Lasting Love*. Josse-Bass Publishing, 2001.

"Fighting for an Awesome Marriage," Rick and Kay Warren. Message delivered at Saddleback Church on October 26, 2014. Watch the 90-minute video at *saddleback.com/ watch/media/fighting-for-an-awesome-marriage*.

"What Does It Take to Make a Marriage Last?" Billy Graham. *Answers*, June 28, 2010. (Accessed at *billygraham.org/answers*.)

"Why Aren't Marriages Lasting Today?" Billy Graham. *Answers*, July 15, 2013. (Accessed at *billygraham.org/answers*.)

"19 People Share What It Actually Takes to Stay Married," Tom Vellner. *BuzzFeed*. Posted on May 31, 2017. Also quotes Dr. Karl Pillemer. (Accessed at *buzzfeed.com/tomvellner*.)

"To Stay Married, Embrace Change," Ada Calhoun. *New York Times*, April 21, 2017. (Accessed at nytimes.com/2017/04/21.)

"The Psychology of Your Future Self," Dr. Dan Gilbert. *Ted Talk*, March 2014. (Accessed at *ted.com/talks/dan_gilbert_you_are_always_changing*.)

Chapter 9. Head Over Heels Forever

"Married 69 Years, Couple Die 40 Minutes Apart," Jamie Sotonoff. *Daily Herald*, April 25, 2017. (Accessed at *dailyherald.com/news*.)

Gary Smalley and John Trent, *Love Is a Decision: Proven Techniques to Keep Your Marriage Alive and Lively*. Thomas Nelson Publishers, 2000. (Recommended website *smalley.cc*.)

Source: *All Pro Dad* article dated September 4, 2014. (Accessed at *allprodad.com*.)

Jim Burns, Ph.D. does marriage conferences. We recommended his website: *refreshingyourmarriage.com*. Also see *apu.edu/seminary/faculty/jmburns/*.

"Marriage Advice: Save Your Marriage with a Getaway?" Krystal Kuehn. *PsychNet-UK*, a psychology and mental health portal. (Accessed at *psychnet-uk.com*.)

"Why Couples Need Vacations," Mike Gropper. *Jerusalem Post*. June 28, 2012.

Robert and Jeanette Lauer, *Marriage and Family: The Quest for Intimacy*. McGraw-Hill Education, 2011.

"Why Couples Stop Talking," Gary Smalley. Originally appeared in the March/April 2014 issue of Focus on the Family's *Thriving Family*. (Accessed at *focusonthefamily.com/marriage*.)

"The Calm, Gentle Rise of Snugglers for Hire," Olga Oksman. *The Atlantic*, December 3, 2015. (Accessed at *theatlantic.com/business*.)

"I'm a Professional Cuddler: Here's What My Job Is Like," Saskia Larsen as told to Judy McGuire. *Prevention*, June 5, 2017. (Accessed at *prevention.com/mind-body/im-a-professional-cuddler*.)

Recommended website for Mark Merrill: "Helping Families Love Well." Check out his excellent resources and blog at *markmerrill.com*.

Rob Grade, *The Cuddle Sutra: An Unabashed Celebration of the Ultimate Intimacy*. Sourcebooks Casablanca, 2007.

"Pat Benatar and Husband Neil Giraldo: We Were Two Missing Pieces That Found Each Other," Erin Hill. *Parade*, published July 14, 2012. (Accessed at *parade.com*.)

Chapter 10. Marriage Tool Kit

"Why Do the Best Athletes Never Stop Getting Better?" Justin Force. Posted April 5, 2016. (Accessed at *theexcellingedge.com*.)

Carol S. Dweck, Ph.D., *Mindset: The New Psychology of Success*. Ballentine Books, 2016.

"Better All the Time," James Surowiecki. *The New Yorker*, November 10, 2014. (Accessed at *newyorker.com*.)

General reference on *kaizen* from: "Kaizen with Six Sigma Ensures Continuous Improvement," Afsar Choudhury. (Accessed at *isixsigma.com/methodology/kaizen.*)

"6 Marriage Mistakes Women Make," Julie Edgar. With feature reviewed by Brunilda Nazario, M.D., on August 22, 2013. Contains quotes by family and marriage therapist Eli Karam, Ph.D. He is an assistant professor at the University of Louisville. (Accessed at *webmd.com/sex-relationships.*)

Made in the USA
San Bernardino,
CA